迹

一位归侨教授的成长与奉献历程

胡新云 编著

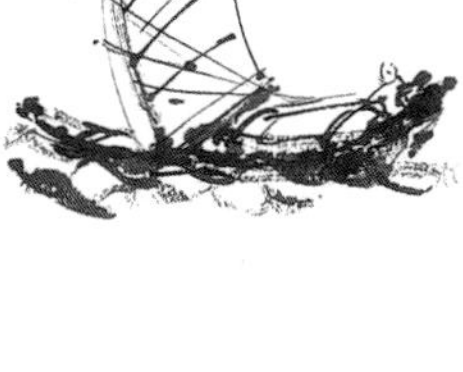

浙江工商大学出版社

图书在版编目(CIP)数据

足迹：一位归侨教授的成长与奉献历程 / 胡新云编著. —杭州：浙江工商大学出版社，2016.2
ISBN 978-7-5178-1285-2

Ⅰ. ①足… Ⅱ. ①胡… Ⅲ. ①英语—教学研究—高等学校—文集 Ⅳ. ①H319.3-53

中国版本图书馆 CIP 数据核字(2015)第 210106 号

足　迹
——一位归侨教授的成长与奉献历程
胡新云 编著

责任编辑　沈　娴
封面设计　林朦朦
责任印制　包建辉
出版发行　浙江工商大学出版社
(杭州市教工路 198 号　邮政编码 310012)
(E-mail:zjgsupress@163.com)
(网址:http://www.zjgsupress.com)
电话:0571-88904980,88831806(传真)
排　　版　杭州朝曦图文设计有限公司
印　　刷　杭州五象印务有限公司
开　　本　710mm×1000mm　1/16
印　　张　19
字　　数　302 千
版 印 次　2016 年 2 月第 1 版　2016 年 2 月第 1 次印刷
书　　号　ISBN 978-7-5178-1285-2
定　　价　56.00 元

浙江工商大学出版社营销部邮购电话　0571-88904970

1953 年摄于马来西亚的砂罗越诗巫

1951 年诗巫圣心学校初中毕业合照

1951 年砂罗越诗巫圣心学校中三学生欢送周师长回国摄影留念

1953 年诗巫圣心英汉学校 Form VI 部分同学欢送我与钱理贤回国升学合影留念

前排右至左：甘佑梨、钱理贤、胡新云、王寿珍

后排右至左：钱良珍、陈信生、陈新同、陈兆杰、黄景文、黄生财

杭州高级中学 1956 届（2）班在灵隐合影

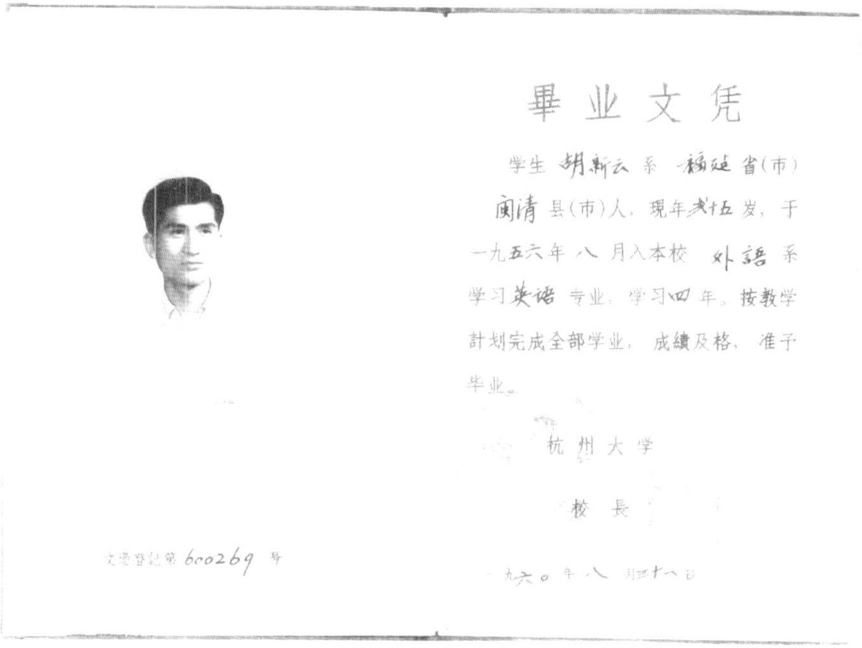
文憑登記第600269号

畢业文凭

学生胡新云系福建省（市）闽清县（市）人，現年贰拾伍岁，于一九五六年八月入本校外語系学习英语专业，学习四年，按教学計划完成全部学业，成績及格，准予毕业。

杭州大学

校長

一九六〇年八月二十八日

1960 年杭州大学毕业文凭

1963 年与吴新娣女士结婚照

1965 年杭州中村军训时我班所在排的解放军教官和四位正副班长合照

1966 年新昌西岭五联社教工作组师生合照

1966 年我们十几位青年教师步行串联井冈山，在黄洋界革命纪念碑前合影

1982—1983年上海外国语学院高校师资英语短训班合照

1986 年中国教育工会杭州大学委员会授予的 1984—1985 年度优秀工会积极分子的奖状

1984 年我偕夫人吴新娣在闽清池园老家与母亲、新平夫妇、新玉夫妇合影

（照片）

持证人：

性别：

出生年月：

民族：

身份证号码：

资格种类：

任教学科：

证书号码：

根据《中华人民共和国教师法》及《教师资格条例》的规定，认定

具备

教师资格。

认定机构（公章）

年　月　日

1988 年晋升副教授，获英国语言学任教资格

1990 年杭州大学丛书教学图书资料工作三十年同志合影

1994 年二哥新平、大姐淑英（前排），与六弟新义、三哥新贵、我（后排）合影留念

1999 年杭州高级中学 1956 届（2）班同学会合照

1999 年我和姚玉英等同学向崔东伯师长献花篮

2007 年杭州大学外语系英语专业 60 届同学会合影

胡伟民　王有根　杜心忱　朱俊杰　历银坤　王志章　支长生　毛颂唐　沈正明

王金凤　金学芳　劳乃先　吴基伦　黄日晶　窦光琳　王烈铮　李新富

汪　怡　林梦玉　范龙华　陈妙留　王碧霞　潘妙英　章莲子　黄丽明　章丁花

钱玲华

杨巧云老师　郭建中老师　姚祖培老师　卢世雄老师　胡新云老师

2008 年我与夫人吴新娣，女儿胡晋、胡蓉，女婿程枫、黄明，外孙女程逸文、黄雨亭的全家福

2010 年杭州大学外语英语专业首届（56 级）同学留影

前排左至右：任绍曾　冯尚理　路丽霞　家属　家属　黄霞萍　徐国华　张合珍　家属　孙中鼎

后排左至右：家属　黄成煌　袁瑞年　卢世雄　毛华奋　朱少华　钱墩　吴文烈　杨森林　张燮泉　谢慎远　胡新云

2012 年杭州大学外语系七七级三十周年庆典合影

2013 年杭州大学外语系 1983 届毕业 30 周年同学会留影

我和程贤政、叶志洪、蒋炳贤、殷惟本在郭庄合影

我与老同学们在曲院风荷聚会并留影

左至右：胡新云　任绍曾　杨森林　袁瑞年　卢世雄　黄成煌　张合珍　家属　路丽霞　陈新琦

上官筱廉　吴文烈　黄霞萍　谢慎远　家属　黄约法　朋友　韩祖铎

我与老同学们在郭庄聚会并留影

左至右：徐国华　黄霞萍　家属　路丽霞　卢世雄　孙中鼎　杨森林　袁瑞年　谢慎远　张燮泉　胡新云　钱炜　吴文烈　任绍曾

序

1934年4月，我出生于马来西亚沙罗越诗巫一个橡胶农家庭，祖籍为福建闽清。时逢第二次世界大战，自小从事橡胶生产劳动的我养成了艰苦朴素、勤俭节约、自立更生、刻苦好学、忠诚老实的品格，逐渐发展成强烈的爱国主义思想，决心回国读书，以报效祖国。

1953年回国后，在党和国家政府的关怀教育下，我经历了长期刻苦的学习和社会磨炼，成长为一个自觉的中国共产党人，一位德才兼备的人民教师。我先后就读于杭州高级中学、浙江师范学院。1958年，浙江师范学院与杭州大学合并，定名杭州大学。1960年，我从杭州大学外语系英语专业毕业。大学毕业后，因需要留系教授英国语言学和阅读基础课，并负责有关的教研工作22年。1982年我赴上海外国语学院进修美国历史一年，回校后，着手自编教材，开设讲授高年级"美国概况"专业课。按理至1995年就该退休了，但其后延聘1年，加上基础课教学22年，我在杭州大学课堂教学第一线奋斗了整整35年。我的专业水平和教学科研成果得到了校系的充分肯定和公正评价。1978年，我被杭州大学教师职务评审委员会评定为讲师，1981年被中共杭州大学党委授权外语系总支接纳成为一名中国共产党员，1986年被中国教育工会杭州大学委员会评为"优秀工会积极分子"，并于1988年被杭州大学职务评审委员会评为副教授，授予高级专业技术资格证书。我和杭州大学同生共长，为祖国的社会主义教育事业的繁荣发展尽力尽职，勤奋工作，奉献了一生，圆了我回国读书、报效祖国的梦。

"英美概况"是杭州大学外语系为英语专业高年级设置的专业课程，也是必修课。我在编写教材《英美概况》"美国概况"部分和摘写其他论文的过程中，注意运用辩证唯物主义和历史唯物主义的观点，观察、分析、处理各种史料，去其糟粕，取其精华，为我创用。《英美概况》涉及历史、地理、政治、经济、教育、文化、宗教史领域的知识，内容丰富，语言标准，通俗易懂，包含英语专业学生必须具备的知识和英语能力。10 多年的教学实践证明，《英美概况》是一部好教材，教学效果良好，为杭州大学外语系培养了一批又一批合格的中高级英语人才。他们奋斗在国内外不同战线的各种领域和岗位，如外交（含联合国）、商贸、金融、科研机构、高校、教育等，为中美关系友好发展、中美友好交流与合作，为我国的改革开放做出了一定贡献。本教材也包含社会上英语工作者所必需的专业知识，曾被浙江省自学考试采用多年，培养了大批英语工作者。

该书的编写和出版获得了任绍曾教授、姚祖培教授、王润中教授和黄遵洸教授的指导、审核、修正和帮助。对此，我深表感谢和敬意！

胡新云

2015 年 3 月 7 日

目　　录

第一部分

第二部分

TRACKS Growth and Devotion of a Refurned Overseas Chinses Professor

第一部分 PART ONE

童年时期

诞生时代背景

1934 年 4 月 20 日,我出生于马来西亚砂罗越诗巫木杰阿十一个橡胶农的家庭里,父胡元安、母林英妹(现均已故)。1927 年至 1936 年,中国共产党领导的工农红军进行了反对帝国主义、封建主义和官僚资本主义反动统治的革命战争,并在战争中不断成长壮大,蒋介石领导的国民党军队则节节败退,逐渐衰败,直至 1936 年 12 月西安事变,蒋介石被迫停止内战,国共两党达成协议,一致对外,全国形成了抗日统一战线,团结抗日。

1931 年日本侵占中国东北三省,1937 年 7 月 7 日卢沟桥事变爆发后,日本开始大举侵犯中国。1941 年 12 月 7 日日军偷袭美国珍珠港,太平洋战争全面爆发,日军迅速占领菲律宾、泰国、老挝、马来西亚、新加坡、缅甸、印度、印度尼西亚等东南亚国家。

1940 年我开始就读诗巫木杰阿十东山小学,1941 年太平洋战争爆发,我被迫辍学,不久日军侵占砂罗越诗巫,实施杀光、烧光、抢光的"三光"政策,到处强占学校、电影院等公共场所和民屋,掠夺民众财物,强征劳役,包括妇女和儿童,修建公路、码头、机场和兵营等,连我三哥这样当时仅 10 岁左右的孩子,都被强征到新珠山建机场。在日军恐怖统治的笼罩下,劳苦大众不堪忍受如此大的劳动强度,挨鞭受饥挣扎在死亡线上。有个邻居童工就被塌崩山岩活活压死,如此惨象,不忍目睹!我和姐姐为了生计常做些糕点、薯干去机场销售,以补贴家用,即买些柴火油盐粮等。在机场附近,每当我们经过由日本兵荷枪实弹把守的新珠湾桥时,总是提心吊胆,尤其更怕姐姐遭到不测。我们总是低着头，偷偷地瞅着日本鬼子的一举一动。有一次，他们喝令我们停下，我们闻声拔腿就跑，避免了被侮辱、被抢劫、挨打，甚至死于非命的命运。这是早年日本侵略者在我心中播下的仇恨种子和造成的不灭伤痕！

第二次世界大战爆发前，父亲回国在福建闽清十一都池园置地造房，以求未来回国谋生，养老定居。他在马来西亚留下我母亲和六个兄弟姐妹，那时我还年幼，长兄年仅15岁。母亲张罗全家生计，其他人不论年龄、力气大小都得通力合作，挥舞刀斧，垦荒种地。我们砍伐野草、灌木、树藤等，晒干后，放上一把火，就出现一片褐色肥沃的土地；再挥动铲、锄挖掉草皮、根茎，然后开沟、松土，平整土地，筑成不同形状板块的种植园，种上蔬菜、水果等。如风调雨顺，经过施肥、松土、除草，这些作物就会茁壮成长，我们等待丰收；若遇干旱或内涝，就会颗粒无收，真有几分人命由天的无奈。

我们在远离住宅的新珠湾河下游沼泽地种植水稻，收割后，乘夜幕手划小木船，小心翼翼、提心吊胆地把稻谷偷偷运回家，以防被日本鬼子发现抢劫，或撞上险滩急流全船覆没。

我们用心血和汗水换来的粮食、副食品、日用品都要秘密存放——粮食放在适温隐蔽处，糖、盐等则放在瓷罐中，埋在地下或塞在树洞里，否则被日本鬼子发现并掠夺，我们就难以维持生计了！

饲养家畜也是我们的生计之一。我们利用剩饭、剩菜和其他饲料，喂养一批又一批鸡、鸭、猪、狗等。狗是用来看家防盗的，是我们的忠实朋友；猪是主要家畜之一，猪肉经济收益好，又是过年过节的佳肴。番薯及其藤叶、剩菜、剩饭是猪的主食，但猪胃口很大，我们还经常上山采摘野菜或潜游河里摘取水草给以补充。

饲养家畜给我们带来不少欢乐和安慰。每天早晚各喂养一次，饱食一顿后，它们就心满意足地自动散开，游玩、栖息或闭眼安睡。公鸡是我们的报时器，每天清晨五时左右准时大叫“喔喔喔，喔……”，提醒我们起来开始一天的工作和生活。每当母鸡下蛋后，它们就会高叫“咯咯咯，咯咯咯……”，向你报喜。当鸡蛋孵出成群的小鸡时，你会感到无限的欢乐和安慰！当你休闲有兴的时候，捉一小鸡握在掌上轻轻抚摸着它的头部，它就会闭眼躺着发出“叽叽叽，叽叽叽……”稚嫩机灵的悦耳叫声，传达着它对你抚养和保护它的谢意！每当此时此刻，我心头都会立即涌起无限的欢慰和高兴！我们彼此之间就是如此和谐相处和依存的！猪则是我们过年过节的主要贡品，大猪屠了，邻里亲戚朋友都可分享一番，作为过年过节的佳肴，庆祝丰收年。如屠只童猪，烘烤后，则是宴席上最上等的佳肴了，皮呈棕黄色，细嫩油光，肉质松脆，香喷喷的，令人垂涎三尺，无一不叫好。因我们全年付出的艰辛劳动，年终时我们都会欢天喜地地准备一年一度的春节团聚盛宴，庆贺新春快乐，祈求阖家平安！

从 1941 年到 1945 年，我经历了第二次世界大战，看清了日本纳粹帝国主义的野心与残酷本质，萌生了爱国的思想。同时，我领悟到自小必须树立刻苦耐劳、艰苦朴素、自力更生的思想观念，养成爱劳动、善读书、懂技术、求发展的理念信仰，才能在与敌人和自然界的搏斗中求生存，求发展，赢得发展和幸福。

童年学习生活

我出身贫穷橡胶农家庭，父母文盲不识字，常说不读书做文盲很苦，做事记账都要借用火柴作标签，成不了大器，这使我萌发了要读书的念头。

1940 年 1 月，我开始就读于村寨的东山小学，很不幸，1941 年太平洋战争全面爆发，日军侵占砂罗越诗巫，我被迫辍学五年之久，于 1946 年 1 月重回东山小学读书。荒废了五年，似乎求知欲望更强烈，我更努力、更认真，效率也更高了。我常在背着的胶丝箩筐里放着课本，边割橡胶，边默念、思考当天的课文内容，如有遗忘，随时拿出课本阅读补正，直至熟记为止，因此年年考试成绩优秀，跳了一级，于 1948 年 12 月提前毕业。

东山小学的校长黄培桃和许志豪等老师都来自福建六都玉泉中学，颇有爱国主义精神和文化知识水平，课程设置合理，教学方法灵活、得体，其启蒙教育对我影响颇大。他们用标准的汉字书写体和普通话进行教学，形式多样，灵活实用，激起了我的浓厚兴趣和求知欲望。校长推荐柳宗元字帖给我，教我如何学好柳体。之后我参加书法比赛，并获奖。许老师教语文和音乐，教唱中国国歌和其他爱国主义歌曲。当日本侵占东北三省，大肆侵害和蹂躏中国人民时，他教我们演唱《满江红》，选我扮演女主角——新娘。演唱时，我怀着沉重的思念感情，唱着："送君送到征途上……打了胜仗快回家，免得小妹相思长……"此时此刻，我的心已经和祖国亿万青年的心完全相通，热血沸腾，只想英勇奋起，奔向战场，与日本侵略军决一死战，保家卫国。

中学生活

风云变幻,世事难料。1947 年,父亲回到诗巫,随后不久,父母矛盾冲突不断,最后母亲不得不离家跟随二兄独立生活,但我还和父亲生活在一起。1948 年 12 月小学毕业后,我到敦化中学读书,离家十几千米,每天骑自行车来回,单程约一个小时,上午割橡胶做生产,下午一点赶到学校上课,五点左右放学回家帮助料理家务。我爱好运动,喜欢打排球,放学途经东山小学时,总要打一两场球,回到家里晚了,父亲经常抱怨和发脾气。一次他赶来学校,半途碰上了我,我跳下自行车掉头就跑,因为生怕回家要被痛打一顿,当晚我跑到敦化中学附近四叔家里躲避。随后我也不敢回家,就在四叔家里住了一个学期,第二学期我转到四叔儿子新金兄就读的卫理英汉学校。第二年我跟随母亲和哥哥生活,又转学到圣心英汉学校。这类英汉学校,上午授英语课,下午授中文课。因经济困难,我必须坚持半工半读,上午劳动,下午读书,直至 1951 年底从圣心英汉学校初中毕业。有初中毕业文凭,就能在小学教书,从 1952 年起我就摆脱了劳累的割橡胶劳动生产,到小学教书,上午读英语,下午教书。三个学期换了三个学校,从诗巫到诗里街圣、安当尼英文学校,到加舒逸的英文学校,再回到圣心英汉学校,从四级(Form Ⅳ)英语读到六级(Form Ⅵ)英语。

综上所述,我在马来西亚的就学轨迹,就是半工半读,“工”是为了挣钱谋生、读书,“读”则是为了更好地工作谋发展。我就是如此孜孜不倦地探索着求知谋发展的人生道路。

离马回国，就读杭高

1949年10月1日，毛泽东主席在北京天安门城楼宣告：中华人民共和国成立，中华民族已经站起来了！我看准了这个机会，响应号召，千辛万苦办妥了回国的一切申请手续。马来西亚政府官员威胁说："你去了中国就永远不能再回马来西亚了！"意指我离开马国就要和父母亲友永别了。但我仍抱着"读书为国"的坚定信念，于1953年7月1日踏上了回国的征途。我们从诗巫码头乘一艘一千多吨的客货轮出发，航行在拉让江上，时而绕过险滩急流，时而穿过弯道漩涡，惊险地驶离马岛进入大洋。孤岛上空不时有群鸟飞翔，发出有节奏的鸣叫声，欢歌雀跃地送离我们；船身两侧排开的浪花中不时涌现成群跃起的小鱼，争先恐后地陪伴我们冲向前方。经过两天两夜既充满惊险又充满喜悦的航程，我们于第三天清晨平安抵达新加坡。

当天傍晚，我们在新加坡换乘一艘约五千吨的客货轮，驶往一望无际的太平洋中国南海海域。夜色已深，顷刻间天空乌云笼罩，狂风刮起大浪，雷电交加，一阵阵狂风、雷雨、大浪向船舱扑来，似乎顿时要把整条船撕裂、吞噬。船随浪峰波谷前后高度颠簸，左右激烈摇晃。多数乘客已晕在床上，疲惫不堪，呕吐不已，只能听天由命。但我还手握护围栏巍然矗立在甲板上，任凭风吹浪打，毫无畏惧，悠然自得，因为我有抗衡如此恶劣环境的特殊能力——决心和毅力。狂风暴雨过后，一切归于平静。翌日清晨，一轮红日从东方升起，照耀着我们乘风破浪，勇往直前。经过五天五夜惊喜兼备的航行，我们终于在7日8日傍晚到达香港维多利亚港湾，四周高楼林立，灯火辉煌，一派繁荣景象。香港是世界最繁华的商贸中心城市之一，当时还未回归祖国的怀抱。

翌日清晨，我乘上火车到达罗湖口边防站，这边挂着英国国旗，对面高高飘扬着五星红旗。当我踏上祖国大地，昂首凝视着中国国旗时，不禁热泪盈眶，激动不已！我的梦想终于实现，我终于回到祖国了！一条崭新的人生道路正等待着我去开拓。

到达广州后，我们受到市政府和侨联的热情欢迎和接待。他们详细咨询了解我们（我和归侨邓本良）的愿望和要求后，分配我们坐火车上北京华侨补习学校，参加各种不同程度的补习班。经过考试评定后，我被分配来杭州高级中学读高中一年级。

杭州高级中学是全省，甚至是全国的一所名校，有众多名人、名师、教授、学者和校友，图书资源丰富，教学设备齐全、先进，教学水平全国一流，历届高考成绩突出，大量考生被名校录取深造。杭高造就了大批建设国家的优秀人才，为社会主义建设做出了重要贡献。我能入读杭高，深感光荣和责任重大。

我在杭高学习初期困难很多。首先是语言关，我在马来西亚虽然学过汉语，即中国语文，但语音、语调不标准，文字书写错误多，语法也不规范，因此很难听懂老师讲课的内容。其次是基础差，马来西亚中文学校的课程少、内容浅，与杭高的课程内容相比难度差别很大，无法衔接，导致我难以理解和接受。我的英语是不成问题的，语文、历史、地理、政治可以勉强应付，但数、理、化对我而言很难，我的化学、物理知识几乎是空白的，连许多符号和公式都不认识，对老师讲课的内容根本无法理解和接受。但学校领导、教师和同学都很关心我，在他们热情且耐心的教导、帮助和鼓励下，我没有气馁。我报效祖国的信念、信心和毅力没有动摇，决心战胜困难取得新胜利！

我们高一(2)班任课老师的水平都是很高的，如崔东伯、王冥鸿、唐魁信、徐士中、任明耀、高育辛等老师。他们讲课深入浅出、重点突出，语言丰富生动、方法灵活多样，图文并茂、扣人心弦，激发了我浓厚的学习兴趣，不断改进我的学习逻辑思维、方法和习惯，使我取得很大进步。

地理、历史、政治课是爱国主义的好课程，这些课让我知道中国是世界国土面积第三大的国家，第一人口大国，是具有五千多年历史文明的古国。

中国的面积有960多万平方千米，东有泰山，东北有大兴安岭，西有喜马拉雅山脉、昆仑山，南有武夷山、天目山等。中国地大物博，矿产丰富。

中国是个多民族的国家，有四亿多人口(1953 年)，中国人民聪明勇敢、奋发有为、刻苦耐劳、勤俭朴素，识礼义、知廉耻、相互尊重、爱好和平。中华民族是个优秀的民族。

中国有两大河流，长江和黄河，源于青海，横贯多省，波涛滚滚流向东方，奔入太平洋。长江流域土地广阔，土壤肥沃，物产丰富，为世世代代中华儿女发展壮大提供了充足的粮食和资源。黄河则是中华儿女的母亲河，炎黄子孙的诞生地，抚育了一代又一代的炎黄子孙，从上古一直到中华人民共和国；从儒家文明到民族复兴，再到现代的社会主义文明。中国有许多不朽的古都和古迹，如北京的天安门、故宫、万里长城，西安的兵马俑，敦煌的莫高窟，杭州的岳王庙等，都记载了中华民族几千年文明发展的历程。这是中华民族的光荣和骄傲！

政治课的高育辛老师简述了现代史。辛亥革命推翻了清王朝君主专制，建立了中华民国，由于执政的国民党官僚资产阶级的软弱性，中国人民仍然遭受三座大山——帝国主义、封建主义和官僚资本主义的压迫和剥削，过着苦难的生活。中国无产阶级革命先辈于 1921 年建立了中国共产党，肩负起推翻三座大山的重任。经过长期浴血奋战，1949 年 10 月 1 日，毛泽东主席在北京天安门城楼宣告："中华人民共和国中央人民政府成立了！"从此中华民族站立起来了，走上了社会主义道路，并开始为强国富民而努力奋斗！

伟大的祖国、伟大的中华民族和伟大的文明历史，潜移默化地培养、充实了我的智慧和爱国主义思想，让我决心为实现祖国的共产主义事业而奋斗终生。高二时，我申请加入了中国共产主义青年团。1956 年 6 月，我圆满完成了高中全部课程学习任务，顺利毕业，参加高考，但报考时犯了错误，报的是我的弱项——工科，未被录取。由于当时中央政府对侨生有特殊照顾政策，省招生办根据我的文科成绩，劝我改报浙师院外语系英语专业，我当机立断欣然同意。经外语系郑儒铖教授面试，我随即被浙师院外语系英语专业录取，开始了大学学习生活的新历程。

大学生活

我很幸运地被浙江师范学院英语专业录取，师从鲍屡平、郑儒鍼、蒋炳贤等教授。他们英语精湛，知识渊博，学贯中西，对古今中外文明都有深入研究；他们治学严谨，教学严肃，认真负责，一丝不苟，甚至连一个标点符号，一点一撇都不轻易放过；他们还经常深入同学中间，耐心辅导，帮助我们克服困难，教导我们增强信心，学好专业。他们言传身教，尽心尽责，对我的心灵和学业都影响很大，至今我仍怀念不已。

除学校课堂教学外，老师还经常带领我们上工厂、下农村，进行学习与劳动生产相结合的教学实践活动。在工厂，我们和工人同住（视厂居住条件而定）、同吃、同劳动，他们刻苦耐劳、献身敬业、勤俭节约、艰苦朴素的思想作风，无时无刻不在影响我们。老师根据实际情况编写教材，边上课边讲解，或组织我们用英语进行交流讨论，把车间或厂房变成课堂，方式多样，方法灵活，学用结合，达到专业学习与思想教育相结合的目的。

在农村，情况也类似，我们和农民实行“三同”。但农村和工厂情况有所不同，农村的劳动生产环境条件比工厂差许多，农民的生活水平比工人低许多。在农忙季节，尤其是抢收抢种时期，劳动强度大，环境恶劣，我们经常要忍受长时间的烈日曝晒，高温田水浸泡，或狂风暴雨、雷电交加的袭击，这对我们的身体和毅力都是一种严峻的锻炼和考验。在生活上，我们和农民一样有什么吃什么，尤其是 20 世纪 60 年代的困难时期，我们和农民常吃不饱，忍饥挨饿，坚持在滚烫的水田里割稻插秧，或从田里挑回两大箩筐（约 100 千克）稻谷。一天劳作后，我感到疲惫不堪，腰酸背痛，坐卧难安，支撑不住，但一想到我来农村是向农民学习的，他们天天如此，我也必须天天坚持下去，做到和农民同甘苦、共患难，和他们打成一片，同心同德，真心诚意为他们服务。这是我下农村劳动锻炼的重要收获。

大学四年(1956—1960)的生活过得很不平静。但我很幸运,未被学校淘汰,于1960年7月如期毕业,当时浙师院已并入杭州大学,因此我被授予由时任杭州大学校长林乎加署名的毕业证书。

在这四年过程中,我反复学习《为人民服务》(*Serving the People*)、《批评和自我批评》(*Criticism and Self-criticism*)、《实践论》(*On Practice*)、《矛盾论》(*On Contradiction*)中英版和其他中央文件。我的收获有以下几点:一、实践是认识的基础,是检验认识的标准,人只有通过实践才能获得真正的认识和科学知识。二、任何事物都是矛盾的统一体,矛盾有主要矛盾和次要矛盾之分,主要矛盾在一定条件下可以转化为次要矛盾,反之亦然。这也符合人的思想意识的转化,如正确和错误、先进和落后等都是相互矛盾的统一体,在一定条件下相互转化。所以我在社会实践中坚持和工农兵打成一片,和他们同甘苦、共患难,在思想感情上和他们融为一体,全心全意为他们服务,不断克服怕苦、怕累、好吃懒做、贪图安逸、自私自利等落后的资产阶级思想。所以,我认为《为人民服务》和《矛盾论》等著作是人们改造世界观、人生观和价值观的有力武器。三、我尊重老师和领导,他们爱国、爱党、爱学生的思想,严谨的教风,敬业精神,严肃认真的工作态度使他们成为我学习的好榜样、好老师。我关心、爱护他们,从不轻易否定他们的工作业绩和奉献。四、我和同学长期同住、同吃、同学习,形成了一个团结友爱、勤奋好学、努力向上的集体,他们的好思想、好作风、好习惯无时无刻不在影响、激励着我,教育和帮助我不断进步。在进行批评和自我批评时,我注意区分敌我矛盾,不随意抓辫子、扣帽子、搞派别斗争,注意团结同学,相互帮助,改正各种不良的思想行动、作风,以求达到新的团结,共同进步。

我经历了大学四年的学习生活和社会实践的考验和锻炼,提高了爱国、爱党、爱人民的思想觉悟,增强了全心全意为人民服务的思想,毕业时决心服从祖国的分配,到最需要的地方去工作,但受校与系领导的信任,得以留校任教,我甚为感激和宽慰。

任教杭州大学外语系

能留在杭州大学外语系任教,很出乎我的预料,因此内心十分高兴和感激,感谢党和政府对我的信任,给予我机会为实现“读书为国”的崇高愿望而努力奋斗。

1960 年杭州大学外语系英语专业招收了 49 名学生,分三个小班,我教一个班的精读基础课,系领导强调英语语言基础知识理论的教学和实践,采用许国璋主编《英语》一至四册,以生活散文为主,辅以原著节选,题材广泛,有正副课文,其中有对话和练习等,着重打好扎实的语音、语调、语法、词汇等方面的基本功和知识理论基础,随后逐步增加外国文学原著和知识的占比。我们的教学小组严格按照每册每课的教学安排和要求,完成各个环节和学期与学年的教学任务。

我在备课、授课时注意三个重点:课文的中心思想、作者及时代背景;语音、语法、句型、词汇等的要点、难点;充分备课,以备解决学生可能产生的疑问和难题。各种作业练习围绕上述要点,重点展开,循序渐进,反复练习,以使学生熟练掌握,达到每课、每学期、每学年的教学目的和要求。

期间,我常阅读参考 Daniel Jones 的 *An Outline of English Phonetics*, *The Pronunciation of English*, 刘炳善的 *A Short History of English Literature*, Randolph Quirk 与 Sidney Geenbuam 的 *A University Grammar of Englsih* 和葛传椝的《英语惯用法词典》等,以便比较准确地传授和指导课文的基础知识理论学习和实践活动,并提高自身的英语基础知识理论储备和实践活动能力,适应和完成一至二年级不断增加难度的教学要求和任务。同时,我深入教室、学生宿舍了解学生的学习和生活情况,及时解决他们的各种困难和问题。这是我初期任教的简况。

随后，我连续接受了几届教学工作，都如期圆满完成任务，为高年级输送了许多合格甚至是优秀的学生。他们毕业后被分配到社会的不同岗位上，成了各行各业的骨干、中坚力量，如杭大的张少伯、章胜强、黄遵洸、王志章等教授，时任杭州商学院党委副书记的胡伟民教授，时任杭州外国语学校校长的毛颂唐……我"读书为国"的梦想开始结出果实，如今桃李满天下，甚感欣慰和光荣。

向解放军学习也是大学生活的一个重要内容。1965 年 8 月我们共约百人赴杭州中村军训，当我们到达营地门口时就看到醒目耀眼的"保家卫国"四个字，不远处在马路两旁的玻璃框架内则是"三大纪律、八项注意"的具体指示。接着我们就到分配好的营房宿舍，床桌、铺盖、用具、枪械等摆放整齐有序，十分大方朴素，呈现出一种严肃、认真、奋发有为的人民解放军军营生活的浓郁气氛，感染着我们每个人的心灵。短暂休息后，我们听令到广场列队集中，听取营部首长的讲话。他布置任务，传达要求、目的，讲解训练计划、组织纪律等，并宣布成立一个营部，下编 2 个连、4 个排、8 个班，每班约 15 人，由一个解放军班长和一正一副师生班长负责管理。我和蒋其宝任正副班长，负责全班每天的起居、生活、训练和学习。

次日，我们正式开始军营生活，6:30 起床，打理床铺，搞卫生；7:00 列队赴餐厅，拿好餐具排队领取饭菜就餐，不浪费，不喧哗，用毕洗好餐具放回原处，等候列队回宿舍；7:30 开始操练，列队是最基础的项目，解放军班长做了示范动作之后，便由我或副班长带领学生操练各个具体动作，如立正、看齐、向左或右转、步行等，视线、体形、双手摆动等都要一一操练到位，人人掌握，做到口令、动作、列队行走一致，完美无缺。经过日复一日的艰辛操练，我班最终达到标准要求，并在全营操练表演比赛中获得了优秀奖。

投弹、射击、伏卧、滚爬等也是我们的必修项目。射击前，我们要先学会开关枪膛，装卸子弹，再学会双脚站立，双手握枪、托枪的要领，保持身、手平稳，用眼睛对准枪眼，将眼、枪眼与靶子形成一直线，扣动扳机，方能准确击中目标。我的射击成绩为优。投弹（手榴弹）一般有站立、跑动和卧式三种。常用的跑动投掷要正确手握手榴弹，配合正确的步伐和速度，合力使用手臂、手腕和腰部的力量，方能达到最佳效果，投到要求的目标和路程。

军训结束前的一个深夜，我们正在甜睡的梦中，突然被一阵紧急的军号令惊醒。我们当即一跃而起，穿上军服、鞋子，戴上帽子，打起背包，背上枪支、水壶等，立即跑到广场列队集合。经检查，全班人数到齐，整装完好，但有个别战士衣未上扣，鞋未结带，被包打结不标准。略做整修后，我报告指挥部，待命出发。在行军途中，我们的队列一直保持整齐、肃穆，斗志昂扬，一切行动听指挥；突然听到紧急号令，我们立刻疏散、埋伏在路途两旁杂草与灌木丛生的荒凉荫蔽处中，三三两两，卧的卧，伏的伏，蹬的蹬，跪的跪，不怕虫叮蛇咬，不顾坑洼、荆棘、木梢、乱石、悬崖，唯恐被前方行进的“敌军”发现和攻击。约过了半小时，军号令响，紧急状态解除，我们又从荒野的灌木林中窜出，列队集合，无一人掉队，继续斗志昂扬、井然有序地行军，直到黎明才圆满结束。

第二天，我们对近一个月来的学习、军训进行了总结。首先，我们按计划认真学习毛泽东著作，如《为人民服务》《愚公移山》《论联合政府》《战争和战略问题》《批评和自我批评》等，培养正确的人生观、世界观和爱国主义思想，树立崇高的革命理想和道德品质，明确人生的方向、目的和要求，做到先人后己，助人为乐，鞠躬尽瘁，死而后已。其次，我们遵守党纪国法，一切行动听指挥，恪守三大纪律、八项注意，做好各项军事训练，掌握各个细小环节的技术和本领，保家卫国。再次，我们全班师生十几人来自不同系科，年龄、经历不同，各有各的优缺点，能自觉开展批评和自我批评，取长补短，相互促进，共同提高，培养我们遵纪守法的意识，做到克己奉公，一切为了强国富民。最后，我们要善始善终，继续保持谦虚谨慎、努力奋斗的态度，戒骄戒躁，认真完成我们的军训任务，从而促进我们未来在各自的学习、工作岗位上求真务实，严谨、认真地搞好学习和工作，为国家做出应有的贡献。此次军训对我的成长裨益匪浅。

1966年，当我任大学二年级老师时，“文化大革命”开始了。杭州大学校园里显得冷清平静，大部分领导干部静观待命，教职员工无所事事，似乎整个学校机制已停止运作。我们共约10位年轻教师商议前往井冈山革命根据地进行徒步“串联”。我们从杭州出发，经衢州、江山入江西，再经玉山、上饶、鹰潭、抚州、吉安到井冈山，后经永新、莲花、萍乡进入湖南醴陵、湘潭、长沙，随后乘火车回杭州，历时28天左右，每天行程约80千米至100千米，从一个县城到另一个县城，经风雨日晒，跋山涉水，攀高峰渡险滩，睡地铺盖披风，吃杂粮喝冷水。每逢困难难忍时，我们便高唱“巍巍井冈山……”等革命歌曲，鼓舞士气，振作精神，日夜兼程继续前进。其间有两次，我的双腿实在不听使唤，乘了公共汽车先到前站等候队友到来，再跟随队伍继续前进；在攀登穿过井冈山黄洋界时，我们前往参观中共创建的井冈山革命根据地，革命先烈建立和领导的工农红军打击土豪劣绅，击退了国民党反动派一次又一次的围剿进攻，开辟了一条以农村包围城市，最后夺取政权的革命道路。

这次徒步“串联”活动磨炼了我们刻苦耐劳、英勇奋斗、勤俭节约、自力更生的精神；我们深入农村目睹了广阔富饶的祖国大地、山清水秀的大好江山，激励了我们爱农村、爱祖国的思想和热情，期盼能早日进课堂培养学生“爱农为国”的思想感情。

1970 年 3 月，工人阶级选派队员进驻全国各类学校领导复课“闹革命”，杭大来了工宣队。杭大外语系英语专业不经考试招收了第一届工农兵学员，约 200 名，按部队编制设 2 个连，每连 3 个班，每班约 30 人。招收的学员只看出身成分，不看文化程度，有的只读过小学，学习很困难，老坐冷板凳，一问三不知。学校实施的教学大纲是工人阶级领导下的复课“闹革命”，以“闹革命”为主，把约 70%的时间和精力花在读毛选和中央文件上，批判资产阶级和修正主义、走资派、反动学术权威和“地富反坏右”，我因有“海外关系”也被列入重点批斗对象。

但我还是要感谢党和人民对我的信任和支持，给了我工作的权利和义务，当了系两个连中一个连的连长，兼一个班的教学和班主任工作，除了领导、组织、安排全连的教学活动（包括备课、上课、考试评定全过程）外，还进行政治学习、军训、锻炼和劳动等工作。

在复课“闹革命”、工人阶级管理和领导下的“文化大革命”背景下，高等学校教育受到了严重诋毁、干扰和破坏，但我们多数老师还是严格遵守老浙大老师传承下来的“实事求是”治学精神，用严谨的教风和学风从事我们的教学和科研工作，出色地完成了教学任务，培养出了不少有用之才，如王选、何刚强、沈长先、林志平、张丽娟等著名人士。

1972 年我兄新平要从马来西亚回福建探望母亲，要我回乡团聚。闻讯，我十分激动：阔别 20 多年，多么渴望能与兄亲相会团聚呀！于是我向校系领导和工宣队申请 20 天的探亲假期，获得批准。我回闽探亲后，陪同兄来杭，经上海北上苏州、南京、北京等地参观旅游。在南京我们拜祭了中山陵。在北京，我们游览了故宫、天安门、天坛、八达岭长城等承载了中华民族五千多年文明精华的历史古迹。我们还参观了卢沟桥，深刻认识到日本军国主义侵华战争所犯下的滔天罪行，欠下中国的累累血债，激发了我们的爱国主义热忱。我们热爱和平，拥护正义。

此次探亲旅游是我们母子兄弟阔别二十几年后，心心相印、血脉相连的再会，加深了母子兄弟的爱和友谊。这是我们归侨，也是我国政府和相关部门做好联络海外华侨，培育爱国感情友谊，团结和保护海外华人的一次很好的尝试。

1977 年全国高校恢复招生，逐步恢复教学秩序和教学制度，高教事业出现了新的希望。

由于我工作信守信念和本分，且经受了长年暴风骤雨的洗礼，受到校系领导的信任。学校委派我负责 1977 年浙江省高考英语试卷命题和考试阅卷的工作。命题组由省教育学院郑恩岳、杭州外国语学校金韵和我组成，其中，我负责具体工作。在省高考办的领导下，我们严肃、认真、负责，合理、科学评估了本省中学英语教学现况、水平和高校招收英语专业学生的要求，按时完成了试卷命题任务。试卷有不同的题型，每种题型有不同的题材和难度、深度、广度：中等难度题约占 70%，符合一般录取线标准；大、小难度题各占约 15%，以求测出学生成绩的优劣，以便高校录取优秀、合格的学生。

1977 年我系英语专业招收约 130 人，完全符合试卷的实际要求标准，是 1959 年创系以来招收的最优秀的一届学生。他们分 9 个班，每班两个任课老师，我任该届一、二年级教学小组组长，负责一个班的教学、授课工作，任务繁重、艰巨，但在全组老师共同努力下，我们出色地完成了任务，向高年级输送了很多合格、优秀的学生，造就了很多优秀人才，留校的有殷企平、姚暨荣、王之光、黄天海等教授，在美国和联合国的有潘大安、唐可青、凌建平、陈依群、叶子南等教授或官员。我的教学工作得到了校系领导的肯定，于 1978 年 12 月被评为讲师，标志着我“读书为国”的贡献。

校系为了健全英语专业课程设置，全面提高教学质量，于 1982 年派我赴上海外国语学院进修美国 Full Bright Program 的美国历史，为期一年。一年中，我认真研读了 John M. Blum 的 *The National Experience*，Edmund S. Morgan 与 Willie Lee Rose 等人的 *An Outline of American History* 和 *Teaher's Guide to the Outline of American History & Selected Documents*。在学习期间，我写了一篇概括了美国政党发展历程的文章。该文阐述了美

国政党的成立、发展和演变，经历三个阶段，从 1789—1827 年的 Federalists vs Democrafic-Republicans，到 1828—1860 年的 Democrats vs National Republicans和 Whigs，再到 1860 年至今的 Democats vs Republicans（the Democratic Pary vs the Republican Party），与此同时，出现了 the Socialist Party, the Populist Party 等第三小党，因各党成员少、力量弱，都无法与民主党或共和党竞争，获得主政地位，但对美国两党制轮流执政产生了一定的社会影响和作用。如今美国两党制的社会制度既相互制约又相互监督和平衡，但无法协调统一美国各民族、各阶层和利益集团之间矛盾和斗争。这种两党制的社会制度并不是所谓的全世界最民主、最完美的社会制度。

我从事英语基础课教学 23 年（1960—1982）和美国概况教学 12 年（1984—1995），还有一年进修和一年延聘。在基础课的教学中，我重视语言与文学基本知识和基础理论及实践能力的培养，包括语音、语调、语法、词汇、写作和有关文学方面的基本知识及阅读能力。在美国概况课的教学中，我注意运用分析、批判的眼光，比较理性、客观地介绍美国的地理、历史、政治、经济、文化、教育等方面的概况，去其糟粕，取其精华，为我所用。我于 1986 年被中国教育工会杭州大学委员会评为“优秀工会积极分子”，并被授予奖状，又于 1988 年晋升为副教授，这是对我的专业水平、教学质量和科研成果做出的公平合理的评价和肯定，圆了我一个爱国华侨回国“读书为国”的梦。

（现将《英美概况》“美国概况”部分和其他论文作为本书第二部分内容，以供参阅。）

信仰和祖国

自1953年7月从罗湖桥跨进祖国大门时，我就感受到了祖国大家庭的温暖和可爱。从在杭州高级中学落脚至杭州大学毕业走向社会，我一直深受祖国、人民和党的关怀，因此我认定我的奋斗目标应是为祖国的社会主义事业奋斗终生，于是我在杭州高级中学的第二年（1954）就申请加入了中国共产主义青年团，直到1966年退团。身为一名团员，我一直遵守和履行中国共产主义青年团章程的宗旨，努力学好专业，锻炼好身体，修好思想道德品质，尽心尽力做好教学工作，在上山下乡劳动、军训和社会主义教育的社会实践中，培养并加深了工农兵劳动大众的思想感情，增强了为他们服务的决心和愿望，决心提出加入中国共产党的申请。经过近二十年的实践、锻炼和考验，我的世界观、人生观和价值观趋于成熟，终于在1981年被批准入党。随后，我遵守和履行党的章程，继续我余生的奋斗历程。

TRACKS Growth and Devotion of a Refurned Overseas Chinses Professor

第二部分 PART TWO

《英美概况》“美国概况”内容

Chapter 1
Brief Introduction to American Geography

Text

Ⅰ. Location and Area

The mainland of the United States lies in central North America with Canada to the north, Mexico to the south, the Atlantic Ocean to the east and the Pacific Ocean to the west. Alaska borders on northwestern Canada, and Hawaii lies in the central Pacific, 3 200 kilometers from the mainland. The continental United States stretches 4 500 kilometers from east to west, and 2 575 kilometers from north to south. Including the states of Alaska and Hawaii, the United States covers an area of 9 327 000 square kilometers and ranks the fourth largest country in the world. Compared with China, it is about 3. 7 million square miles smaller. (Russia is the largest country in the world and Canada comes the second.)

Ⅱ. *Physiographic Regions*[1]

Physiographically, the United States may be divided into six major geographic sections—*the Atlantic and Gulf Coastal Plain*[2], the Appalachian Highlands, the Central Lowlands, the Great Plains, *the Rockies and the*

Pacific Borderlands[3]. Although each of these regions has a great deal of uniformity, the geographic variety of the continental United States appears endless.

The Atlantic and Gulf Coastal Plain, or East Coast, is the lowland bordering the Atlantic seaboard of the United States from Maine in the north to Florida in the south. The plain is extremely narrow in the north but broad in the south. The northern part of the plain is rocky and barren and it is not good for farming. Owing to the stony soil and short growing seasons, early settlers *turned to other productive pursuits*[4], such as commerce, industry and fishing. The sea off the northern coast is one of the world's richest fishing grounds. It is rich in cod, lobsters and whales. In the south the broad coastal plain and fertile soil *lent itself to a plantation economy*[5]. It depended mainly on tobacco, cotton and indigo which drained the soil quickly, causing numerous problems. Though a diversified economy is developing today, there are still large farms with their dependence on the above staple crops. In the southeast there is a peninsula called Florida. The weather is usually good and there is plenty of rain, though sometimes there are big storms, which they call hurricanes in America. Citrus fruits such as oranges, lemons are grown well all the year round. Florida is a good place for merry-makers, the famous Miami Beach is the merry-making center. Besides, the John F. Kennedy Space Centre is located here. The Gulf states make up *the Cotton Belt*[6] where the climate is especially good for growing cotton. There are 180 days free from frost that kills the cotton.

In this area there are deep rivers and water bays which *provided excellent facilities for the building of shipyards, ports, cities and the development of industry, commerce, trades, transportation, etc*[7]. By the time of the American Revolution nine out of every ten Americans lived along this coastal plain. Here was England's frontier in North America and the eventual foundation for an American nation.

The Appalachian Highlands run in a southwesterly direction from

New England to central Georgia and include the Piedmont region east of *the Fall Line*[8] and two mountain chains—the Appalachians and Alleghenies on its west. In the north there are the Green Mountains of Vermont and the White Mountains of New Hampshire. The highest peak of the Appalachians is the Mount Mitchell(6 684 ft. in N. C.). Here is a region with fertile valleys and rich beds of coal, ore and deposits of petroleum. Pittsburg sprang up as the center of iron and steel industry in America. The Appalachian and Allegheny mountain chains prevented early settlers on the Atlantic plain from migrating westward. Eventually the colonial settlers found three trails—*the Wilderness Road, the Pennsylvania Road, and the National Road*[9] that gave them access into the Trans-Appalachian area and the Central Lowlands.

The Central Lowlands was the great interior valley of North America, known today as the Middle West. It stretches from the Appalachian Highlands on the east to the Great Plains on the west. During *the Ice Age*[10] glaciers flowed over North America and made the land almost flat with rich soil, abundant rainfall, making it an excellent agricultural area and *the Corn Belt*[11] of America. The glaciers also determined the size and drainage of the Great Lakes and changed the direction of the Missouri River. Water, timber and minerals combined to make the area an industrial center as well. The main artery of the region is the mighty Mississippi River, which cuts through the interior and provides a water highway. This river, along with its important branches, the Missouri and the Ohio, provided the pioneers with convenient waterways for transportation. This relatively flat area was quickly settled, but settlement slowed substantially at its western edge—the Great Plains.

The Great Plains, a semiarid belt, was an area long considered *unfit for cultivation and habitation*[12]. Neither could settlers survive themselves nor could crops be grown here. Over the years the view of the plains had changed little. But much of the area has been given over to wheat and corn, and even the arid high plains has been brought under cultivation by

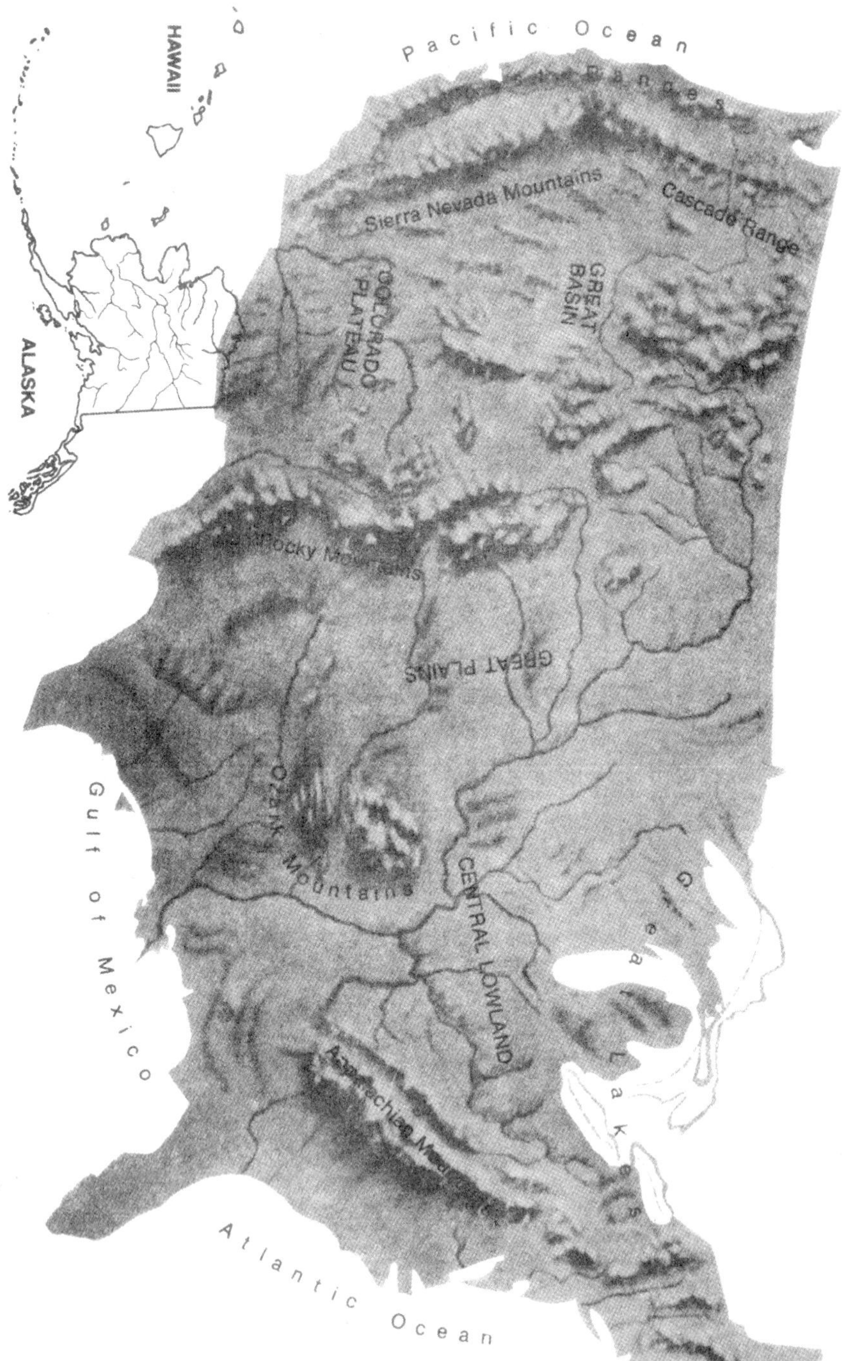
Pacific Ocean
Sierra Nevada Mountains
Cascade Range
GREAT BASIN
COLORADO PLATEAU
Rocky Mountains
GREAT PLAINS
Ozark Mountains
CENTRAL LOWLAND
Great Lakes
Gulf of Mexico
Atlantic Ocean
HAWAII
ALASKA

a process called "dry farming". Kansas leads the country in the production of wheat; cotton is the second important crop and corn the third. Life here, both animal and human, has been shaped by the lack of water. Found here also was *the "dust bowl" region*[13], where terrible wind storms literally removed the top soil overnight. Now it is *the land of sodhouses, cowboys and cattle drives*[14]—a land characterized by the deficiency of water.

The Rocky Mountains comprise the western border of the Great Plains and stretch from northern New Mexico through Canada into Alaska. The Rockies have been known as *the "Continental Divide"*[15], because all the rivers east of the Rockies flow into the Atlantic while those on the west flow into the Pacific. Like the Appalachian Highlands, the Rockies blocked further expansion in the west. But the Rockies were *a much mote forbidding barrier, with their rugged terrain and majestic peaks*[16] which can rise more than 14 000 feet above sea level. Pioneers spent much time and effort getting through them. Today, *interest in the Rockies centers on its mineral deposits and its vacation potential*[17]. The Rockies are rich in gold, copper, lead and silver. Bingham is the largest open-pit copper mining center in the United States.

The Pacific Borderlands stretch from the Rockies to the Pacific Ocean. This region is *a jumble of mountains, arid plateaus and basins with well-watered mountains and valleys*[18]. Between the Rocky Mountains and the Sierra Nevada and Cascade ranges are the Columbia and Colorado plateaus with extremes in temperature and few cities. Yet the natural landscape is panoramic, for example, the Grand Canyon of the Colorado River, one of the world's natural wonders, and Death Valley, the lowest point in the United States. Lying west of the Sierra Nevadas and Cascades is a series of coastal plains and valleys bordering the Pacific Coast. There are the Great Pacific Valley in the north and the Great Valley of California in the south. Here were built the important cities of the Far West, such as Los Angeles and San Francisco. Due to its location, the Pacific Borderlands is frequently looked upon as the last frontier, as well as the land of golden opportunity.

Alaska

Alaska was purchased from Russia in 1867 and admitted into the Union in 1959. It adjoins on northwestern Canada, and stretches from the Arctic Ocean to the Pacific. It is an area covered with ice masses with extremes in temperature. Though the midnight sun sets on Alaska from early May to early August, the sun can never melt the icy soil more than two-thirds of a meter down. In central Alaska, there are the Brooks Range and the Alaska Range, *where Mount McKinley*[19] rises 6 187 meters—the highest peak in North America.

Alaska is rich in coal, oil, copper, gold, fish and timber. It is becoming more and more important in America's economy.

Hawaii

Hawaii was annexed by the Americans in 1898 and admitted into the Union as the 50th state in 1959. It is made up of eight islands and over one hundred small islets, lying 3 200 kilometers out in the middle of the Pacific Ocean. Though it is located in the tropical zone, its climate is comfortable all the year round.

Of all the eight islands Hawaii is the biggest. but the best known is the third largest island called Oahu, where Honolulu, the capital and largest city of the state, is located, and Waikiki Beach is a world-famous scenic spot where people from all parts of the world go merry-making. Besides, Hawaii is famous for its pineapples.

Ⅲ. Climate

Climate in the Unite States *is affected by latitude, altitude, distance from oceans and winds*[20]. The size of the country, the variety of surface features and the great extent from north to south result in many different kinds of climate.

The climate varies from extremely cold in Alaska to semitropical in southern Florida and Hawaii. The coasts of Oregon and Washington are among the rainiest places in the world. The Mojave Desert in Arizona and California is one of the driest regions. The West Coast is affected by winds that blow inland from the Pacific, where temperature changes little between winter and summer. In some places, the average difference between July and January is as little as 10 degrees centigrade. But in the north central part of the country, summer and winter are worlds apart. The difference between July and January is 36 degrees centigrade and more violent extremes are common. The coldest January days may be 40 degrees centigrade below zero, and the hottest July days may rise to 45 degrees centigrade.

On the East Coast the climate is humid and continental. In New England states, it is cold and snowy in winter, and it is warm in summer. Near the Gulf of Mexico the climate is humid and subtropical.

The Central Basin is open to passage of air currents. Alternating north and south winds sweep over this region causing great changes in temperature. In the northern part of the region it is very cold in winter and hot in summer. In the southern part it is mild in winter and hot in summer.

One of the most important geographic boundaries in the United States is *the 50-centimeter rainfall line*[21], which runs north and south almost through the middle of the country. East of the line, there are more than 50 centimeters of rain falls annually; rain is plentiful and farming is relatively easy. West of the line, there are less than 50 centimeters of rain falls, and as little as 12.7 centimeters of rain falls annually. But in Oregon and Washington there are 250 centimeters of rain falls a year.

Ⅳ. Rivers and Lakes

The Mississippi River is one of the world's greatest rivers. It has been called the "Father of Waters". It has two major tributaries, the Ohio on its east and the Missouri on its west. Together with the Missouri, the Mississippi flows some 6 400 kilometers from the Rocky Mountains to the Gulf of Mexico. As it is very important to the life of the American people, there are many plays, stories and songs about life on the Mississippi.

Mark Twain *based on his rich experience as a pilot on the Mississippi his famous stories*[22], *The Adventures of Tom Sawyer*, *The Adventures of Huckleberry Finn* and *Life on the Mississippi*. *Old Man River* is a famous Negro folk song about the Mississippi.

The Rio Grande, about 3 200 kilometers long, forms a natural boundary between Mexico and the United States.

The Colorado is about 2 300 kilometers long. *It is enormously wild, restless and furious, cutting through deep desert rocks, and emptying into the Gulf of California.*[23] On the Colorado there is a magnificent, deep gorge called the Grand Canyon.

The Columbia rises in western Canada and continues in the United States for about 1 900 kilometers west of the Rocky Mountains.

The Yukon is another important river, flowing about 3 166 kilometers through Alaska into the Bering Sea.

The Hudson and the Potomac are well-known rivers to the east of the Appalachians. The Hudson, about 400 kilometers long, pours into the Atlantic Ocean at New York City, and the Potomac borders the national capital at Washington.

Note: 1. Missisippi; 2. Missouri; 3. Ohio; 4. Columbia; 5. Colorado; 6. Rio Grande; 7. Potomac; 8. Hudson; 9. Tennessee; 10. Lake Superior; 11. Lake Michigan; 12. Lake Huron; 13. Lake Erie; 14. Lake Ontario

North of the Central Basin, extending for about 1 600 kilometers are the five Great Lakes—Lake Superior, Lake Michigan, Lake Huron, Lake Erie and Lake Ontario, emptying into the St. Lawrence River. They are joined into the Mississippi River and the Hudson River, providing *the world's longest inland transportation waterway*[24]. Between Lake Erie and Lake Ontario lies *the Niagara Falls forming one of the natural wonders*[25].

Ⅴ. Population

The United States is a country made up of many ethnic groups originating from all parts of the world. It has a population of 250 million people.

Originally, the North American continent was inhabited by about eight million native Indians. Under colonialism, the Indians had a sad history. They were constantly threatened, robbed and driven off their lands and large numbers of them were killed. *The genocide of the Indians*[26] was completed in the 19th century, and the Indians were reduced to only about one million making up less than 0.5% of the country's population.

The first settlers arrived in the 17th and the 18th centuries from England and the Netherlands. They were *White Anglo-Saxon Protestants* (*WASPs*)[27] and even today they constitute the dominant ethnic group in America.

WASPs brought with them black slaves upon whom the South depended for production. The first group of blacks was brought to America in 1619. Now there are about 21 million black people, forming more than 12 percent of the population. And about 60 percent of black Americans live in big cities, such as Washington, New York, Chicago, etc.

In the 19th century arrived other ethnic groups from eastern and western Europe, such as *Irish peasants fleeing famine at home*, *political refugees from Germany*, *impoverished Italian tenant-farmers*[28], and in the early 20th century, large numbers of Eastern European *Jews forced by pogroms to leave their home countries*[29].

Because Mexico had owned vast region of the West and Southwest until the 1840s and the 1850s, large areas of the United States were originally settled by Spanish-speaking people known as *Hispanics*[30] (including Cubans and Puerto Ricans who speak Spanish). Since then they have been entering the United States both legally and illegally, and now constitute the second largest ethnic minority in the country.

The Chinese immigration began in the 18th century. They worked as coolies in the mines and on the building of railroads. They have always been a small community, numbering about one quarter of a million, to be exact, 236 000. They suffered most exploitation and oppression. Today most Chinese Americans live in California, New York and Hawaii.

In recent years there have been small but noticeable ethnic groups of Fillipinos, Koreans, Vietnamese, Laotians, Cambodians and overseas Chinese migrating into the United States.

In a word, the United States is made up of many ethnic groups coming from all parts of the world. Some historians today would rather call America a "tossed salad" than a "*melting pot*"[31].

Ⅵ. Principal Cities

1. *Washington D.C.*

Washington D.C. is the capital of the United States. It lies between Virginia and Maryland on the Potomac River. The city was carefully planned and built as a government city. Many of the buildings are government offices. The most important buildings are the Capitol where Congress meets, *the Pentagon*[32] where the Department of Defense has its offices and the White House where the President lives. It is the ninth largest city in the United States with a population of about 3 million people of which 60 percent are black.

2. *New York City*

After the Erie Canal was completed in 1825, New York quickly became the largest city in the United States. *It is made up of five boroughs—Manhaltan, Queens, Bronx, Richmond and Brooklyn with Manhattan as its heart*.[33] In the first place, it is a huge industrial city and seaport. New York is the center for money where Wall Street is known as the symbol of capitalism. It is also the center for the theatre, radio, television, advertising and newspapers. By the side of the East River stand the United Nations buildings. And in the harbor *stands the immense Statue of Liberty holding high her torch of freedom*[34].

3. *Chicago*

Chicago, on the southern end of Lake Michigan, is the second largest city in the United States with a population of about 3.5 million. It is a railway center, Great Lakes shipping center, a link between east and west, and *famous for stockyards and grain elevators and meat-packing industries*[35]. Nearby there are great steel-making cities. Chicago has had a stormy history *where originated the International Labour Day*[36].

4. *Los Angeles*

Los Angeles is the third largest city in the United States with a population of about 3 million. It is an important shipping and commercial centre in the Far West. Nearby there is Hollywood where motion pictures and many television shows are made.

5. *San Francisco*

San Francisco, a fine land-locked harbor, is an important commercial and trading seaport. Cargoes of fish, timber and fruit are shipped from here to the Orient countries. *Chinatown is the largest Chinese community in the United States*.[37]

6. *Philadelphia*

Philadelphia is the fourth largest city with a population of about 2 million people. It is the place where the Declaration of Independence and the Constitution were drawn up and signed.

7. *Boston*

Boston is the port that sent forth fishermen, whalers and ships that sailed the China seas. It was one of the first settlements and major cities and is the heart of the New England states. It is the largest leather, shoe and wool market in the United States.

8. *Detroit*

Detroit was the birth place of mass production of motor cars and today it is the headquarter of the country's car manufacture. *The famous Ford Company, General Motors and Chrysler are located here.*[38] It is interesting to note that more than half the population are black.

Ⅶ. Natural Resources

1. *Water*

Water has played a very important part in America's growth. In America there are many mighty rivers and great lakes. such as the Mississippi, the Missouri, the Ohio, the Hudson, the Colorado and the Great Lakes. These rivers and lakes have made possible not only the development of prosperous agriculture but also the development of many industrial bases. They have also been an important means of transportation since the earliest days. Today they provide large amounts of fresh water for city use, irrigation and the production of electric power. Besides, the United States has been actively developing practical ways to convert ocean water into fresh water.

2. *Forests*

About a third of the land area in the United States is covered with forests. Forests not only prevent the wearing away of soil and flooding but provide forest products of all kinds. There are 154 National Forests covering 187 million acres. They serve not only as areas for recreation but also protection of wildlife. In the West, more than 3 600 000 cattle, horses, swine, sheep and goats graze on the open lands of the National Forests.

3. *Metal and Minerals*

The nation's chief mineral resources are ore, coal, oil, gas, etc. The country produces about 100 million tons of iron and 200 000 iron and steel products a year for its manufacturing industries. Minnesota near Lake Superior is the largest ore-mining area, providing three-quarters of the ore. Coal is the second major mineral resource found in large quantities in the Appalachians, the Central Plains and the Rockies. There are sufficient reserves to last hundreds of years. Most of the coal is used by electric plants and chemical industries. Oil is third important, more than 370 million metric tons of petroleum are produced a year. The production, processing and marketing of petroleum products make up one of America's largest industries. Texas leads the country in oil production, next come the Gulf of Mexico and Alaska. Natural gas supplies more than 33 percent of the nation's power. Gas is carried by huge pipelines from oil or gas fields thousands of kilometers to cities and towns to heat homes and to service industries.

Other basic minerals mined on a large-scale are zinc, copper, gold, silver, and phosphate which is used for fertilizers.

Notes

1. physiographic regions

自然地理地区

2. the Atlantic and Gulf Coastal Plain

大西洋和墨西哥海湾沿岸平原

3. the Rockies and the Pacific Borderlands

落基山脉和太平洋沿岸边疆

4. turned to other pursuits

转向其他生产事业

turn to ... 转向

5. lent itself to a plantation economy

适宜于种植园经济

lend itself to ... 适宜于……

6. the cotton belt

棉花带 由南卡罗来纳、佐治亚、亚拉巴马、密西西比和路易斯安那等州组成。

7. ... provided excellent facilities for the building of shipyards, ports,

cities and the development of industry, commerce, trades, transportation, etc.

……为建造船坞、港口、城市和工、商、贸、运输的发展提供了优越的便利条件。

provide facilities for ... 为……提供便利条件

8. the Fall Line

瀑布线 源于此线以东的瀑布、河、川均流向大西洋。

9. the Wilderness Road, the Pennsylvania Road, and the National Road

荒野通道、宾夕法尼亚通道和国家通道 荒野通道,始于弗吉尼亚州的东北部,经过弗吉尼亚州、肯塔基州和田纳西州交界处的昆布兰山口(Cumberland Gap Pass),通往西南部;宾夕法尼亚通道,始于该州境内,沿着俄亥俄河进入西北部;国家通道,始于东海岸,沿着哈德逊河,经过伊利运河区进入西北部。

10. the Ice Age

冰河时代 约 10 000—25 000 年前。

11. the corn belt

玉米带 由俄亥俄、印第安纳、伊利诺伊和艾奥瓦等州组成。

12. unfit for cultivation and habitation

不适宜于耕作和居住

13. the"dust bowl"region

长期干旱和尘暴的地区

14. the land of sodhouses, cowboys and cattle drives

布满着草根泥房、牛仔和放牧羊群的大地

15. the"Continental Divide"

大陆分水岭 落基山脉以东的河川流向大西洋,以西的河川流向太平洋,可见落基山脉构成了北美大陆的分水岭。

16. a much more forbidding barrier, with their rugged terrain and majestic peaks

一个由崎岖不平的地形和雄伟壮观的山峰构成的屏障更加令人生畏,望而却步

17. interest in the Rockies centers on its mineral deposits and its vacation potential

对落基山脉的兴趣集中在它的丰富的矿藏资源和度假旅游潜力的开发利用

center on ... 集中于……

18. a jumble of mountains, arid plateaus and basins with well-watered mountains and valleys

一个由山脉、干旱高原和峡谷、山峦盆地所构成的复杂地质、地貌结构的地区

a jumble of ... 一个复杂的……

19. Mount McKinley

马金利山 北美洲最高峰

20. be affected by latitude, altitude, distance from oceans and winds

受纬度、高度、与海岸距离和风的影响

21. the 50-centimeter rainfall line

50厘米降雨线 此线大致从南到北穿过大平原和中央平原的分界线，线以东年降雨量多于50厘米，以西少于50厘米。

22. based on his rich experience ... his famous stories

在密西西比河当水手的丰富经历为基础创作了他的著名小说

（文中句子的结构为倒装）

base ... on ... 以……为基础

23. It is enormously wild, restless and furious, cutting through deep desert rocks, and emptying into the Gulf of California.

它（科罗拉多河）极其汹涌澎湃，波涛滚滚，穿过深山峡谷，直泻加利福尼亚海湾。

24. the world's longest inland transportation waterway

世界最长的内陆运输水路 始于纽约港，经哈德逊河、伊利运河、俄亥俄河和密西西比河等，直泻墨西哥湾。

25. the Niagara Falls forming one of the natural wonders

尼亚加拉瀑布形成自然奇观之一

26. the genocide of the Indians

对印第安人灭绝种族的大屠杀 在一个世纪里，印第安人自从在东部被英国殖民者剥夺土地，赶出家园之后，就一步一步地被赶往西部，

最后到达保留地，西南部最贫困的亚利桑那等州。途中，大量印第安人被害致死，由原来的约800万减少到约100万，这就是对印第安人灭绝种族的大屠杀。

27. White Anglo-Saxon Protestants(WASPs)

白人新教徒

28. Irish peasants fleeing famine at home, political refugees from Germany, impoverished Italian tenant-farmers

逃离家园饥荒的爱尔兰农民，来自德国的政治难民，陷入穷困的意大利佃农

29. Jews forced by pogroms to leave their home countries

由于大屠杀被迫离开他们本国的犹太人

30. Hispanics

讲西班牙语的民族　包括讲西班牙语的古巴人和波多黎各人。

31. melting pot

熔炉　指外国移民到达美国后逐步被同化为美国公民，所以称美国为熔炉。

32. the Pentagon

五角大楼　因大楼建筑为五角形而得名，为美国国防部所在地。

33. It is made up of five boroughs—Manhattan, Queens, Bronx, Richmond and Brooklyn with Manhattan as its heart.

它由以曼哈顿为中心的曼哈顿、皇后区、布朗克斯和里士满五个行政区组成。

34. stands the immense Statue of Liberty holding high her torch of freedom

直立着高举自由火炬的巨大的自由女神钢像

35. famous for stockyards and grain elevators and meat-packing industries

因牲畜围场、谷物仓库和肉类加工业而出名

36. where originated the International Labour Day.

国际劳动节发源于此地(芝加哥城)。

originate　发源于

37. Chinatown is the largest Chinese community in the United States.

唐人街是美国最大的华人社区。

38. The famous Ford Company, General Motors and Chrysler are located here.

著名的福特公司、大众汽车公司和克来斯勒公司坐落于此地(底特律)。

Exercises

Ⅰ. Fill in each blank with the right word or expression from the text:

1. Mount ________ is the highest peak in North America.
2. Of all the canyons in the United States, the best known is ________.
3. The United States has an area of ________ square kilometers and a population of ________.
4. New York is made up of five boroughs, namely, ________, ________, ________, ________ and ________.
5. The five Great Lakes are ________, ________, ________, ________ and ________.
6. The car-manufacturing center in the United States is ________.
7. The largest seaport in the United States is ________.
8. The city that is most important for meat-packing industry in the United States is ________.
9. The city where is located the headquarters of the Boeing Company is ________.
10. ________ is the center for motion pictures and television shows in the United States.
11. The Mississippi River is ________ kilometers from ________ to ________.
12. In the United States, the longest inland transportation waterway starts from ________, via ________, ________, ________, ________, ________ to ________.
13. The birth place of the International Labour Day is ________.
14. The birth place of jazz in the United States is ________.

Ⅱ. Questions for discussion:

1. What is the size of the United States? Where is its location?

2. What are the major geographic features of the United States?
3. What are the regions which the United States may be divided into? What are the special features of each region?
4. What is the climate like in America?
5. What is meant by the"50-centimeter rainfall line"?
6. What are the major mountain ranges, rivers and lakes in the United States? What do you know about them?
7. What does WASP stand for?
8. What are the major minorities in the United States?
9. What do you think are the most important cities in the United States? Why?
10. What are the important natural resources in the United States? Where are they deposited or produced?
11. What do you know about forests in the United States?

Chapter 2

The U. S. Constitution and U. S. Government

Text

The United States of America is a capitalist republic, whose political power belongs to monopoly capitalists. It is a federal union of 50 states. The District of Columbia is the seat of the national government. The form of the government is based on the Constitution adopted on September 17, 1787, which came into effect on March 4, 1789.

Ⅰ. The U. S. Constitution

The Constitution is the fundamental law of the state, reflecting the balance of forces within the country. It determines the social system of the state, the form of the government, the basic principles under which the state organs are to perform their functions, and the fundamental rights and obligations of the people.

The Federal Constitution consists of the Preamble, seven articles and twenty-six amendments, the first ten of them collectively called *the Bill of Rights*, and adopted under the popular pressure in 1791. The constitution outlines the framework of the national government, and specifies its powers and activities. The fundamental features of the Constitution are *the federal system and the"separation of powers"*[2].

1. *The Federal System*

The United States is a union of 50 states. There is a division of political power between two levels of government—state and national. The constitution says that all powers not granted to the central or federal government are to be kept by the individual state government. The central government is allowed to deal with problems that are national, such as general taxation, foreign affairs, foreign and interstate trade, the armed forces, postal service, coinage, weight and measures, etc.

These are *the delegated powers*[3]. The state government is left free to handle matters that are of local concern, such as raising taxes for state uses, regulating industry and commerce within a state, maintaining law and order, directing education, relief, transportation and communication, supervising local governments, etc. These powers are called *residual powers*[4]. And those that are exercised by both the state and national governments are called *concurrent powers*[5].

After the Civil War and especially during the 20th century there has been a steady rise in the influence and authority of the federal government. In order to push the policies at home and abroad, the ruling class has gradually strengthened the position of the federal government and assumed direct control.

The shift of power from the state to the central government is not only the result of the political ideologies and conspiracies, but is caused by the inexorable pressure of economic crises or depressions, new means of communication, urbanization, industrialization, technology and all other factors that have shrunk the size of the world and created problems so big and urgent that people have *thought fit to push them up to the nation level for handling*[6]. This shift of power is still growing today.

2. "*Separation of Powers*"

"Separation of Powers" means that the political power of the federal and state governments is divided into three branches: the executive, the legislative and the judiciary. Congress exercises the legislative power, the President the executive power, and the Supreme Court the judicial power. *This is a system of "check and balance" based on the theory of "separation of powers"*.[7] It is the power of Congress to make laws; it is the power of the President to exercise laws but he has a *veto*[8] on laws passed by Congress; and the Supreme Court is vested with the authority to declare a law to be constitutional or unconstitutional. Each branch has its respective power but each would be tied into the other two branches and share the power together with them, so that each tries to prevent any one of them from taking over the supreme power. Under this federal system, the central government acts on the people without going through the state government. The system of "check and balance" or the "separation of powers" is in essence a means of softening the conflicts within the ruling class.

Ⅱ. The U.S. Government

1. *The Executive Branch*

The Constitution vests the executive power in the President. It also provides for the office of Vice President, *who succeeds to the Presidency in case of the death, resignation or incapacitation of the President*[9]. The Constitution entrusts specific duties and powers to the President, but it does not specially delegate any such powers to the Vice President or any high-ranking officials.

In addition to the power of his succession, the Vice President is made the presiding officer of the Senate. An amendment adopted in 1967 describes the specific condition under which the Vice President is empowered to take over the office of President if the President should become incapacitated. It also provides that the President shall resume his office in the event of his recovery. In addition, the amendment enables the President to name a Vice President with congressional approval, when the second office is vacated.

The Constitution gives Congress the power to establish the order of succession after the Vice President. In the event that both the President and Vice President should vacate their offices, the Speaker of the House of Representatives would resume the Presidency. Next comes *the Presideut pro tempore of the Senate*[10] (a Senator elected by the Senate to preside in the absence of the Vice President), and then Cabinet officers in designated order.

The Constitution requires the President to be a native-born American citizen at least 35 years old and resident in the country for 14 years. Candidates for the Presidency are chosen by political parties several months (from June to August) before the presidential election is held every four years on the first Tuesday after the first Monday of November.

In the election, American citizens of each state do not actually vote directly for the President and Vice President. Instead, they elect Presidential electors, equal to the number of Senators and Representatives (respectively 100 and 435 members all told) which each state has in Congress. The electors of all 50 states and the District of Columbia—a total of 538 persons—comprise *the Electoral College*[11]. To be successful, a candidate for the Presidency must receive 270 votes. If no candidate has a majority, the election shall be made by the House of Representatives, with all members from a state voting as a unit; each state and the District of Columbia would be alloted one vote only.

The presidential term of office is four years beginning on January 20 following the November election. The President starts his official duties with an inauguration ceremony, traditionally held on the steps of the U.S. Capitol, where Congress meets. The President publicly takes an oath of office. After the oath-taking ceremony the new President makes an inauguration address, in which he outlines the policies and plans of his administration.

1) Presidential Powers

The office of the President of the United States enjoys the greatest power of the three branches. The Constitution says that the President must "protect the Constitution and *take care that the laws be faithfully executed*"[12]. To carry out his responsibility, he presides over the executive branch of the federal government, and in addition, he has important powers in legislative and judicial matters.

Being head of the executive branch, the President has broad powers to manage national affairs and the workings of the federal government. He can issue rules, regulations and instructions called executive orders, which have the binding force of law upon federal agencies. He is Commander-in-Chief of the armed forces of the United States, and may *call in federal service the state units of the National Guard*[13]. In times of war or national emergency, the President has even broader powers to manage the national economy and protect the security of the United States. He has the power to appoint the heads of all executive departments and agencies, together with hundreds of other high-ranking federal officials.

Under the Constitution, the President is the federal official primarily responsible for the relations of the United States with foreign nations. He appoints ambassadors, ministers and consuls, and receives foreign ambassadors and other public officials. He can send out "*personal agents*", "*special envoys*" or "*secret emissaries*"[14] on diplomatic missions without asking the approval of the Senate. With the help of the Secretary of State, he manages all official contacts with foreign governments. On occasion, he may personally *participate in summit conferences where chiefs of state meet for direct consultation*[15]. The President is empowered to negotiate treaties with other nations with the approval of two-thirds of the Senate or executive agreements without the consent of the Senate.

Despite the Constitutional provision that "all legislation powers" shall be vested in Congress, the Presideut as the chief policy-maker, has a major legislative role.[16] He can veto any bill passed by Congress, and unless two-thirds in each house vote to override the veto, the bill does not become law. Much of the legislation made by Congress is drafted or proposed by the executive branch. Every year the President makes a speech called *the State of the Union Message*[17] soon after Congress meets every year. In the message he outlines his general program and makes recommendations for legislation to carry out. He also delivers to Congress a Budget Message, an economic report and other special messages. Once the messages are discussed and approved by Congress, they become laws.

Besides, presidential powers are also felt in judiciary. A new President may appoint as many as thousands of officers to positions in the federal government and in the state. The most important officers are heads of all government departments, ambassadors and judges of the Supreme Court. Another significant power is that of *granting a full or conditional pardon to anyone convicted of breaking a federal law—except in a case of impeachment*[18]. This pardoning power includes the power to shorten prison terms and reduce fines.

2) The Executive Offices

The day-to-day enforcement and administration of federal laws is in the hands of the various executive departments created by Congress to deal with specific areas of national and international affairs. The heads of the departments, chosen by the President and approved by the Senate, form a council of advisers generally known as the Cabinet. In addition to 13 departments, there are a number of executive offices of the President. Such as the White House, the National Security Council, the Bureau of Management and Budget, the Office of Emergency Planning, etc.

The nucleus of the President's administration is the Cabinet made up of the heads of the major departments and other persons chosen by the President. They discuss and advise the President on important problems concerning the administration of national affairs. In addition, there is the National Security Council with the President as its chairman. It includes the Vice President, the Secretaries of State and Defense and a few other important persons chosen by the President. *The Central Intelligence Agency*[19] is under its control and provides necessary information for its work, which is to advise the President with respect to the integration of domestic, foreign and military policies relating to national security. *The Special Assistant to the President for the National Security Council*[20] is to help the President in this respect. This Council does not make decisions but give suggestions to the President. Once the suggestions are accepted by the President, they become policies of the government. Therefore the National Security Council is in a sense the highest policy-making body of the U.S. government. The President often calls a meeting of the Council rather than the Cabinet whenever a serious situation arises.

The White House serves the President in the performance of the many detailed routine activities. The staff of the office include Director of the White House, Press Secretary, Director for Communications, Assistant for Congressional Relations and other assistants and advisers. The various chief assistants to the President are his personal aides, who assist him in such matters as he may direct. One of the chief functions is to maintain communication with Congress, the individual Congressmen, the heads of the executive departments and agencies, the press and the general public. In short, these men are eyes, ears, monitors and advisers for the President.

The job of the President's office is to keep the President fully informed, to help him monitor the departments and agencies, to help develop his program, to help decide what he should do and what he should not do, to help decide what he should do first and what he should do next. In short, the Office offers the President the administrative means to be head of the government in fact as well as in name.

3) The Executive Departments

There are thirteen executive departments that are responsible to the Presidency. They are the Departments of State, Treasury, Defense, Justice, Interior, Agriculture, Commerce, Labour, Health and Human Services, Education, Housing and Urban Development, Transportation and Energy. Of these Departments, the Department of State, the Department of Treasury and the Department of Defense are most important.

The Department of State is headed by the Secretary of State, the highest-ranking executive officer next to the President and Vice President. He is the President's principal adviser on foreign affairs. The State Department helps maintain contacts and friendly relations and interests between the United States and foreign countries, supervise the foreign service of the United States, negotiate and enforce treaties and other agreements with foreign countries, issue passports to U. S. citizens or foreign visitors, protect foreign trade, commerce, American citizens and their property abroad.

The Secretary of the Treasury is the second-ranking Presidential Cabinet officer. The Treasury Department manages the financial affairs of the United States, collecting taxes, issuing bonds, paying the government's debts, supervising the issuance of money, and regulating international financial transactions. Besides, the Treasury Department has a wide range of other responsibilities. *The operation of the secret service is part of its work, such as the protection of the president*[21], Vice President and their families and other principal candidates for the Presidency and Vice Presidency.

The Department of Defense is made up of the Army, the Navy and the Air Force and the Joint Chiefs of staff. It is responsible for all matters relating to the nation's security, providing unified direction of the armed forces under civilian control. *The Joint Chiefs of Staff*[22] consists of the Chairman and the Chiefs of the Army, the Navy and the Air Force. The Pentagon is the location of the Headquarters of the U.S. Armed Forces.

2. *The Legislative Branch*

The legislative branch of the national government is *the Bicameral Congress*[23]. Its principal function is the making of laws. Congress is composed of two chambers, the Senate and the House of Representatives.

The Senate is composed of 100 members, two from each state, who are elected directly by the people to serve a term of 6 years in even-numbered years. Hence one-third of the Senators require reelection every two years.

The number of Representatives from each state is determined by population. At present, there is one Representative for about 480 000 people, but a state with a less population is entitled at least to one Representative. A large state is divided into the same number of congressional districts as that of Representatives it is entitled to, and a Representative is elected from the district he lives in. Now the total number of Representatives is

435. The membership of the House may be redistributed among the states to make it suit the changes in their population after a national census is made every ten years.

Both the Senators and the Representatives must be residents of the states from which they are chosen. In addition, a Senator must be at least 30 years old and a citizen of the United States for at least 9 years; a Representative must be at least 25 years old and a citizen for at least 7 years. No Senator or Representative can, during his service in Congress, be appointed to any office under authority of the U.S. and likewise no person holding any such office can be a member of either House during his continuance in office.

Congress is the highest law-making body of the U.S. government. It has the power to make whatever laws necessary and proper. Its chief powers are: to regulate commerce, both foreign and interstate; to coin money and protect the monetary system; to establish post offices and postal roads to the Supreme Court; to declare war; to raise and maintain an army and navy; to authorize the President to enforce federal laws. Congress may propose amendments to the Constitution but the amendments must be ratified by three-fourths of the state legislatures.

The Senate has the power to ratify all treaties with foreign countries by a two-thirds vote, and approve the President's appointments by a majority vote. In case the House *brings charges of impeachment*[24], the Senate sits as a jury to hear the evidence and determines the question of guilt. The Senate elects a Vice President in case the Electoral College fails to give any candidate a majority of the vote.

The House has the power to *propose revenue bills*[25]. The House has the power to propose impeachments against the President, Vice President and all civil officers of the U.S. government, but the impeachments should be tried by the Senate. The House has the power to elect the President in case the Electoral College fails to give any candidate a majority of the vote.

The business of Congress is done mostly in different committees. Congress meets at least once a year. The Vice President is the Chairman of the Senate. In his absence, a president pro tempore elected by the Senate takes over his duties. The House of Representatives elects its own Speaker.

In both houses there are a number of standing committees, such as Appropriations, Foreign Relations, Finance, Armed services, Judiciary, Agriculture and Forestry, Interstate and Foreign Commerce of the Senate and Appropriations, *Ways and Means*[26], Foreign Affairs, Interstate and Foreign Commerce and Government Operations of the House. They deal with foreign affairs, taxation, appropriations, armed services, banking and money, commerce, labor, government operations, and the law coutts.

Besides standing committees, there are special committees set up from time to time to investigate a certain matter both Houses are interested in.

The procedure of law-making is rather complicated. After a bill or a resolution is introduced, it is assigned to a standing committee for discussion. If it is favorably considered, the bill is reported to the Senate or the House in its original form or with amendments for debate. After a bill is passed in one House, it is sent to the other House to go through the same process. If differences over the bill occur in the two Houses, a joint committee may be formed to effect a compromise. After both Houses have finally approved it, the bill is signed by the Speaker or the Vice President, and then it is presented to the President, who should veto it or sign it within ten days. If he holds it for ten days without signing, it also becomes law when Congress remains in session. If he vetoes the bill, it cannot become a law unless it is passed by a two-thirds vote of both Houses.

3. *The Judicial Branch*

In the United States there are two systems of laws and courts, federal and state. Each is independent of the other. Federal courts enforce federal laws while state courts enforce state laws.

The Constitution says that the judicial power of the U.S. shall be vested in one supreme court, and in such lower courts as Congress may establish. All the judges are appointed by the President and confirmed by the Senate, they shall hold their offices during good behavior. The Supreme Court hears and decides cases arising under the Constitution, laws and treaties of the U.S.; cases relating to commerce between states; disputes in which the U.S. is involved; disputes between two and more states, or between citizens of different states. Other cases and disputes are heard and decided by state courts.

The Supreme Court is headed by *a Chief Justice and eight Associate Justices*[27]. They are appointed by the President with the consent of the Senate. The Supreme Court meets from October until June next year. All cases affecting ambassadors, ministers and consuls, and those in which a state is involved, can go straight to the Supreme Court. In other cases it acts as a court of final appeal. The decisions of the Supreme Court are final in all cases.

The Supreme Court has the power to interpret the Constitution and declare a law passed by Congress to be unconstitutional and unlawful. This law is known as *judicial review*[28].

The second highest level of the federal judiciary is made up of *the courts of appeals*[29], which facilitate the disposition of cases and ease the burden on the Supreme Court. The U.S. is divided into 11 separate appeal regions, each served by a court of appeal with three to fifteen judges. They review decisions of the district courts within their areas.

Below the courts of appeals are the district courts. The 50 states are divided into 89 districts so that cases may be decided and tried within easy reach. Additionally there is one district court in the District of Columbia and one in the Commonwealth of Puerto Rico.

The state courts have judicial power over all civil and criminal cases arising under state laws. The state court system is similar to the federal system to the extent that it also has a number of trial courts and intermediate courts, and a single court of last resort.

Ⅲ. Parties and Elections

1. *The Two-party System*

U.S. politics *has been characterized by a two-party system or a "spoils" system*[30]. The two major parties have ruled the country by turns since the founding of the United States.

Soon after the United States was born, two parties came into being. *The Federalists virtually took shape in 1782*[31] with Alexander Hamilton as its head representing the interests of the wealthy merchants, industrialists, businessmen, and the upper class. It favored a strong central government. *The Democratic Rupublicans*[32] was formed in 1796 under Thomas Jefferson making up an alliance between bourgeois democrats, small farmers and city workers representing the interests of the broad masses of workers and farmers, the southern slave-holders and the middle class in the North. It favored a decentralized democratic government. The Federalists dominated the country from 1789—1800 while the Democratic Republicans from 1800—1828.

By the time of Andrew Jackson (elected President in 1828), the Democratic Republican Party had become dominant and was named the Democratic Party in 1828. Meanwhile the Federalists had lost their strength and was disbanded in 1820. Many of its remnants joined the northern capitalists to form the Whig Party in 1836, which sought to reduce the presidential dower.

The Whigs won two presidential elections of 1840 and 1848. But it came to a steady decline, it was finally replaced by the Republican Party in 1854.

Meanwhile the Democratic Party had undergone a deep change. As a result of the planters' control over the party since the 1830s, the Democratic Party was no longer a party with a democratic tinge, but had become a tool of the slave owners. With its dominant position, in Congress and its successive victories in presidential elections, the party firmly stood for and wanted to extend the slave system throughout the country. On the eve of the Civil War, the Democratic Party was completely identified with the interests of the slave owners. This enraged the people and gave rise to a nationwide antislavery movement.

The northern capitalists saw the need for a new political organization capable of rallying the antislavery forces around itself so as to stop the Democratic advance. Thus the Republican Party came into being in July 1854. It absorbed most of the dissenters from the dying Whig Party. *The Free Soilers*[33], an agrarian party opposed to slavery, and many of the small farmers and workers who had broken from the Democratic Party also joined its ranks. On the eve of the Civil War, the Democratic Party and the Republican Party were the two major parties.

After the Civil War, the slave owners were defeated, slavery was put an end to and the Democratic Party was kept out of office for some seventy years except for two Democratic Presidents—Grover Cleveland (1884—1888, 1892—1896) and Woodrow Wilson (1912—1920). The economic depression from 1929—1933 caused widespread discontent among the American people with the governing Republican Party, and consequently, the Democratic Party won the election in 1932 with Franklin D. Roosevelt as the President. He led the Democrats with his "*New Deal*" *programme*[31] involving federal and state intervention in the economy and the beginnings of governmental social services. In the next forty years the Democrats pushed these policies further, particularly by Presidents Kennedy and Johnson. Hence the "welfare society".

The Republicans during the same period tend to be more conservative than the Democratic Party. They oppose too much government intervention in the economy; have little enthusiasm for new social programs; practise conservative foreign policies. But they maintain high responsibility of the individual and of state and local autonomy. This party is associated with free enterprise economy and is strongly supported in the rural and suburban areas of the North, the Middle West and the West.

The Democratic Party tends to protect the civil rights of the people so as to promote progress and freedom while the Republican Party tends to protect the ownership of property, business and wealth of the people so as to promote progress and freedom.

2. *Presidential Election*

Both Parties are election-oriented.[35] Party election is held every four years. In the election there are two stages, *primary and national convention*[36]. Primaries are statewide intraparty elections: their basic purpose is to give voters the opportunity to select directly their party's candidates for the presidency, vice presidency and various other offices. The national convention is held in summer several months before the general election. It has to work out the party's platform, a statement of the party's general policy, but its main job is to select a Presidential candidate. After the candidate is chosen, he is allowed to choose his *running mate*[37], a candidate for the Vice presidency. After the convention the whole party will help its candidates run the election all over the country. The general election is held on the first Tuesday after the first Monday of November in each election year. The President is elected by the Electoral College. Following the November general election the presidential inauguration ceremony takes place before the U.S. Capitol Building on January 20.

Notes

1. the Bill of Rights

《权利法案》

2. the federal system and the "separation of powers"

联邦制和"三权分立" 联邦制指美国中央政府和州政府两级，中央政府享有美国宪法赋予中央政府的权力，州政府享有美国宪法规定属于州政府的权力。

"三权分立"指中央和州政府均分设行政、立法和司法三个部门。

3. the delegated powers

赋予中央政府的权力

4. residual powers

属于州政府的权力

5. concurrent powers

归中央政府和州政府共同行使的权力

6. thought it fit to push them up to the nation level for handling

认为把这些问题提交中央政府处理是合适的

7. This is a system of "check and balance" based on the theory of "separation of powers".

这是一个以"三权分立"理论为基础的"制约和平衡"的制度。

... based on the theory of or on the basis of the theory of ...

以……理论为基础;在……的理论基础上

8. veto

否决权　指美国总统有权否决国会通过的任何议案

9. who succeeds to the Presidency in case of the death of ... of the President

假使总统死亡、辞职或不称职，他(副总统)继承总统职位

succeed to ...　继承……

in case of ...　假使……

10. the President pro tempore of the Senate

参议院的临时或代理主席

11. the Electoral College

选举团　美国总统和副总统由选举团选举产生，选举团由538名成员组成，其名额比例按参、众两院的人数名额选举产生，其余3名由华盛顿区选举产生。

12. take care that the laws be faithfully executed

谨慎地使法律得到忠实的贯彻执行

take care that ...　谨慎地;小心地

13. call in federal service the state units of the National Guard

征召州国民警卫队为联邦服役(文中句子结构为倒装)

call ... in the service of ...　征召……为……服役;号召……为……服务

14. "personal agents", "special envoys", or "secret emissaries"

"私人代表""特使"或"密使"

15. participate in summit conferences where chiefs of state meet for direct consultation

参加国家首脑会晤、直接磋商的最高级会议

16. Despite the Constitutional provision that "all legislation powers" shall be vested in Congress, the President as the chief policy-maker, has a major legislative role.

尽管美国宪法规定"一切立法权"归于国会，总统作为主要的政策制订者有重要的立法作用。

17. the State of the Union Message

国情咨文　总统每年向国会做一次国情咨文报告，提出执政纲领，并向立法部门推荐并予以贯彻执行。

18. granting a full or conditional pardon to anyone convicted of breaking a federal law—except in a case of impeachment

给予任何破坏联邦法律的犯罪分子，除非在被弹劾，全部或有条件的赦免

grant/give pardon to ...　给予……赦免

19. the Central Intelligence Agency

中央情报局　直辖于国家安全委员会，并为其提供信息情报和决策。

20. the Special Assistant to the President for the National Security Council

国家安全委员会总统特别助理

21. The operation of the secret service is part of its work, such as the protection of the President.

秘密保安工作的运作是财政部的工作之一，如总统的安全保卫工作。

22. the Joint Chiefs of Staff

参谋长联席会议　由陆、海、空三军司令和会议主席组成，负责国防安全和三军的统一指挥。

23. the Bicameral Congress

两院制国会　由参议院和众议院组成。

24. bring charges of impeachment

提出弹劾指控

25. propose revenue bills

提出税收议案

26. Ways and Means

赋税委员会(议会中的)

27. a Chief Justice and eight Associate Justices

一位首席法官和八位副首席法官

28. judicial review

司法审查　法院审查法律是否符合宪法，政府官员行为是否违反宪法。

29. the courts of appeals

上诉法院　美国全国分11个区，各设一个上诉法院，以便于案件的分布并减轻最高法院的负担。

30. has been characterized by a two-party system or a"spoils"system

以两党制或政党分赃制为特征

be characterized by ...　以……为特征

31. The Federalists virtually took shape in 1782 ...

联邦制拥护者或联邦党实际上在1782年形成……　主张建立一个坚强的中央联邦政府，优先发展工、商业。

take shape　形成

32. the Democratic Republicans

民主共和党人或民主共和党人　主张建立一个非中央集权的民主政府，维护州权，优先发展农业。

33. the Free Soilers

自由土地者(为农民组织的政党)　主张民主改革，争取土地自由。

34. "New Deal" programme

"新政"纲领　于1932年罗斯福总统上任后提出并经国会批准的一系列法令和政策，以解决经济大萧条的危机，这些法令和政策统称"新政"。

35. Both parties are election-oriented.

两党都以选举为目标。　两党的目标就是竞选总统和副总统，一旦总统和副总统由选举产生，两党就停止活动。

36. primary and national convention

初选和全国选举　各党的总统候选人先由各党在各州初选产生，后参加该党的全国选举产生该党的总统候选人。

37. running mate

竞选伙伴　由各党的总统候选人选为参加竞选的副总统候选人。

Exercises

Ⅰ. Fill in each blank with the right word or expression from the text:

1. The two fundamental features of the U. S. constitution are ________ and ________.
2. The principal function of the U.S. Congress is ________.
3. The power of the President to reject a bill passed by Congress is called ________.
4. Cases of impeachment are proposed by the ________, but are heard and decided by the ________.
5. In 1791, Congress adopted the first ten amendments to the Constitution known as ________.
6. The two major parties of the United States are ________ symbolized by ________, and ________ symbolized by ________.
7. The power to declare federal and state laws and actions unconstitutional is known as ________.
8. In case the Electoral College fails to give any candidate a majority of the vote, the President is elected by ________, and the Vice President by ________.
9. The Federalists represented the interests of ________ in favour of a ________ government and the prior development of ________ while the Democratic Republicans represented the interests of ________ in favour of a ________ government and the prior development of ________.
10. The U. S. Constitution provides an elaborate system of ________ based on the theory of ________.
11. The U.S. Congress is composed of ________ with ________ determined by ________ and ________ with ________ determined by ________.

Ⅱ. Questions for discussion:

1. Why is the U. S. Constitution the fundamental law of the United

States?

2. What is meant by "separation of power"?
3. What are the prescribed qualifications for the President? What powers does the President have?
4. What are the main executive offices directly responsible for the President? In what ways are they responsible for the President?
5. How many executive departments are there in the federal government? What do you think are the most important departments? Why?
6. What does Congress consist of? How is each house formed? What requirements must a Senator or a Representative meet? What are the main powers of each house?
7. What is meant by judicial review?
8. What is the federal court system?
9. What is meant by the two-party system or the "spoils" system in the United States?
10. How is the U.S. President elected?

Chapter 3

American Education

Text

Americans are well aware of their commitment to education.[1] It can be traced back to the early colonial days. As soon as the Puritans settled along the New England coast, they "recognized the importance of schools as agents of religion and made their central purpose knowledge of the word of God", and they were determined that their children should receive sufficient education to read the Bible and participate in religious services. As early as 1635, the first formal educational institution, the Boston Latin School, was established in Massachusetts. A year later, the first college, Harvard College was founded to "advance the learning and perpetuate it to posterity".

In 1647 the Massachusetts General Court enacted *the Old Deluder Satan Law*[2] requiring every town of 50 households to support an elementary school and every 100 households to set up a grammar school to prepare youth for the university. The compulsory and equalized taxation of all for all town charges laid down the foundation on which the American system of public education has been based.

No sooner was the new republic born than the Founding Fathers were fully aware of the indispensable role of education in a free nation. They had thought of establishing a national university. Thomas Jefferson said in 1816 "If a nation expects to be ignorant and free, in a state of civilization, it expects what never was and never will be". Since then education has been accepted as a primary requisite of a free nation.

The Industrial Revolution in the 19th century had far-reaching effects on American education. More institutions were founded and the range of education was widened. In addition to religion and the classics, practical subjects were conducted not only in Greek, Latin, English, history and writing, but also in mathematics, science, gardening, agriculture, commerce, drawing and bookkeeping, etc. The first mechanic's institute was set up in Boston in 1745. Colleges like Harvard and Yale also added applied science to their curricula. The continuous development in industry and technology gave a stimulus to the steady development of education both in quantity and in quality for strengthening further American commitment to education.

New demands were made on education when millions of immigrants poured into the United States from all over the world, bringing with them their own culture, customs and values. How to "*Americanize*"[3] them became a problem of serious concern. Education was to be the means by which the immigrants and their children would be Americanized. Now they became Americans having the common ways of life, the same language, English, and the same nationality. Hence the melting pot of the United States.

Massive immigration further consolidated their commitment in another way. Most immigrants came to "the land of opportunity" with little means to start a new life. Besides hard work, they depended on education for success. A good education would open vast opportunities in life. Many did climb out of the abyss of poverty and others reached their heights in society. Their success stories in turn encouraged enthusiasm for education. This attitude towards education has greatly influenced the whole nation. Today Americans believe that their prospects of success in life depend on their education more than on any other single factor. So there is an ever-increasing demand for educational opportunities. At the same time, it is generally recognized that even from the material point of view economic development up till now has owed much to the skills and abilities which grow through education, and for the traditional Americans, *respect for learning is reinforced by a doctrine that it is an investment that brings the community an economic return as well as social and cultural improvement*[4].

The central government does not provide a federal system except for some basic rules. *Constitutionally, education is the responsibility of each state*.[5] Usually a state has a state board of education whose members are either appointed by the governor or elected, a state superintendent of schools appointed by the board, and a state department of education. Though, in the final analysis, the local school communities have the highest say in decision-making in education, "most states now have regulations and standards regarding most aspects of operations, such as courses of study, textbooks, teacher certificates, compulsory attendance of pupils, length of the school term, the school census, transportation of pupils, health of pupils, school architecture and the auditing of funds."

At the local school community, the school board controls educational policy and performs other related functions. It also appoints a superintendent who administers school affairs. In recent years, school communities have been consolidated to improve the teaching quality and teaching facilities.

Every elementary and secondary school is administered by a professionally trained principal. The Parent-Teacher Association (PTA) assists in the administration and frequently lobbies for specific issues, such as busing and school expenditure. Colleges and universities are governed by boards composed of private citizens who are not professional educators, while the daily administration is the responsibility of the president or chancellor.

Closely linked with administration is financing. *In the United States, public schools are supported mainly by states and local communities out of property taxes*.[6] This has resulted in the vast difference in the amount of funds available to schools in different neighborhoods and consequently the difference in quality of schools between schools both in facilities and in quality. Since the late 1950s, the federal government has been following a policy of increasing its financial contribution to education, providing free lunch, textbooks, library materials, special training, research programs and various kinds of educational aid. The National Defence Education Act of 1958 enabled students to borrow money to help with their expenses, provided that they needed the money and had a good academic record after a period of study. The Higher Education Act of 1965 was an important new development, allowing students to receive loans in their first year at college, on the basis of need alone. Students may take up to eleven years to repay the loans, though those who themselves become teachers in public schools only have to repay a portion of the loan. Those who teach in depressed areas are specially favoured and each year of the depressed area teaching wipes out fifteen percent of the loan received.

School education in the United States can be divided into three stages—elementary, secondary and higher education.

Elementary education begins at the age of five or six and ends at the age of 11 or 12. At this level most teachers are women. Pupils learn spelling, reading, writing, arithmetic, history, geography, music, drawing, etc. Besides this travel and sports are much emphasized. For the sake of pupils' schooling, a "School Bus" system has been established. The school bus travels along a fixed route picking up pupils at prefixed points in the morning and unloading them in the afternoon.

Secondary education is conducted by high schools or secondary schools. This high school is further divided into three years of senior high school and three years of junior high school, ending at the age of 17 or 18. At a comprehensive high school, its major objectives as James Bryand Conant says in "The American High School Today" are: "firstly, to provide a general education for all the future citizens; secondly, to provide good elective programs for those who wish to use their acquired skills immediately on graduation; thirdly, to provide satisfactory programs for those whose vocations will depend on their subsequent education in a college or university." The comprehensiveness naturally varies from school to school depending on the community where the school is located. A high school in a wealthy suburban neighborhood will certainly emphasize the academic programs to prepare its pupils for college, while *one in a black ghetto will have more vocational training*[7]. In some cities there are special schools for handicapped children, vocational training and special subjects such as art and music.

In addition to public schools, there are schools run and operated by the Catholic Church and some other religious denominations where the churches can preach God's teaching and train clergymen, because the U.S. Constitution prohibits the teaching of religion in public schools.

The best of the elementary and high schools are the expensive, private boarding schools, also called "prep" schools.[8] They are financed by the rich who want to prepare their children for the best universities. These schools have extremely good equipment and better qualified teachers, but the number of this kind of schools is very small.

Extracurricular activities are an important part of high school life. Students organize various clubs and societies. There are orchestras and brass bands. Sports are especially popular. Almost every high school has a football team, a basketball team, a baseball team and others. Students are encouraged to participate in all kinds of physical and recreational activities.

The higher education in America is done at universities or colleges. The difference between them is that a university includes a number of colleges. Even colleges are divided into two kinds. In addition to large colleges run by the state or big cities, which provide four-year degrees, there are colleges run by smaller cities and counties. These colleges award two-year degrees in vocational training such as computer programming, hotel and restaurant management, or practical nursing. Now there is a strong tendency for two-year colleges to become four-year colleges, because the demand for skill and knowledge has become greater with the development of science and technology.

Different states run their own state universities. These universities are founded by the state and no admission examination is required for the residents within the state. They grant both undergraduate and graduate degrees. A state university may include different schools, such as schools of medicine, law or business management. This often makes a state university rather large. The University of California, for example, has 9 separate campuses and tens of thousands of students. The best known of them are at Los Angeles and Berkeley. *Berkeley is near San Francisco and is famous for the number of the Nobel Prize winners among its teachers.*[9] Many students from Asia, including China, are studying here.

Most prestigious of all are the older, private *Ivy League*[10] schools such as Harvard, in Cambridge near Boston, Yale, in New Haven which is between New York and Boston, Princeton, in New Jersey, and Columbia, in New York City. Since these universities are private ones and do not enjoy tax support, students have to pay a high tuition, which may amount to several thousand dollars for each student each year. It is almost beyond the reach of common American families. Good marks are also very important for entrance into these universities. Since they enjoy high prestige and have better qualified professors and extremely good equipment, many American youth are eager to contest for admission.

A university student must attend a certain number of courses. In his first year (as a freshman) and second year (as a sophomore), he usually takes courses in a wide range of subjects. In his third (junior) and fourth (senior) years, a student may specialize in his main subject. A typical course consists of 3 classes per week for one semester (a half year term). *A bachelor's degree*[11] requires about 36 courses, each lasting one semester. For every course that he takes a student is given certain credits. When his credits amount to the required number, he gets a bachelor's degree. That's about four years' study at university. Higher degrees require further study.

Because most American universities do not have entrance examination, the first two years in a college or university are looked on as a trial period during which students must study a certain number of compulsory subjects and reach a certain scholastic level. If a student fails to do so, he may be dismissed unless he finds a way to repeat the courses. In a big university there may be several thousand students taking a compulsory subject at the same time. They have to be divided into several classes. This also makes it desirable to employ closed-circuit and two-way television techniques. Students hardly know their professors well since it is the teaching assistant who answers their questions and marks their exam pagers.

In the third and fourth years, a student may devote himself to an intensive study of his special field. He usually consults his teachers on his choice, but he has also to take a look at the labour market. Many students choose to study medicine, law, veterinary science or engineering, because these professions are among the highest paid in America. It usually takes four years to complete the courses required for a Bachelor of Arts or Bachelor of Science (B. A.) degree. A *Master of Arts or Master of Science (M. A.) degree*[12] needs one or two additional years of study. *The highest academic degree is the Doctor of Philosophy (Ph. D.).*[13] It may take any number of years to complete the original research work necessary to obtain this degree.

American universities normally honour class discussion. In preparation for each class, the class teacher first asks his students to read several pages. Then in the following class students may put their questions to the teacher for explanation. Students are usually quite ready to give their opinion on any subject.

College students have their residence halls which were called dormitories in the past. But many of them do not live in their school. Meals are provided in students' cafeteria-type campus restaurants where the food is usually cheaper than outside. Authorities concerned see to it that the food be up to the required quality.

It has always been common for American students to earn money, not only in vacations but also by doing odd jobs during term-time. Some of them work for the college, such as in the library or restaurants, others work outside, such as in a supermarket as porters. Not only the poor, even the rich also do this. No one will look down upon it and nearly all of them feel proud of the money they earn. Some students may borrow money from the Federal Government. They are allowed to take up to 11 years to pay the loan.

Disciplines in universities are not strict. It certainly does not mean there are no hard-working students in America. Since a student's grades in college are likely to be examined by his prospective employers, he is almost always conscious of the need for good marks. The normal scene is that they are extremely busy on week-days, with few going outside for pleasure or shopping, but at weekends, almost all of them become lost in seeking pleasure.

In addition to the various two-year course colleges and special schools, America has more than 2 000 universities and other such institutions. There are some 11 million students studying in various colleges and universities. They make up half of American youth. By law, all American youth have the right to receive higher education, but serious inequality still exists. The blacks have the lowest proportion to the black population. Among the whites, families with a higher income are more likely to send their children to university than the families with a lower income. What is remarkable is that the Chinese Americans have the highest level of education in America, higher than that of the whites.

America as a whole shows much respect for education, although teachers are not among the highest-paid in the country. All traffic, for example, has to stop and make way for school buses which are carrying pupils from their homes to schools. *Many Americans regard education as the only way to ensure national defence and solve scientific problems which affect the development of modern society.*[14] A public survey in 1973 showed that about 68 percent of the American adults picked out attributed U.S. influence in the world to its technological know-how and scientific creativity. About 92% of the public agreed with the statement "technological know-how is largely responsible for the standard of living in the U.S.". Physicians and scientists received the highest degree of confidence from a cross section of the public in a 1980 study. About 60% of the Americans want their government to spend much money on research and development. The successful launching of the first man-made satellite by the Russians in 1957 produced a great shock to the Americans. They were worried to see that the Russians were equalling or even surpassing them in certain fields. America thus raised their total public expenditure on education from 25 billion in 1960 to 120 billion dollars in 1975. Some universities have top class research centers.

American education faces some problems. More and more wealthy people are moving to the suburbs. The inner areas of big cities are left to the poor and this leads to the poor conditions of the schools there. Juvenile delinquency has become more disturbing. Children are spending more and more time watching television which is full of crime, violence and pornography. Some students even take drugs. Inflation has made it harder for many students to go on to university. Some professors are more interested in research than in teaching. To have all the students of different academic records in the same class can be a cost to efficiency. Many Americans complain that "equal opportunity for all" in education is being interpreted to mean "the same education for all" regardless of differences in ability and need of the students. American society places a great stress on college education as the pathway to success in business. It is true that American education requires students to develop the mind rather than memorize mere facts, but the problem of what courses are more relevant or useful in the students' future work is still under debate. It is not easy to solve all these problems satisfactorily.

Notes

1. Americans are well aware of their commitment to education.

美国人民对教育所承担的义务认识很深刻。

2. the Old Deluder Satan Law

老骗子撒旦法　1647年由马萨诸塞议会颁布，它要求每50户的镇或市区设立一所小学，每百户的镇或市区建立一所语法学校为大学培养学生，这种城镇主管的义务和平摊的税收为美国公立教育体系奠定了基础。

3."Americanize"

"美国化" 指美国人民如何用他们的政治、思想、文化、习惯和价值观等来教育、同化外国移民，使他们成为美国公民。

4. respect for learning is reinforced by a doctrine that it is an investment that brings the community an economic return as well as social and cultural improvement

尊重学习受到一种思想的推动，即教育是一种给社会带来经济和社会、文化进步的投资

5. Constitutionally, education is the responsibility of each state.

宪法规定教育是每个州的责任。

6. In the United States, public schools are supported mainly by states and local communities out of property taxes.

在美国，公立学校主要靠州和地方社团公众财产的税收来支持。

7. one in a black ghetto will have more vocational training

在黑人区的学校要进行更多的技术训练

ghetto 为城市中少数民族集中的居住区，故有黑人区(black ghetto)，犹太人区(Jewish ghetto)，华人区(Chinese ghetto)等。

8. The best of the elementary and high schools are the expensive, private boarding schools, also called "prep" schools.

中小学中最好的学校是费用昂贵的私立寄宿学校，又叫"学龄前或入学前"学校。 这些学校由富人赞助，为培养他们的子女成为一流大学的学生。

9. Berkeley is near San Francisco and is famous for the number of the Nobel Prize winners among its teachers.

加州大学伯克利分校靠近旧金山，因教员中诺贝尔奖获得者人数之多而著名。

10. Ivy League

常青藤联合会 由美国最古老的、最有声望的私立大学组成，如波士顿近邻剑桥的哈佛大学，在纽约和波士顿之间新哈芬的耶鲁大学，在新泽西的普林斯顿大学和在纽约城的哥伦比亚大学。

11. a bachelor's degree

学士学位　要取得该学位要修完约36门课程。

12. Master of Arts or Master of Science degree (M. A. or M. S.)

文学硕士或理科硕士　取得这种学位要修一至二年的课程。

13. The highest academic degree is the Doctor of Philosophy (Ph. D.).

最高的学位是博士。　获得该学位需要几年的时间完成原先的研究工作。

14. Many Americans regard education as the only way to ensure national defence and solve scientific problems which affect the development of modern society.

很多美国人把教育看作保障国防安全、解决影响现代社会发展的科学问题的唯一途径。

Exercises

Ⅰ. Fill in each blank with the right word or expression from the text:

1. The earliest college founded in the United States was ________.
2. Americans believe that their prospects of success in life depend on their ________ more than on any single factor.
3. School education in the United States can be divided into three stages: ________, ________ and ________.
4. Elementary education begins at the age of ________ or ________ and ends at the age of ________ or ________, and secondary education ends at the age of ________ or ________.
5. The higher education in America is done at ________ or ________.
6. Ivy League is mainly composed of ________, ________, ________ and ________.
7. A first-year university student is known as ________, a second-year one as ________, a third-year one as ________, a fourth-year one as ________.
8. A university normally offers the degrees of ________, ________ and ________.
9. American universities normally honor ________ in class.

Ⅱ. Questions for discussion:

1. Give a brief account of the development of education in American history.
   Describe its principal purposes in different historical stages.
2. What is Americans' attitude toward education?
3. What is the elementary and secondary educational system in the United States?
4. How is a local elementary or secondary school administered? How is it financed?
5. Into what stages can school education be divided and how is higher education conducted in the United States?
6. What are the most important ways of study and life at college or university in the United States?

Chapter 4
The Press

Text

The press is an important means of communication, and its function is taken very seriously. Many universities provide courses in journalism, and the journalist is usually a graduate with special training in the duties of the newspaperman to inform the public, to offer reasoned argument and comment without distortion of facts, and to offer honest guidance. The press provides the U.S. people and the world people with news and information from the United States and from the world.

The United States is so large that no single newspaper can compete on a nation-wide basis against local newspapers. As a result, America has about 1 700 newspapers. Usually people buy newspapers printed in their own state. There are some important newspapers which can be regarded as something like national newspapers.

The most important newspaper is *The New York Times*[1], which is sold all over the United States, especially to the upper or upper-middle class. *The New York Times* has a reputation for its serious attitude and great bulk. Its Sunday edition may be over 200 pages. The reader has to select what he needs.

Another important newspaper is *The Washington Post*[2] often quoted, but it cannot be regarded as a single means of expression covering the nation as a whole.

Some other important newspapers are *The Wall Street Journal*, *New York Daily News*, *The Christian Science Monitor*, *and Los Angeles Times*[3].

Two genuinely "national" weekly journals of information and opinion, *Newsweek* and *Time*[4], are important throughout the United States and indeed all over the world. *U. S. News & World Report*[5] is also well known to the country.

Reader's Digest and *Playboy*[6] are monthly.

The press in the United States is particularly important because it is recognized as having a responsible role to perform in relation to one aspect of the process of government.[7] *The press conference*[8] is an American invention, and it began to be important in the form of a meeting between President and journalists in which the President replied to questions. Press conferences take place all over the world now, but the presidential press conference is an institution which gives the U.S. a key to the special role America assigns to the press and to the newspapermen. The British Parliament has its question time when each day Members of Parliament address questions to ministers in charge of executive department, and some European parliaments have something of the same kind. There is no possibility of such device in the United States Congress because heads of executive departments are not members of it. Thus the executive has no political platform through which to expound its views and give information. President Franklin D. Roosevelt showed the advantages of using the press for such purposes when he called regular meetings of newspapermen at which he invited questions.

This device is still regularly used, and although the press has no formally recognized role one cannot give a broad picture of the American governmental process without mentioning the part that the press has to play in its contacts with the President. A newspaperman attending the presidential press conference is there not just as an employee of the newspaper for which he works, but as a representative of the American public entrusted with the task of conveying information; his role in doing this has a real significance in the democratic political process. The same could be said of press conferences involving heads of departments or visiting foreign statesmen or people in the news. The American scene would be unimaginable without these occasions. The press conference has become an institution and an indispensable element in the world system of public communication.

The American newspaperman's public responsibility goes beyond the reporting of political facts, beyond even comment on the facts. His role becomes heroic when he discovers crimes about which the police knew nothing, and more still when he produces evidence of corruption or misbehavior by police officials. However democratic the electoral process, there have been many local officials who have made themselves rich by scandalous means, and a journalist *who finds out the discreditable truth, relentlessly pressing his inquiries and courageously publishing the results in the face of wicked menaces, expresses one of the highest ideals that the press sets before itself*[9]. And the press as a whole deserves some credit for the marvellous openness of public life, which is one of the special features of American democracy. Many things which in other countries are hidden away are quickly made known in America. That is partly due to the dedication of the press to its task, together with the prestige that it has earned as a protector of the public interest.

Investigative journalism had its greatest triumph with the unravelling of *the whole Watergate affair*[10]. Journalists worked relentlessly to produce proof that there was something suspicious about *the handling of this petty break-in without theft*[11]. It was their persistence which led to the formal inquiry by a congressional committee, and to the gradual uncovering of evidence that Nixon's closest advisers, and even the President himself, had not behaved in accordance with the highest standards. Yet this journalistic triumph also ensured that for some months together America was without a proper government. It led to the destruction of a President who, for all his faults, had been both successful and endorsed by the people for his success. An immediate effect was the replacement of Nixon by Ford for two and a half years; its less immediate effect was the humiliation of America in the world, together with an unprecedented decline in America's confidence in itself.

The journalists' achievement was spectacular. It perhaps ensured that future Presidents would behave more "decently" than Nixon. They gained their triumph without risk of persecution; that is to America's credit. That's why the press in the United States is particularly important.

Notes

1. *The New York Times*

《纽约时报》

2. *The Washington Post*

《华盛顿邮报》

3. *The Wall Street Journal*, *New York Daily News*, *The Christian Science Monitor*, *Los Angeles Times*

《华尔街日报》《纽约每日新闻》《基督教科学箴言报》《洛杉矶时报》

4. *Newsweek* and *Time*

《新闻周刊》和《时代周刊》

5. *U.S. News & World Report*

《美国新闻与世界报道》

6. *Reader's Digest* and *Playboy*

《读者文摘》和《花花公子》

7. The press in the United States is particularly important ... to one aspect of the process of government.

在美国，新闻尤其重要，因为它被认为在与政府工作进程方面有关的运作中负有责任。

8. the press conference

记者招待会

9. who finds out the discreditable truth, relentlessly pressing his inquiries and courageously publishing the results in the face of wicked menaces, express one of the highest ideas that the press sets before itself

记者在发现不可信的问题时，坚持不懈地进行调查，面对凶恶的恐吓勇敢地公布结果，体现了新闻界自身树立的崇高理想

10. the whole Watergate affair

整个水门事件

11. the handling of this petty break-in without theft

处理这种卑劣的非盗窃的破门而入行为　意指白宫内部卑劣的窃听行为。

Exercises

Ⅰ. Fill in each blank with the right word or expression from the test:

1. The two most important newspapers in the United States are ________ and ________.
2. Two genuinely "national" weekly journals in the United States are ________ and ________.
3. The most popular U.S. monthly journal to the Chinese readers is ________.
4. The press conference is the form of a meeting between ________ and ________.

Ⅱ. Questions for discussion:

1. What is the press? What is its role in the United States?
2. What are the most popular newspapers and weekly journals in the United States?
3. What is the press conference? Why has it become an institution and an indispensable element in the world system of public communication?
4. Why is the press particularly important in the United States?

Chapter 5
Transportation

Text

The United States has one of the most highly developed transportation systems in the world. It can be said that there is no part of the country that is not easily accessible by car, by train, or by air, and more often than not by all the three of them.

The transportation revolution began at the beginning of the nineteenth century in the United States. Private companies started to build toll roads called *turnpikes*[1]. By 1830, the milage had reached 27 800. The federal government also joined in the effort. In 1806, Congress authorized the building of the National Road from Cumberland on the Potomac, Maryland to Wheeling on the Ohio, Virginia, and then it was extended to Vandalia, Illinois.

However, by the 1830s, canals overtook turnpikes. The Erie Canal was completed in 1825 and became the major waterway that linked Lake Erie to the Atlantic Ocean. After the Erie-Ohio Canal was constructed, a complete waterway starting from New York City through the Hudson River, the Erie Canal, the Erie-Ohio Canal, the Ohio River and the Mississippi River to New Orleans came into use. With the use of steamboats, this waterway played a very great role in transportation from the Middle West to the Atlantic coast.

After the Civil War, waterway transportation gradually gave way to railroad transportation. In 1825, the world's first commercial railroad, the British Stockton and Darlington line, went into operation. Three years later, construction began on the first American railroad—the Baltimore and Ohio. By 1860, trackage had grown to 30 626 miles, exceeding the combined total of Britain, France and Germany.

The golden age of American railroad construction, however, came after the Civil War.[2] The construction of the first transcontinental railroad was started jointly by the Central Pacific and the Union Pacific in 1863. The Central Pacific built eastward from San Clemanto, California, while the Union Pacific built westward from Omaha, Nebraska, across the plains. They met at Promontory Point, Utah, on May 10, 1869. In the next quarter of a century, four more transcontinental railroads were built across the continent from east to west. They ran roughly parallel with the first transcontinental railroad, with the Southern Pacific and the Santa Fe to its south, and the Great Northern and the Northern Pacific to its north. By 1916, the milage had reached an all time record of 254 037 miles which carried 77 percent of all the nation's intercity freight traffic and 98 percent of all its intercity passenger business. The roaring of *the Iron Horse*[3], as the steam-powered locomotive was called, could be heard by almost every American wherever he lived.

No one could have foreseen the rate at which railroads increased, nor the role they played in the Westward Expansion at the mid-nineteenth century. Abraham Lincoln thought it might take a century to settle the western frontier. But before the century drew to a close, the western frontier had disappeared as rapid rail construction moved well ahead of the frontier line and brought millions of Americans to the West.

However, the golden age of American railroad ended after World War Ⅰ when it met with strong competition first from automobiles and highways, then from airplanes, and to a lesser extent from pipelines. By 1980, the railroad trackage had shrunk to about 200 000 miles and the railroad share of intercity freight traffic had dropped to 35 percent. In passenger services the decline is even worse. Long-distance passenger trains have become something of the past. Besides commuter lines serving cities, only a few intercity passenger routes of relative short distances now exist between major cities. In 1971, *the government established the National Railroad Passenger Cooperation known as Amtrak*[4], which provides a federally subsidized and much reduced passenger service over about a tenth of the national railroad network. Still, the railroad's role in passenger transportation is almost negligible, accounting for less than 1 percent of the nation's total passenger traffic.

With the decline of the railroad transportation, came the age of the automobile. *Nothing is more expressive of the American way of life than the automobile*.[5] It means more than a mere means of transportation, it has become an American institution.

The first successful American gasoline automobile was built by the Duryea brothers in 1893. Two years later, they established the first automobile firm in the United States, but progress was very slow. It was not until 1908 that the auto industry took to revolution. In October that year, Henry Ford began to manufacture the famous Model T. mass production of cars and prices were reasonable and lowered year after year, and many common Americans could afford to buy them.

Since then the auto industry has developed into a massive industry. Car manufacturing has been further revolutionized and improved in style and in variety, in quantity and in quality. Today, there are 130 million passenger cars in the United States, averaging 1.5 per household, and every American drives an average of 7 767 miles a year. Private automobiles are responsible for about 83 percent of all intercity passenger traffic. Directly or indirectly, the auto industry provides jobs for one out of every nine American workers.

The car has become a necessity rather than a luxury in American life. Americans drive to their jobs, to big shopping centers which are often inaccessible by other means, to holiday-making places for the weekend or vacation, to wherever their fancy takes them. The car provides them with the highly valued freedom of movement in a comfortable and convenient way. Most cars are now airconditioned, many are equipped with automatic gears, CB radios, and other creature comfort devices. The majority of Americans would find it hard to imagine what life would be like without a car.

In addition to cars, there are over 30 million trucks and buses in the United States. Buses are used not only for passenger service within cities but also for long distance intercity travel. On long distance routes, buses are comfortably outfitted, complete with a toilet. The best known bus company is the *Grey-hound*[6], whose buses with a large running grey hound on the sides can be seen all over the country. In 1972, buses carried 15 percent of intercity passenger traffic compared with 5 percent for railroads and over 75 percent for airlines. Trucks play a very important role in cargo transportation in the United States. In 1983, trucks carried 23.6 percent of all the intercity freight traffic, next to only railroads (35.9 percent) and pipelines (25 percent).

For the easy movement of over 150 million cars, buses and trucks, the United States has built a complete and complex national road network of 3.8 million miles, which literally extends to every corner of the country. *No visitor is not impressed by the divided multi-lane super highways with controlled access, clear road signs, and good lighting at night, stretching straight beyond the horizon.*[7]

At first, the construction of modern highways lagged behind the production of automobiles in the United States. But from 1935, large-scale modern highway construction began when President Franklin D. Roosevelt established the Works Progress Administration (WPA) to provide jobs for the unemployed during the Great Depression. By 1943, 600 000 miles had been completed. Then in 1956, the government started *the National System of Interstate and Defense Highways*[8] with 90 percent of the total costs. A system of 42 500 miles was intended to be completed by 1990 to serve major centers of population and industry with a network of high capacity highways built to the latest and safest design standards. Now the system is open to traffic. Travel on such roads is not interrupted bv stoplights or intersections. *Interstate 80*[9], for example, is a double ribbon stretching 5000 miles from Manhattan in the East to San Francisco

Bay in the West without any stoplight.

Another type of super highway is the high capacity toll roads known as turnpikes. Construction of the first modern turnpike, the Pennsylvania Turnpike, was begun in 1937 and completed in 1940. Since then, more than $ 7.2 billion has been invested in building modern turnpikes and more than 4 400 miles are now in use. Just like on the old turnpikes at the beginning of the last century, the driver is required to stop at certain fixed points to pay a toll of a few dollars for the use of such roads.

Along with the development of the automobile and the highway, other facilities have also been developed. Thousands of motels are set up by the roadside to provide drivers with comfortable overnight stops. Drive-ins make life very convenient for the motorists, who can watch a movie, have a meal, or draw money at the places while remaining seated comfortably in his car. Besides, water and electricity are provided at trailer camps.

With millions of vehicles on the road and a vast network of roads, problems inevitably abound. Large cities are plagued by traffic congestion. Traffic accidents take a heavy toll of human lives. But the worst problem is the smog caused by car fumes which seriously pollutes the air in the United States.

The United States ushered in the era of aviation at the beginning of the twentieth century. In December, 1903, Orville Wright and his brother Wilbur made the first successful flight in an air-plane. In 1927, Charles Lindbergh made the spectacular non-stop flight from New York to Paris in 33 hours and 20 minutes in the Spirit of St. Louis. His success touched off an aviation boom. In the following years, 27 airlines were opened and carried 53 000 passengers. In 1930, the Boeing Company first introduced air hostess service on the route between San Francisco and Chicago. By 1939 the U.S. airlines were carrying about 3 million passengers annually, and their service extended to every major city. The jet plane first appeared in the forties; by the sixties all U.S. airlines were equipped with jet planes; and in the seventies *Jumbo jets*[10] like Boeing 747 with a maximum capacity of nearly 500 passengers went into worldwide service. With the increase in speed the world has grown smaller and smaller. Now a transcontinental flight from New York to San Francisco takes only about five hours; in about seven hours a Boeing 747 can fly from New York across the Atlantic Ocean to Paris without any stop, and the *supersonic Concord*[11] needs just half of that time to cover the same distance.

In the United States today, air travel has become not only the fastest means of transportation but also a very convenient one. In addition to numerous regular flights, airlines also provide *shuttle services*[12] between major population centers, such as New York and Washington shuttle flights operate more like municipal buses; planes leave every hour during most time of the day, and during the rush hours, a plane takes off as soon as it is fully loaded; passengers buy tickets after they get on board rather than book in advance. Such services make it possible for people who live in New York to work in one of the government departments in Washington.

Apart from the automobile, the airplane has become the largest carrier of passenger traffic in the United States. According to the 1984 statistics, there are over 230 000 civilian planes and 15 000 airports. The airlines fly 252.7 billion passenger miles compared with the railroad's 11 miles—a ratio of almost 23 to 1.

Another important means of U. S. transportation is the pipeline, which carries petroleum and natural gas in large volumes at a lower cost than any other means. The United States began to build pipelines on a continental scale in the 1930s, and the work was accelerated during World War Ⅱ. By the mid-1970s, the nation had established a vast network of pipelines, totaling about 1 200 000 miles, including 977 000 miles for natural gas and 222 000 miles for crude oil and products. Today, pipelines carry about a quarter of the country's total intercity freight traffic. Some of the major pipelines are the "Big Inch", 1 341 miles, running from

Longview, Texas, to Phoenixville, Pa., with branches to Linden, N.J., and the Philadelphia area; the "Little Big Inch", 1 475 miles, running from Beaumont, Texas to Linden, N. J.; the network of 4 300 miles carrying natural gas from Texas to the New York City area; and the trans-Alaska pipeline extending from Prudhoe Bay on the Arctic coast to Valdez on the southern coast.

Water transportation, today, still plays an indispensable role in cargo transportation. There are 25 543 miles of inland waterways including canals and rivers, which carried a cargo volume of 410. 8 billion short-ton-miles in 1984 compared with railroads' 919 billion short-ton-miles. In the network, the Mississippi River system is by far the most important. The Great Lakes, connected with the rivers and, through the Saint Lawrence River, with the Atlantic Ocean, also handle a large portion of freight traffic. As improvements are made in waterways, their traffic has been on the increase. Besides, the United States has a merchant marine of 6 437 vessels with a total dead-weight tonnage of 29 295 000.

In short, the United States transportation system has, over the last two centuries or so, evolved into a highly developed multiple network. Within the network, the automobile and the airplane are the two latest and most important developments, while the railroad, the ship, and the pipeline are necessary components, making their own respective contributions to the development of a highly mobile country. This pattern will remain largely unchanged in the near future though space shuttles have opened up the possibility for the ordinary man to travel into space and back.

Notes

1. turnpikes

收税路　使用这种马路驾驶员要在一定的地点付一定的路费，故叫“收税路”。

2. The golden age of American railroad construction, however, came after the Civil War.

然而，美国铁路建设的黄金时代开始于内战之后，到第一次世界大战之后结束。

3.the Iron Horse

火车头

4. the government established the National Railroad Passenger Cooperation known as Amtrak

美国政府建立了美国铁路客运公司，称“美铁”(American Track)

5.Nothing is more expressive of the American way of life than the automobile.

汽车最能表达美国人民的生活方式。

6.Grey-hound

灵猩　一种体瘦、行动快捷的狗。

7.No visitor is not impressed by the divided multi-lane super highways with controlled access, clear road signs, and good lighting at night, stretching straight beyond the horizon.

所有的游客都对分开的多车道高速公路有深刻的印象，这种公路是全封闭的通道，路标清晰，夜灯明亮，笔直地延伸至地平线以外。

8.the National System of Interstate and Defense Highways

美国州际和防务公路体系

9.Interstate 80

80 号洲际公路　从东海岸的曼哈顿直达西海岸的旧金山湾没有一个交通指示灯。

10.Jumbo jets

大型喷气客机

11.supersonic Concord

超音速协和式客机(英、法合制)

12.shuttle services

穿梭班机服务　在人口密集的中心城市提供的短距离班机服务，每小时都有班机，交通高峰时间，班机一客满就起飞，机上售票。

Exercises

Ⅰ. Fill in each blank with the right word or expression from the text:

1. Toll roads are known as _______.
2. The Erie Canal links _______ to _______.
3. The longest complete waterway starts from _______, through _______, _______, _______, _______ and _______, to _______.
4. The Iron Horse means _______.
5. The Grey-hound is _______.
6. The most successful and influential airline company in the United States aviation industry is _______.
7. Shuttle services are _______.
8. Pipelines carrying _______ and _______ are important in freight traffic.
9. The necessary components of the U.S. transportation system are _______, _______, _______, _______ and _______, but _______ and _______ are the most important ones.

Ⅱ. Questions for discussion:

1. Give a brief account of the historical development of the U. S. transportation system.
2. What are the major components of the U.S. transportation system?
3. What components are the most important ones of the U.S. transportation system? Why?
4. Give a brief account of the U.S. waterway transportation system.
5. What do you mean by "Nothing is more expressive of the American way of life than the automobile"?
6. Give a brief account of the U.S. airplane traffic.
7. Give a brief account of the different roles played by the different components of the U.S. transportation system.

Chapter 6
Colonial America

Text

Long before Columbus discovered the New World, *Europe endured the gradual decay of medieval ideas and institutions*[1]. New forces stirred and modern civilization began to develop. Europe became full of vigour and vitality; it was to expand aggressively through conquest, colonies and commerce and stamp its culture throughout the world.

European Expansion

Medieval Europe was *a religion-dominated society that restricted individualism*[2]. The Roman Catholic Church viewed life on earth as preparation for life after death and discouraged aspirations to better human conditions in the world. Europe's painful transition from "medieval" to "modern" was brought about by three inter-related movements: 1) *the Culural Renaissance*[3], 2) the Religious Reformation, and 3) the Commercial Revolution.

The Cultural Renaissance revived classical Greek culture, encouraged inquiry, and stimulated dissatisfaction with existing conditions. Medieval thinkers insisted that nature was a mystery which God had not permitted man to know. Renaissance thinkers believed that through reason man could understand nature. They began to experiment, measure and question—eventually producing modern science. With the invention of printing, books were published and new ideas about the world were spread. *The humanistic spirit of the Renaissance also contributed secular and critical attitudes toward religion by restoring man to a more central place in the universe*.[4]

The Religious Reformation hastened Europe's transition from medieval to modern. In 1517 a German monk named *Martin Luther*[5] led a successful revolt against the Catholic Church, the dominant Christian church in Europe in the Middle Ages, and the Protestant Reformation began. Soon followed other religious revolts, such as those led by *John Calvin and King Henry Ⅷ*[6] of England. The Protestant Reformation sought to reform the Roman Catholic Church, asserting that individual faith rather than obedience to Church rules was the source of salvation. *It rejected the authority of the Church for the authority of the Bible*.[7] In the process, the Reformation broke up the unity of the Christendom and glorified personal enrichment, both spiritual and economic. Even before the discovery of the New World many Protestants wished to leave Europe for a holy place where they could practise their new faith in peace. The discovery of the New World answered the prayers of many Protestants.

The Commercial Revolution accompanied changes in intellectual and religious attitudes. The Revolution created new classes, such as traders, bankers and merchants. Long-distance trade was developed, joint-stock companies were created and free capital flowed in commercial ventures, and as a result new world exploration was hastened.

1. *Early Exploration*

In 1096 *the Crusades*[8] attempted to recover the Holy land from the Moslems. Though the Crusades failed they did enforce the Europeans out of their isolated world and into contact with a new culture.

In the 1200s travellers such as Marco Polo travelled deep into Asia and returned with stories of the wealth of the Orient. Polo wrote: "The Lord has a great palace which is entirely roofed with fine gold, just as our churches are roofed with lead." Polo's stories stirred up European exploration.

The late 15th and early 16th centuries brought about great voyages of exploration and discovery. Portugal took the lead in the exploration. In 1486, Bartholomew Dias sailed around the tip of Africa, the Cape of Good Hope. In 1498 Vasco da Gama sailed round Africa and arrived in India. Large-scale exploration resulted in a Portuguese overseas empire.

They dominated the sea lanes and trade routes to the Orient and set up trading posts here and there in Africa and Asia.

2. *Columbus' Discovery of America*

On the morning of Oct. 12, 1492, Columbus discovered the New World. Columbus had proposed to the Portuguese Court his plan *to find a direct ocean route to the Indies by sailing due west*[9], which the Portuguese rejected, then he sought help from Queen Isabella and King Ferdinand of Spain. They agreed to finance a small fleet for his westward expedition.

He set sail from Spain, crossed the Atlantic, and after six weeks' journey his ships arrived at San Salvador in the Bahamas on Oct. 12, 1492. Columbus did not proclaim that he had found America, for he believed that this was part of the Indies and that the inhabitants should be called"Indians". Though it is universally acknowledged that it was Columbus who had discovered America the New World was named for *Amerigo Vespucci*[10]. Amerigo Vespucci, an Italian sailor, sailed for the New World in 1497. After he reached and explored the coast of South America in the region of the Guianas, he wrote lots of reports back and proved it was a big continent and indicated that India could be reached by crossing another ocean. In 1507, a German professor published a map of the New World on the basis of Amerigo's voyages and called it America.

3. *Spanish Exploration*

After Columbus the Spanish swarmed from the Caribbean islands to the mainland. In 1513 de Balboa cut his way across the Isthmus of Darien and is considered to be the first European to sight the Pacific Ocean. Balboa's discovery led to a new research for the southwest Passage—a waterway through south America. In 1519 Magellan, a Portuguese, sailed around the tip of South America by way of the strait that today bears his name. He travelled for 14 weeks across the Pacific and eventually arrived in the Philippine Islands where he was killed by one of his seamen. His lieutenant continued his voyage and returned to Spain. Magellan is regarded as the first man to have sailed around the world.

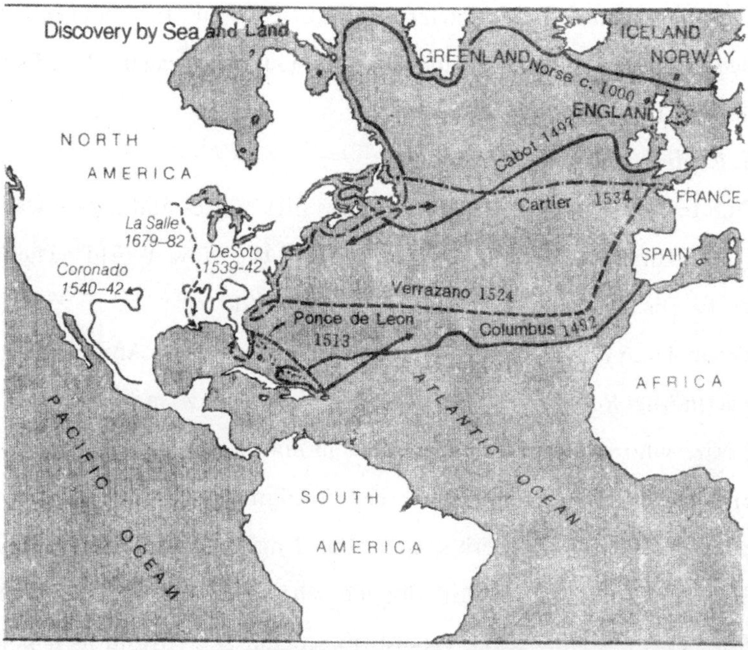

Encouraged by these discoveries, the Spanish swarmed over the Caribbean islands and onto the mainland of North and South Americas. They conquered Peru and Mexico, then they explored Florida, southern California and marched into the Southwest and the Mississippi Valley. By 1600, the Spanish had set up a vast empire in North America stretching from southern California through the Southwest to Florida.

4. *French Exploration*

Unlike the Portuguese and the Spanish overseas empires, the French started colonization in the New World on the basis of fishing and fur trade. The French came in small groups to fish on the Newfoundland banks or to barter for furs with the Indians.

It was Samuel de Champlain who pioneered the French empire. After exploring the Gulf of the St. Lawrence, he erected a fort at Quebec in 1698 which soon became *the permanent trapping and trading centre*[11]. Then the French penetrated into the Great Lakes area and beyond the Mississippi River. They sailed down the Mississippi River and when they got to the mouth of the Mississippi River in 1682 they claimed all the area along the river and its tributaries for France. Thus far the French had occupied a vast amount of area including the Gulf of Mexico, the Mississippi and the St. Lawrence.

5. *English Exploration*

Due to internal political and religious difficulties and a long war with Spain, the English were the last to colonize the New World. Then why did the English want to settle in the New World?

When Henry Ⅷ defied the pope in order to marry Anne Boleyn, *he broke with the Roman Catholic Church*[12]. The new marriage bore him Elizabeth, who was England's greatest monarch. Under Elizabeth's rule England became strong enough to seek foreign markets and build a New World empire. In Elizabeth's time the English attacked the Spanish successfully by pirating its ships loaded with gold and silver from South America. This encouraged the English to see the New World as a potential source of riches. Henry's break with Rome also gave impetus to a Protestant movement which was already under way secretly. The Calvinists, also known as Puritans, *became increasingly discontent with the incomplete reformation of the Anglican Church*[13]. Many of these Puritans went to America in the hope of completing reforms there.

The Enclosure Movement[14] of the 1500s also stimulated English colonization. This was a movement by large landowners to turn agricultural fields into sheep pastures. This agricultural shift led to thousands of farm workers' losing their jobs and to an increase in the urban population. America, of course, would bc a good place for those unemployed.

1) Early Attempts

In 1578 Humphrey Gilbert acquired a charter from Queen Elizabeth granting him a tract of land in the New World. He set sail from England and reached Newfoundland in 1583. After two weeks' stay there, he cruised southward and on his return trip he ran into a heavy sea and was drowned.

After Gilbert's death, his half brother, Sir Walter Raleigh carried on his career. In 1584 he got a charter from Queen Elizabeth and sent out a reconnoitering force. They reached the lower reach of the Chesapeake Bay. When they returned, Raleigh named it Virginia in honour of Elizabeth, the Virgin Queen. In 1585 Raleigh sent an expedition to settle the Roanoke Island, near the present boundary between Virginia and North Carolina. *For short of timely supplies, relief and money, no settlers survived*.[15] Though Raleigh failed he did lead the way to the settlement of Virginia.

2) Founding of Jamestown

When Elizabeth died in 1603, King James I sponsored a joint-stock company, the Virginia Company of London. It was given a charter to monopolize much of the Atlantic coast of the present United States. They set sail in three ships carrying 104 settlers and reached the mouth of the James River. After exploring they founded Jamestown in 1607 on the lower reach of the Chesapeake Bay. After settling down, they met with lots of troubles, hardships and attacks from the native Indians. However, *John Smith had nerve enough to take command*[16]. They managed to survive on by planting corn, tobacco, erecting houses and fortifications. Then they saw the need of a local self-government, and *the House of Burgesses*[17]—a local assembly—was established in July 1619, helping improve the affairs of Virginians.

3) Founding of Plymouth and Other Colonies

After Virginia, the next successful settlement was Plymouth founded by a group of Pilgrims. In the fall of 1620, a group of 35 Pilgrims and 70 non-Pilgrims set sail aboard the ship "Mayflower" for northern Virginia. But after making their landfall at Cape Cod and exploring the coast, they began a settlement named Plymouth. Knowing well they were out of any legally constituted government, on their voyage they drew up the famous "*Mayflower Compact*"[18]. Under Bradford, the Pilgrims liquidated the debt owed to the English merchants and established for themselves a self-supporting community. An enslaved Indian named Squanto taught them how to grow Indian corn and where to hunt and catch fish. After the Pilgrims harvested a good crop in the autumn of 1621, a feast of thanksgiving was held on the last Thursday in November to thank God for His protection. That's how *the Thanksgiving Day*[19] has come down and why the Day has been observed as one of the great occasions celebrated every year in American history.

In 1628 another group of Puritans bought their way into the New England Company. The company obtained a charter authorizing settlement in the Massachusetts Bay. Under John Winthrop the Puritans transformed the Company into a commonwealth. *They admitted "freemen" into a general court, in fact an assembly of elected representatives to help with public affairs.*[20]

As more and more immigrants entered into Massachusetts colony, problems began to arise, and religious disputes became serious. Those who could no longer endure the life and *theocracy*[21] in Massachusetts began to move off. They migrated into areas beyond Massachusetts and established their own colonies, New Hampshire, Connecticut and Rhode Island. Together with Massachusetts, the colonies were collectively called New England. After independence, Maine and Vermont were also included.

New York was first founded by the Dutch in 1621. It was conquered by England in 1664 and was given to the younger brother of Charles Ⅱ, the Duke of York. Thus New York came into being as *a proprietary colony*[22]. Then part of New York was given to another proprietor who named it New Jersey. Delaware was first colonized by the Swedish and it was also taken by England by force and became one of the 13 colonies.

Pennsylvania was a remarkable experience in idealism. It was said to reflect the ideas of William Penn, a rich and powerful *Quaker*[23]. He believed in the idea of peace through brotherly love and freedom of worship. His liberal ideas attracted people of many nationalities and many religions. He received the colony from Charles Ⅱ in 1681 in satisfaction of a debt owed to his father. Penn was left free to draft the first laws on a consciously moral plan which provided liberty of conscience for all. He placed the legislative power in a council and an assembly, both elected by the freeholders. Attracted by the prospect of good land, free government and religious liberty, English, Irish, Welsh, Dutch and German Quakers flocked into the colony. Under William Penn's government, Pennsylvanians enjoyed full religious and civil liberty. Therefore Pennsylvania *was regarded as the most "American" of colonies*[24].

Maryland was granted by Charles Ⅰ to his friend Lord Baltimore as a refuge for English Catholics because Catholics had been having a very hard time in England after the Religious Reformation.

South Carolina and North Carolina were originally given by Charles Ⅱ to his close supporters. They were so faithful to him that they followed him to France in exile during *the English Bourgeois Revolution*[25]. After Charles Ⅱ was restored to the throne, he awarded them with large tracts of land in what are now South Carolina and North Carolina.

Georgia was the last of the 13 colonies set up in 1733 by a group of philanthropic proprietors. They sympathized with the religiously persecuted prisoners in England and asked King George Ⅱ for a charter granting a tract of land for putting the prisoners. The King agreed and the criminal colony Georgia was set up in the South as a barrier against the Spanish.

Between 1607 and 1733 the 13 British colonies had been established along the east coast of North America. They were Virginia, New York, Massachusetts, New Hampshire, New Jersey, Maryland, Pennsylvania, Connecticut, Rhode Island, Delaware, North Carolina, South Carolina and Georgia. According to distinctive characteristics, the colonies fell into three types: the Crown colonies, the proprietary colonies and *the autonomous colonies*[26]. In 1775 there were eight Crown colonies—New Hampshire, Massachusetts, New York, New Jersey, Virginia, South Carolina, North Carolina and Georgia, three proprietary colonies—Pennsylvania, Delaware and Maryland, two autonomous colonies—Connecticut and Rhode Island. The Crown colonies were controlled by governors directly appointed by the King; the governors of the proprietary colonies were the proprietors who served their own interests and benefits while the governors of the autonomous were elected by the colonial legislatures. The form of the colonial government was based on the council or the assembly, the former was equivalent to the British House of Lords and the latter to the House of Commons.

According to geographic, social and economic features, the 13 colonies might be divided into three regions: New England, the Middle Atlantic states and the South. New England was mountainous and rocky with short summer and long winter, so it was not good for farming. Early settlers turned to other pursuits, such as fishing, trade and shipbuilding. Boston quickly developed and became the center of New England. The South was quite different. Here the plains were wide and fertile and the climate was warm. Most southerners were devoted to agriculture, working large plantation farms. The plantation owners depended on slaves for producing grain, cotton and tobacco for exports. These staple crops quickly exhausted the soil, causing lots of troubles and hardships in the South. The slave owners who fattened on slave labour lived an extravagant life and made up the most backward upper class in American history while the slaves led the poorest life in all the colonies.

The Middle Atlantic colonies *were far more varied, cosmopolitan, tolerant*[27]. By the end of the colonial period, there were 30 000 people made up of different ethnic groups and nations. They engaged in farming, weaving, shoe-making, shipbuilding and other crafts. Trade and commerce also thrived quickly. As a result, these colonies became the center of the development of colonial America.

The early settlers in the 13 colonies were from different European countries, but most of them came from England generally known as the White Anglo-Saxon Protestants (WASPs). Religious dispute caused these people to flee to America. The Anglican Church not only persecuted the Catholics but also the Protestant extremists, such as the Puritans. Many of these religious people went to the New World to seek freedom of belief.

Countless poor British people also poured into the New World. As a result of the Enclosure Movement, thousands of farmers and workers became jobless and impoverished. As they could no longer endure their sufferings and hardships, they went to the New World to earn a living as *indentured servants*[28]. They had to labour for the company or merchants from 5 to 7 years for the pay of their voyage transportation. After the term was over, they became freemen or citizens.

These early settlers were usually energetic individuals. They all settled in the colonies for individual aims and purposes. Part of them wanted a strong government to keep peace and order so as to ensure private ownership of property; part of them wanted to set up holy places where they could abide by their own religious beliefs; many of them wanted the greatest possible freedom for individuals in which each could develop in any way he liked. Thus individualism became their principle and belief and played an important role in shaping American politics.

Large numbers of immigrants also came from France, Germany, Switzerland and other countries. They all adopted the English language but their own cultures did not disappear completely. These immigrants lived together and created the American culture which was a blending of European cultures under new circumstances. Once a French-born agriculturist wrote: "What then is the American, this new man? He is either a European, or the descendant of a European, hence that strange mixture of blood, which you find in no other country ..., I could point out to you a family whose grandfather was an Englishman, whose wife was a Dutch, whose son married a French woman, and whose present four sons have now four wives of different nations. He is an American ..."

In religion, the colonies had *to adopt a policy of tolerance*[29]. Different religious sects grew freely along with the different immigrants with different religious beliefs. Any attempt to enforce people to worship God in a way which they did not like would often drive them to other places. This practice grounded the separation of church from government in America, a marked development in human history.

The colonies also developed education. The Puritans were firm believers in education. They tried hard to establish enough schools for their children. The schools were not only to spread literacy but also to train clergymen. The first college, Harvard, was set up in Massachusetts in 1636. By the mid-eighteenth century several other well-known colleges were founded, including Yale in Connecticut, Columbia in New York and Princeton in New Jersey.

Notes

1. Europe endured the gradual decay of medieval ideas and institutions

欧洲经历过中世纪思想和制度逐渐衰败的过程　中世纪(the Medieval Age or the Middle Ages)指欧洲史上约5世纪末至15世纪中叶的时间。

2. a religion-dominated society that restricted individualism

一个教会统治的社会，限制个性发展

3. the Cultural Renaissance

文艺复兴　指欧洲13世纪末至16世纪的文艺复兴，始于意大利，逐渐扩展到其他欧洲国家，标志着中世纪文艺向现代文艺的过渡。

4. The humanistic spirit of the Renaissance ... to a mere central place in the universe.

文艺复兴的人文主义精神对宗教的世俗批判做出过贡献，把人置于宇宙的中心位置。

5. Martin Luther

马丁路德(1483—1546)　德国神学家，宗教改革的领袖，创立了路德派。

6. John Calvin and King Henry Ⅷ

约翰·加尔文(1509—1564)和亨利八世(1491—1547)　前者是法国宗教改革的领袖，创立了加尔文派(基督教);后者是英国国王，也是宗教改革的领袖，与罗马天主教分离之后，在英国创立了英国国教(the Anglican Church)。

7. It rejected the authority of the Church for the authority of the Bible.

新教改革运动拒绝罗马天主教作为主宰圣经的权威。

8. the Crusades

十字军　中世纪罗马教皇领导的天主教会和世俗封建主合伙建立的军队，从1096年至1291年，先后八次东征镇压各国人民，以图从穆斯林手里夺回圣地。

9. to find a direct ocean route to the Indies by sailing due west

向西航行寻找一条直达东印度群岛的海洋通道

10. Amerigo Vespucci

雅马利格·维斯浦奇(1451—1512)　意大利的航海家，曾三度航海至美洲大陆，探察了圭亚那等地区，做了详细记载和报告，指出南美洲是一个大陆，并可另找一条海路通往印度，这为麦哲伦的环球航行成功所证实。

11. the permanent trapping and trading center

永久捕猎和经营皮货的中心

12. he broke with the Roman Catholic Church

他断绝了与罗马天主教的关系

13. became increasingly discontent with the incomplete reformation of the Anglican Church

对英国国教改革的不彻底性越来越感到不满意

14. the Enclosure Movement

圈地运动　在14—15世纪，随着养羊业的发展，英国领主用栅栏、篱笆把农民的公有地围起来作为牧羊场，造成大批农民失去赖以生存的土地，沦为乞丐或城市无业游民。

15. For short of timely supplies, relief and money, no settlers survived.

由于缺少及时的补给、救济和资金，定居者无一生还。

16. John Smith had nerve enough to take command.

约翰·史密斯有足够的勇气担当起领导、指挥的任务。

17. the House of Burgesses

下议院　指美国革命前，弗吉尼亚和马里兰两洲所建立的下议院。

18. the Mayflower Compact

“五月花”契约　在1620年的秋季，一批清教徒(Pilgrims)从英国移民“新世界”，在航海的途中制订了该契约，实行自治。

19. the Thanksgiving Day

感恩节　英国清教徒移民在1621年的秋季获得谷物好收成后，于11月的第四个星期四举办一个宴会，感谢上帝对他们的保护，这就是感恩节的由来，并成了美国每年都要庆祝的重要节日之一。

20. They admitted “freemen” into a general court, in fact an assembly of elected representatives to help with public affairs.

他们吸纳“自由民”组成众议院，实际上是一个由选民组成的议会(或众议院)协助处理公务。

21. theocracy

神权统治 指当时清教徒在马萨诸塞州殖民地所实行的严密的宗教统治，排斥、打击持有政教分离观点的人。

22. a proprietary colony

英王特许领主独占的殖民地

23. quaker

贵格会教徒(或称公谊会，教友会) 属于基督教的一个教派。

24. was regarded as the most“American”of colonies

被看作是最美国化的殖民地 该殖民地议会由选民自由选举产生的上议院和下议院组成。

25. the English Bourgeois Revolution

英国资产阶级革命 亦称“光荣革命”，是17世纪初，英国资产阶级、新贵族与封建专制、教会之间的矛盾和革命斗争。经过反复较量，新兴的资产阶级取得胜利，建立了君主立宪政权，确立了资产阶级的统治。

26. the autonomous colonies

自治殖民地 殖民地的议会由殖民地人民自由选举产生，实行自治。

27. were far more varied, cosmopolitan, tolerant

更具有多样性、世界性和容忍的特点 多样性主要指工、农、商、贸等多种经济的综合发展；世界性主要指来自世界各国不同移民、文化和宗教等；容忍则指这些殖民地采用一系列的容忍政策，允许各国种族团体移民、文化和宗教和谐相处，共同发展。

28. indentured servants

契约工 17—19世纪，许多英国贫民移居美洲，他们十分穷苦，无力偿付路费等费用，便与公司或商人签订契约，到达美洲后为公司或商人服役5—7年，以偿还债务。

29. to adopt a policy of tolerance

采用容忍政策 因为美国移民来自世界各国，语言、宗教和文化又各异，所以采用此政策。

Exercises

Ⅰ. Fill in each blank with the right word or expression from the text:

1. The New World was named for ________.
2. The doctrine that motivated British colonization in the New World was ________.
3. ________ was the second English settlement in the New World.
4. The last English colony founded in the New World was ________.
5. The first college established in the colonies was ________.
6. According to distinctive characteristics, the 13 colonies fell into three types: ________, ________ and ________.
7. According to geographic, social and economic features, the 13 colonies might be divided into three regions: ________, ________ and ________.
8. The region, ________, became the center of the development of colonial America.
9. WASPs refers to ________.

Ⅱ. Questions for discussion:

1. Give a brief account of the three important movements that brought about Europe's gradual transition from "medieval" to "modern".
2. What was the significance of Columbus' discovery of the New World?
3. What were the different sections of English immigrants who migrated into the New World? For what different purposes?
4. Give a brief account of the different types of the English colonies in America.
5. What was the early colonial life like in America?
6. What were the important English heritages or values that grew in colonial America?

Chapter 7
American Revolution

Text

Americans remained colonial for one and a half centuries (from 1607 to 1776) before they quite suddenly became revolutionary. During most of that long period, England adopted a *mercantilist policy*[1] towards the colonies but the colonies enjoyed "*salutary neglect*"[2] and all colonists in America became Americans.

The first settlers established local governments based on their English experience, but the role of the colonial legislatures changed and expanded over decades of constant friction with English authorities. Crown officials often had little understanding of American conditions. Royal governors represented the interests of the Crown, executed orders coming from England and therefore opposed many natural colonial demands. However, such Royal government proved ineffective and most colonies were left largely dependent on their own colonial legislatures to manage themselves politically, economically and culturally.

Colonists had the view that each colonial legislature had the same position as did the English Parliament. They insisted on their rights and liberties within the British empire. British officials naturally emphasized the responsibilities and duties of the colonists to the British empire. Thus arose the conflicts and contradictions between the mother country and the colonies, between the colonialists and the colonists. Colonialism and anti-colonialism became the major contradiction between England and the colonies. This grounded basically the rise of the American revolution.

Ⅰ. Mercantilism

Mercantilism was the economic philosophy which motivated British colonization. Mercantilist policy was the core of the British imperial policies towards the colonies. According to this policy, a major purpose of any colony was to increase the wealth of the mother country. Colonies were desirable both as markets for the products of the homeland and as source of essential raw materials. The rules and regulations imposed on the 13 colonies were designed to promote British interests rather than those of the colonies. *The Navigation Acts*[3] were the typical ones that ensured the interests of the British empire.

Actually, for over one hundred years (1660—1763), *the English Board of Commissioners for Trade and Plantations*[4] handled colonial matters haphazardly. American colonies obeyed those laws and regulations they approved of, while English authorities looked the other way when Americans disregarded other laws and regulations. This policy of "salutary neglect" ended in 1763 following England's victory over the French in he Seven Year's War. In order to exert direct control of the Ohio Valley, the British government launched a war against the French which lasted seven years and ended in England's victory. The French lost almost all her American holdings. After the war, England moved toward direct imperial control and taxation of the colonies. The following reasons seemed to justify England's change in policy. England had to pay the war debt and people's financial burdens were heavy. Administration of the enlarged British empire now cost five times more than before the war, having thirty-three colonies to defend and millions of colonial officials to support.

Right after the end of the War, the English Parliament issued a series of acts against the colonies. The Proclamation of 1763 prohibited colonial settlement west of the Appalachians. Lands west of the Appalachians were barred off as a Crown domain, and no Indians' lands were to be sold except to the Crown. The Sugar Act of 1764 placed heavy taxes on sugar imported from Spanish and French West Indies, thus threatening the profitable trade of New England merchants. By the Currency Act of 1764, the colonies were not allowed to issue their own paper money, thus putting colonial debts under the control of English creditors. The Quartering Act of 1765 required the colonies to provide food and living quarters for the British soldiers to live in. All these acts were against the interests and sovereignty of the colonies. Therefore distrust and hatred began to take root in the hearts and minds of the colonial people and prepared for resistance against the British Acts.

Ⅱ. Stamp Act of 1765 & Sons of Liberty

One of the new policies taken by the British government was the Stamp Act of 1765, which provided for a direct tax paid by affixing a stamp to every sort of document or article. The colonists objected because they thought Englishmen had no voice in the levying. Postmen resigned; the "Sons of Liberty" was formed to burn or tear down post-offices; merchants joined the opposition to boycott English goods, and English trade with the colonies dropped off by over one-fourth. In addition, a congress was held in New York in October 1765 to discuss the Stamp Act. *The congress affirmed the principle of no taxation without representation.*[5] Due to colonists' pressure, Parliament repealed the Stamp Act in March, 1766.

Ⅲ. Townshend Act & Boston Massacre

Soon after the Stamp Act was repealed, Parliament resorted to another new measure. A new Chancellor of the Exchequer, Charles Townshend *pushed through Parliament a series of import duties on lead, glass, paper, paint and tea at colonial ports*[6]. Again Americans rioted, organized boycotts, reaffirmed the unconstitutionality of taxation without representation. To protect the Customs officials, British troops had to be sent to Boston. The presence of the British troops in turn led to the *Boston Massacre*[7] of March 5, 1770, in which British soldiers fired on colonial demonstrators and made heavy casualties.

Ironically, on the same day a new English government ordered the Townshend Act repealed except for a tax on tea. There remained relatively calm for three years. However, American radicals continued to insist on their equality within the empire with England. Led by Samuel Adams, Patrick Henry, Thomas Jefferson, they started *Committees of Correspondence*[8], which established permanent contact among all colonial leaders, informed people in one area of what happened in another, and provided concerted action against new English acts. They were ready in 1773, when the English government *botched another crisis*[9].

Ⅳ. The Boston Tea Party

The East India Company kept stores of tea in warehouse in England for the American market. Colonists smuggled most of their tea directly from Holland. As a result, the company built up a vast oversupply of tea in England. To aid the financially-troubled company, Parliament in 1773 passed the Tea Act, which gave the Company a monopoly on all tea exported to the colonies and provided also that tea shipped to America would have the English import duties in America for about one-half what it cost in England. The British government assumed that Americans would take advantage of the new low price and use up surplus inventory of the Company. But from colonists' point of view, buying tea would weaken their arguments agaist taxation, *since the tea still carried the low tax left over from the Townshend Act to keep up the right*[10]. Once again merchants resorted to non-importation agreements. Men dressed in homespun clothing, women found substitutes for tea. Students used colonial-made paper. Houses went unpainted. Ships loaded with tea were forced to return to England. In Charleston several shiploads were placed in warehouses because no one would pay the tax. A mob burned a ship and its tea cargo in Annapolis. Mass meetings in Boston resulted in the most famous example of reaction. Some 50 men dressed as Indians boarded ships and threw all the tea overboard. This was known as the *Boston Tea Party*[11].

The British government reacted quickly in a series of Parliamentary coercive measures called the Intolerable Act by the Americans.[12] Parliament ordered Boston's harbor closed until the destroyed tea was paid for. It changed the charter of Massachusetts to restrict popular participation in government. Governors were empowered to requisition vacant buildings for quartering Royal troops. General Thomas Gage was appointed the new governor of Massachusetts for reinforcement. However, these Coercive Acts only served to unite the colonies in opposition to British coercion.

Ⅴ. The First Continental Congress

During this crisis the Massachusetts leaders called for a meeting of all colonies. Support of Massachusetts was so strong that twelve colonies responded to the call for a national congress. So the First Continental Congress met in Philadelphia in September, 1774, to plan concerted resistance. Fifty-five representatives from twelve colonies recognized that if Boston's government could be suspended and its chief port closed without opposition, then other colonies might as well yield. In a *Declaration of Rights and Grievances*[13], the representatives asserted their rights to life, liberty, and property and declared that only their own elected assemblies could tax them. They took a long step toward ultimate union with the formation of the *Continental Association*[14] which pledged to stop almost all trade between England and the colonies. Under the Association the colonies were more united than ever before in their resistance against English tyranny and monopoly.

Ⅵ. Battle at Lexington—Outbreak of the Revolution

In the meantime, the people of Massachusetts moved rapidly toward armed rebellion. The colonial militia (called "*minutemen*"[15]) laid up arms and ammunitions in strategic locations around Boston in preparation for war, when General Gage set out to destroy the stockpile at Concord, warnings spread rapidly in advance of the British march. At Lexington the first blood was shed as the 700 British regulars brushed aside 70 colonial militiamen, but more rebels gathered as the march toward Concord continued. There the British came under attack from three to four hundred colonists and were forced to retreat to Boston. During the fight the British lost 273 men, while the Americans lost only 93. More significant for the future, New England responded instantly. Gage's forces in Boston found themselves surrounded by an angry force of approximately 20 000 men.

Ⅶ. The Second Continental Congress

At this critical juncture Americans elected delegates to the Second Continental Congress, which met in Philadelphia in May, 1775. Radical leaders attempted to push through a declaration of independence, but could not yet win suffcient following. Instead they issued a *Declaration of the Causes and Necessity of Taking Up Arms*[16], in which they justified the colonial position and petitioned the king again for redress of grievances and warned that unless the king straightened matters out to the satisfaction of the colonists, independence would surely follow.

In the meantime, Congress took the militia into continental service and appointed George Washington Commander-in-Chief of the American forces. It also decided to seek help from other countries, especially France, a rival of Britain. All these were important steps toward armed struggle for independence.

The king and his ministers, however, determined to crush the rebels. In late August, 1775, they officially declared Americans in "open and avowed rebellion" and sent heavy military reinforcements to America. Americans for their part began to demand total independence. Early in 1776, Thomas Paine punished a significant book entitled *Common Sense*[17], which argues that Americans should overthrow royal power and establigh a republican government. He called for immediate separation, thorough and complete independence from England. He said in his pamphlet: "The Sun never shined on a cause of greater worth. 'Tis not the affair of a City, a County, a Province, or a Kingdom; but of a Continent—of at least one eighth part of the habitable globe. 'Tis not the concern of a day, a year, or an age; posterity are virtually involved in the contest, and will be more of less affected even to the end of time, by the proceedings now. Now is the seed-time of Continental union, faith and honour. Everything that is right or reasonable pleads for separation. The blood of slain, the weeping voice of nature cries, 'Tis Time to part." Within a short time nearly 500 000 copies had sold to men who not only read the book but read it aloud to men who could not read. Meanwhile, the Second Continental Congress took warlike actions by declaring American ports open to all nations except England and advising the individual colonies to create governments outside the authority of King and Parliament.

Ⅷ. Declaration of Independence

In June 1776 the Congress began serious debate on the question of independence and in early July twelve delegations supported the act of separation and issued the *Declaration of Independence*[18]. The Declaration of Independence consists of three parts: 1) a profound and eloquent statement of political philosophy—the philosophy of democracy and freedom; 2) a statement of 27 specific grievances designed to prove that George Ⅲ had subverted American freedoms; and 3) a solemn statement of independence and pledge of support for that policy. In the Declaration, they declared that "*all men are created equal, that they are endowed by their Creator with certain unalienable Rights, that among these are Life, Liberty and the pursuit of Happiness. That to secure these rights, Governments are instituted among Men, deriving their powers from the consent of the governed*"[19]. John Adams later remarked that the Revolution was effected before the war commenced. The revolution was in the hearts and minds of the "people". By then Americans had moved a period of ten years from loyalty to defiance and to rebellion. It now remained for them to win recognition of their independence in the battlefield and then to define the character of their new nation.

Ⅸ. War of Independence

The war for American independence took seven long years. During most of the time, the British retained the initiative, but the American patriots survived and triumphed because the struggle was clearly a people's war.

At the outset of the war the British outnumbered the Americans by four-to-one, drew upon the resources of the world's most powerful empire, controlled the world with the world's greatest navy and possessed a well-trained and well-equipped army of seasoned troops and mercenaries. They lacked, however, the will to institute and successfully execute a broad strategy for dealing with the rebellious colonies. They seemed outwardly superior, but they never had sufficient forces in America to subdue a continental rebellion. They failed to solve the problems of supplying an army 3 000 miles from its base, nor did they effectively coordinate military and naval operations. *These irremediable weaknesses grounded the doom of the British colonialists*.[20]

At the outset of the war, Americans were neither fully united in rebellion nor consistently able to field an effective army. But they possessed desire for freedom and will to win that grew in the face of defeat as in victory. Due to the genius and correct leadership of the Commander-in-Chief, George Washington, the Patriot forces grew in strength and endured to the end of the struggle. The overall American strategy was to survive and, in the process, to make the war too costly in man, materials, and money for the British to continue. Time and terrain also aided the Patriot cause. Dependent upon ocean and river supply lines, the British could neither long hold inland areas nor pursue elusive Patriot armies over great distances. The vast forests, innumerable rivers, and untenable mountains became the Patriots' chief resources for defense.

Still, Americans might not have won their independence but for the assistance of France. By 1777 the British had formulated a master plan. General John Burgoyne was to lead a large army down the St. Lawrence, via Lake Champlain and the Hudson to Albany. But on October 17, 1777, Burgoyne was forced to surrender at the Battle of Saratoga after suffering very heavy losses. The Battle of Saratoga was considered the turning point of the war. It not only changed the American mood to

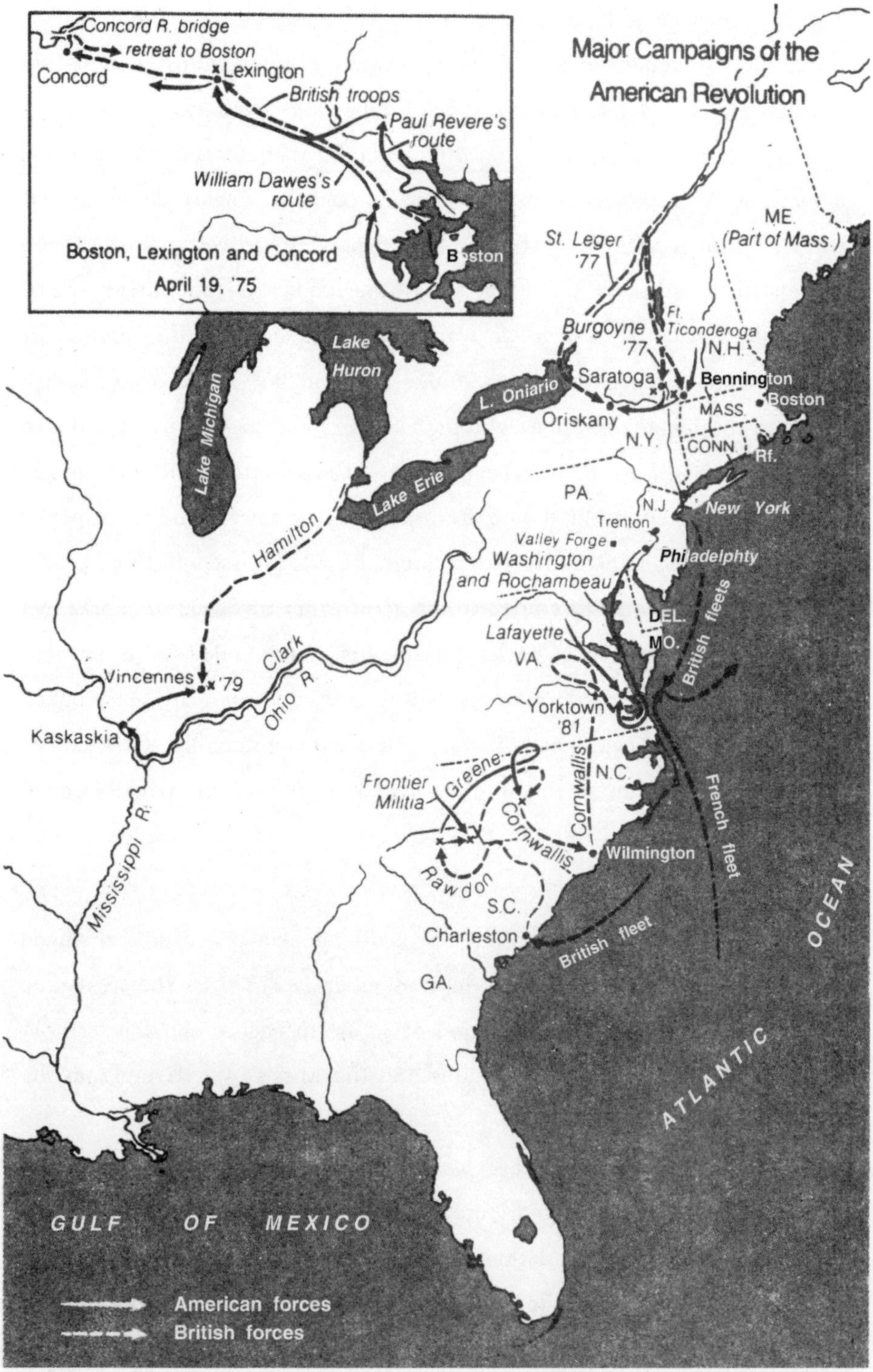
Major Campaigns of the American Revolution
Concord R. bridge
retreat to Boston
Concord
Lexington
British troops
Paul Revere's route
William Dawes's route
Boston
Boston, Lexington and Concord
April 19, '75
St. Leger '77
Burgoyne '77
Ft. Ticonderoga
ME. (Part of Mass.)
N.H.
Saratoga
Bennington
Boston
MASS.
CONN.
Rf.
Oriskany
N.Y.
L. Ontario
Lake Huron
Lake Michigan
Lake Erie
PA.
N.J.
New York
Trenton
Valley Forge
Philadelphty
Washington and Rochambeau
DEL.
MO.
Lafayette
VA.
British fleets
Yorktown '81
Hamilton
Clark
Vincennes
'79
Ohio R.
Kaskaskia
Mississippi R.
Frontier Militia
Greene
Cornwallis
Cornwallis
N.C.
Wilmington
Rawdon
S.C.
Charleston
British fleet
French fleet
GA.
ATLANTIC OCEAN
GULF OF MEXICO
American forces
British forces

optimism but caused foreign countries to stand on their side. After Burgoyne's surrender at Saratoga, the French Foreign Minister signed on February 6, 1778, *two treaties, one of amity and commerce, and one of military alliance*[21]. The military alliance made available French officers, money and naval power to the Americans, brought an English declaration of war on France, and forced England to disperse its forces against French threats to the empire. Spain and the Netherlands also took advantage of England's difficulties and made war against England. In the summer of 1781, twenty French warships, under Admiral de Grasse arrived with orders to coordinate operations with the mainland Franco-American forces. In August Washington and his French ally, the Comte de Rochambean, moved their troops from New York and Newport toward the Chesapeake Bay, where they joined with troops landed by de Grasse and those of the Marquis de Lafayette to confront a British army of 8 000 at Yorktown under the command of Charles Cornwallis. Surrounded by a Franco-American army of 16 000 men and with his escape route by sea blocked by the French fleet, Cornwallis' position became untenable. On October 19, 1781, Cornwallis surrendered his entire army, which virtually ended fighting on American soil.

Ⅹ. The Treaty of Paris

General Cornwallis' surrender brought about a peace talk arranged in Paris and a treaty was signed on September 3, 1783. By the treaty the United States won formal recognition of its independence and the territory between the Appalachian Mountains and the Mississippi River from the Great Lakes to Florida.

The War of Independence was a historic event. By smashing the fetters of the British colonial rule, it gave the Americans a chance for free development of their nation. It was the first large-scale revolutionary movement of the American people against national oppression and for political and economic independence. It helped rouse the middle class in Europe against feudalism. Several years later, the *French Revolution*[22] broke out in 1789. Then the Spanish colonies in Americas rebelled. Following the example of the American people, the French people overthrew their king, and the Spanish colonies in Americas rose one after another to overthrow Spanish colonial rule.

Now Americans had won their independence and started a new era in American history. They were confronted with such new problems as how to organize their new nation and how to establish their new government.

Notes

1. mercantilist policy

重商主义政策　15—16世纪，随着资本主义的发展，重商主义开始产生和形成，英国殖民主义者通过重商主义政策扩大对殖民地的贸易、投资、出口工农业成品换取殖民地的廉价资源和原材料，以达到富裕母国的目的。

2. "salutary neglect"

"有益的疏忽"　指殖民主义时期，英国对殖民地统治软弱无能，不能有效地推行重商主义政策，这对殖民地的独立和发展十分有益，所以被殖民地人民看作是"有益的疏忽"。

3. The Navigation Acts

《航海法令》　是重商主义政策的典型，因为它禁止英国以外的其他一切国家和殖民地通商；禁止一切货物用英国船只以外的别国船只运回殖民地；禁止殖民地向英国以外的其他任何国家出口商品。

4. the English Board of Commissioners for Trade and Plantations

英国贸易和开发专署　负责英国对殖民地的贸易和开发事业。

5. The Congress affirmed the principle of no taxation without representation.

国会重申了如果殖民地在英国议会里没有代表资格，英国议会就没有权力向殖民地征税的原则。

6. pushed through Parliament a series of import duties on lead, glass, paper, paint and tea at colonial ports

通过议会，通过了在殖民地港口实行对铅、玻璃、纸、油漆和茶叶等一系列的进口税收

7. Boston Massacre

波士顿惨案　被看作美国革命的首轮较量。

8. Committees of Correspondence

通信或联络委员会　该组织的建立是便于各殖民地之间互通情报，协调步骤，统一行动，共同抗英。

9. botched another crisis

笨拙地制造了又一个危机

10. since the tea still carried the low tax left over from the Townshend Act to keep up the right

因为茶叶仍然保留汤森法案遗留下来的低税收，以维护英国向殖民地征税的权力

11. Boston Tea Party

波士顿茶会　为了抵制英国茶叶税，马萨诸塞州的人民伪装成印第安人，冲上停泊在波士顿港口满载茶叶的英国货轮，把全部茶叶倾倒入海，故名波士顿茶会。

12. The British government reacted quickly in a series ... the Intolerable Acts by the Americans.

英国政府迅速做出反应，议会通过了一系列强硬措施，这些措施被美国人称为“不可容忍的法令”。

13. Declaration of Rights and Grievances

《权利宣言与怨由陈情书》　宣言中阐明了殖民地人民的权利，并向英国抗议、请愿，以获得他们与英国的平等权利和地位。

14. Continental Association

大陆联盟　通过该组织，殖民地人民正式联合起来，在该组织的统一领导下统一计划、统一步骤、统一行动，共同抗英。

15. minutemen

随时准备立即应召的民兵

16. Declaration of the Causes and Necessity of Taking Up Arms

《关于拿起武器的原因和必要的公告》　公告重申了殖民地与英国的平等地位，并再次向英王申冤，请求改正错误，否则殖民地人民就要拿起武器，进行争取独立的武装斗争。

17. *Common Sense*

《常识》 劝说美国人民务必武装起来，开展独立战争，推翻英国皇家政权，建立一个共和政府。为号召殖民地人民武装起来，进行革命战争起了重要作用。

18. Declaration of Independence

《美国独立宣言》 阐明了美国人民独立战争的原因和理论根据，痛斥了英国殖民主义者所犯下的滔天罪行，殖民地人民宣誓坚决支持、拥护、参与独立战争，不获全胜，决不放下武器。

19. all men are created equal, that they are endowed by their Creator with certain unalienable Rights, that among these are Life, Liberty and the pursuit of Happiness. That to secure these rights, Governments are instituted among Men, deriving their powers from the consent of the governed

人类生而平等，造物者赋予他们若干不能出让的权利，其中如生命、自由和幸福的追求。为了保障这些权利，人类之间建立政府，而政府之正当权力，是经被统治者的同意而产生的。

be endowed with ... 被赋予……

20. These irremediable weaknesses grounded the doom of the British colonialists.

这些无法克服的弱点注定了英国殖民主义者的灭亡。

ground ... 把……基于……之上

21. two treaties, one of amity and commerce, and one of military alliance

两个条约，一个是友好通商，另一个是军事同盟 1778年，美国人民在萨拉托加战役取得胜利后，法国与美国签订了这两个条约，支持美国抗英独立战争。

22. French (Bourgeois) Revolution

法国(资产阶级)革命 亦称“法国大革命”，是1789—1794年法国人民推翻封建制度，确立资产阶级制度的革命。18世纪末，法国封建制度极端腐败，阶级矛盾日益尖锐，农民、城市市民和资产阶级纷纷起来反对僧侣、贵族的封建专制统治，摧毁了法国封建制度，建立了资产阶级政权，沉重地打击了欧洲封建体系，推动了欧洲和拉丁美洲各国的资产阶级革命和民族解放运动。

Exercises

Ⅰ. Fill in each blank with the right word or expression from the text:

1. Mass meeting on board the ships to throw all the tea overboard in Boston harbour was called ________.
2. The War of Independence broke out in ________ (year) at ________ (place).
3. The principal author of the Declaration of Independence was ________.
4. In January 1776, ________ published a pamphlet entitled ________, in which he urged complete independence.
5. Cornwallis' surrender at ________ (place) in ________ (year) virtually ended the War of Independence.
6. ________ was the economic philosophy which motivated British colonization of the New World.

Ⅱ. Questions for discussion:

1. What is meant by "mercantilism"?
2. What were the basic causes for the American Revolution?
3. Give a brief account of the Boston Tea Party.
4. Why was Lexington famous in American history?
5. Why was the Declaration of Independence significant in American history?
6. What was the significance of the American Revolution?

Chapter 8
The Formation of the Nation

Text

Ⅰ. The Formation of the Union

After they won independence, the Americans were faced with the problem of how to create a new nation—*should it be a strong union or a loose confederations?*[1] Union seemed indispensable to winning and preserving American independence, but many Americans had no desire to build a strong central government.

Ⅱ. *Critical Period*[2]

Shortly after the issuance of the Declaration of Independence, the Second Continental Congress appointed a committee under John Dickinson to draft a written constitution. "*The Articles of Confederation*"[3] was submitted in November 1777 to the states for ratification. However, it was not ratified until February 1781. The long delay resulted not from dissatisfaction with the Articles, but *from dissension over the status of western land claims*[4]. Seven landed states claimed western lands, yet the other six "landless" states with fixed boundaries argued that all western lands should be surrendered to Congress. In response to popular pressures and a congressional recommendation, most landed states ceded in 1780—1781 their claims to Congress. By this concession the United States secured for the public domain some hundred million acres for future expansion, which Congress promised would be "settled and formed into distinct republican states". Having settled the western land problem, "The Articles of Confederation" was ratified and became the law of the land On March 1, 1781.

The Articles created a de jure government in place of a de facto government.[5] Under the Articles each state retained complete sovereignty, independence and freedom, while the Confederation Congress acted merely as the administrative agency for the states. The Articles made no provision for a national executive or judicial branch, but provided for a unicameral legislature in which each state had a single vote. Passage of important measures required complete agreement. Congress could declare war and make peace, draft treaties and alliances, regulate currency, manage Indian affairs and maintain a postal service, but these powers were often denied by states. And the powers to tax, to coin and to regulate commerce were preserved by the states. It was the intention of the designers of the Articles that ultimate power be vested in the states as a precaution against the emergence of a strong central government. The Articles was written on the basis of the colonial experience and the theory of democracy and freedom which held that local self-government desirable and trustworthy.

During the Confederation period (1781—1789, also known as the (Critical Period), the new nation made the difficult transition from war to peace; the states remained united, though loosely, despite serious tensions; the spirit of nationalism spread and intensified, and Congress took action that had far-reaching effects. The major contribution of Congress to future development of the American cause was the passage of *the Northwest Ordinance of 1787*[6] by which the land between the Ohio and Mississippi Rivers would be divided into no less than three, or no more than five territories which would eventually enter the Union on an equal basis with the original states. In the beginning, Congress would appoint the governor and judges for each territory, but when the population reached 60 000 the territory could frame a constitution and petition Congress for statehood in the Union. The Ordinance also provided a bill of rights, guaranteeing settlers personal and religious freedom and forbidding slavery and involuntary servitude. Eventually five commonwealths—Ohio, Indiana, Illinois, Michigan, and Wisconsin—were formed out of the western territory.

The disadvantages of a weak government became increasingly apparent to Americans. Lacking power to tax, the Confederation Congress could not

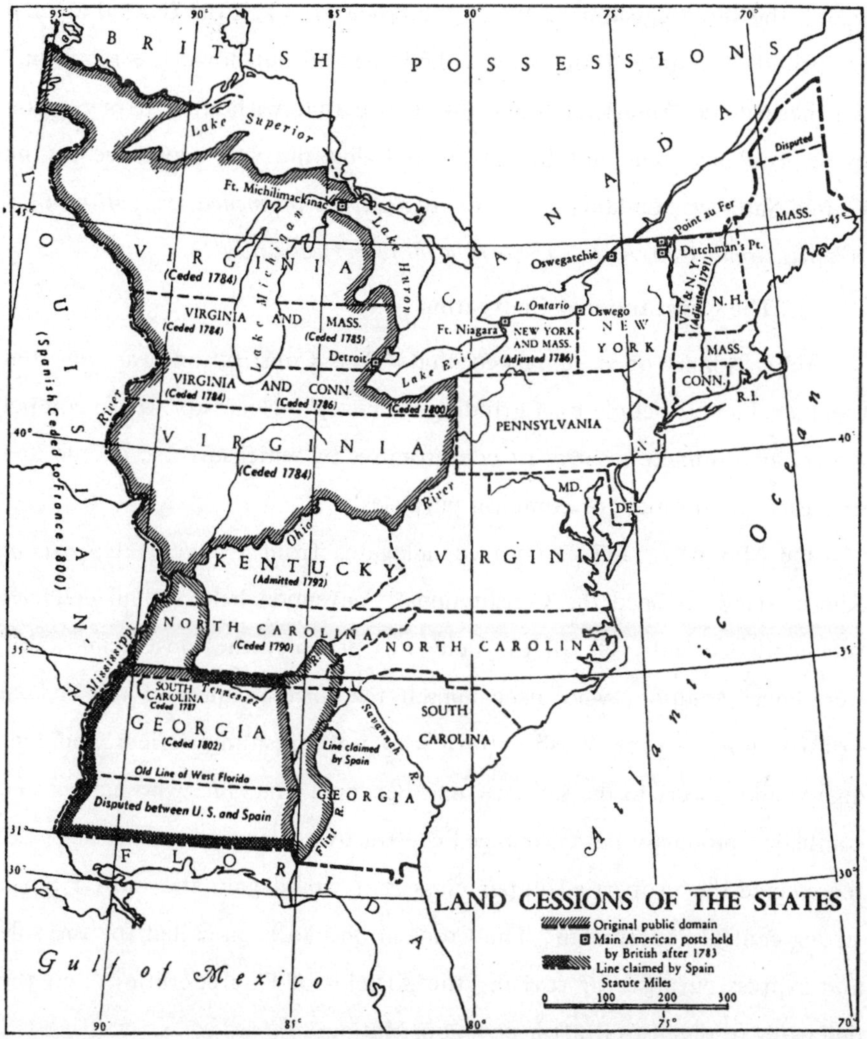

exercise even the meager authority granted by the Articles. The government could not support an armed force for national defense and security. Lacking power to regulate foreign and interstate commerce, Congress could neither negotiate favorable trade agreements abroad nor prevent domestic commercial rivalries. Besides, Americans were confronted by economic dislocations, internal conflicts, diplomatic frictions and frontier clashes. Things were particularly bad in Massachusetts. Mounting debts, depreciation of currency, high taxes, inflation and bankruptcy gave rise to *Shay's Rebellion*[7]. The insurgents dispersed the courts, opened the debtors prison and demonstrated against the state legislature. When the rebels attacked the federal arsenal at Springfield, state troops were called out and put down the rebellion. All these made Americans come to realize that without a strong union these problems could not be solved and that the very existence of the United Sates was endangered. *This realization prompted the calling of a Constitutional Convention to form a more perfect union.*[8]

Ⅱ. The Constitutional Convention

John Adams once remarked that "The Constitution was extorted from a reluctant people by a grinding necessity". Necessity would compel Americans to make a series of compromises by which diverse people and interests might unite for common purposes.

On May 12, 1787, fifty-five delegates from twelve states except Rhode Island attended the Constitutional Convention held at Philadelphia's Independence Hall. Of all the delegates present, the most remarkable were James Madison, who made himself the chief architect of the Federal Constitution, George Washington, who was presiding officer and lent dignity and respect to the sessions, and Benjamin Franklin, who harmonized conflicting proposals and encouraged constructive compromises. All delegates represented the propertied upper class that would gain the most from a strong central government. The Convention had been called for the sole and express purpose for revising the Articles of Confederation, but the delegates resolved to draft a new constitution.

At the Convention different proposals for drafting the Constitution were made. Virginia presented a proposal for a national government made up of two-house legislature, the lower house and the upper house. Both houses would be apportioned according to population and voting in the legislature would be by individuals. This plan held that larger states should have larger representation. New Jersey countered with a federal plan representing the small-state view and calling for a one-house legislature elected by the states regardless of population. This plan proposed that a small state should have the same voting as a large state. However, most delegates preferred a compromise and supported the proposal of Connecticut made by Roger Sherman. By the Connecticut Compromise, Congress would consist of two houses: a Senate in which each state would have two Senators and a House of Representatives in which each state would have at least one representative, with the number of other representatives to be determined by population, approximately one for every 30 000. This compromise reconciled the federal and national principles, and hence the "*Great Compromise*"[9].

Slavery itself did not become an issue at the Convention, *but controversy arose over the status of staves for taxation and representation*[10]. Since slaves were considered property rather than citizens, Northerners argued that slaves should be counted as equal to whites for purposes of taxation but ignored when apportioning representatives to the states on the basis of population. Southerners naturally reversed the argument, numbering slaves with whites for representation but not for taxation. The delegates eventually compromised by counting three-fifths of the slaves in determining both representation and taxation. In another compromise, Congress received authority to levy import taxes and to regulate interstate and foreign commerce but was expressly forbidden to impose export duties. This agreement assured national protection to Northern mercantile and maritime interests and non-interference with the Southern export economy. After the above controversial issues were settled, the Constitution was virtually shaped and became the "supreme law of the land" which compels obedience to the national government from the state governments, binds state officials to enforce Acts of Congress, and gives federal judges jurisdiction over all cases arising under the supreme law.

According to the principle of separation of powers, the U.S. government was set up with separate legislative, executive and judicial branches.[11] The legislative power was vested in Congress, the executive power in the President and the judicial power in the Supreme Court. Congress had the power to inaugurate laws, the President the power to veto any law passed by Congress, and the Supreme Court the power to interpret constitutionality of the law. Each branch shared its own respective power but was checked by the others, preventing each of them from taking over the supreme power. The Constitution also provided a division of powers between the federal government and the state government. The federal government exercised those federal powers under the supreme law while all other powers were reserved to the states respectively. However, the nation took precedence over the states.

The Convention decided that the Constitution would take force when ratified by nine states. After the Constitution was signed unanimously at the Convention on September 17, 1787, it was duly referred to the states for ratification.

Ⅲ. Ratification of the Constitution

The ratification debate in the country raged furiously and cut across economic, sectional and class divisions.[12] Opponents of the Constitution were called Anti-Federalists. They feared the potential for tyranny of a strong government and popular liberties would not be secured unless a bill of rights guaranteed them. Some farmers and debtors disliked restriction of the state's power to issue paper money, while some wealthy land-owners feared heavier taxation. Some westerners feared eastern indifference to the Mississippi navigation problem, while some southerners feared northern interference with their export economy. These fears seemed to justify their opposition to the ratification of the Constitution.

The champions of the Constitution were called Federalists.[13] They argued that the Constitution would create a strong but responsible government. The new government would be powerful enough to provide for national defense, financial solvency, Indian problems, protection of industry and commerce, dignity and respect at home and abroad, but not strong enough to interfere with states' rights and popular liberties. Thereby, they calmed many fears of the Anti-Federalists with a compromise to add a Bill of Rights to the Constitution, which formed the first ten amendments of the federal Constitution. These amendments guaranteed to citizens of the United States freedom of religion, speech, press and assembly. Notwithstanding, the ratification struggle was very close. Delaware and New Jersey ratified unanimously and Pennsylvania secured a two-to-one majority. Georgia and Connecticut ratified the Constitution without much contest. But in Massachusetts the Federalists won by a narrow margin. By June 21, 1788, Maryland, South Carolina and New Hampshire also ratified. With the approval of nine states the Constitution was technically in force. However, there could be no real union without Virginia, North Carolina and New York, which together had over 35 per cent of the population and which by geographical location split the nation into three distinct parts. Virginia accepted the Constitution by a narrow vote of 89 to 79 on June 26, 1788. The New York convention was almost evenly divided; North Carolina held out until November, 1789, and Rhode Island until May, 1790. However, the Constitution Congress declared the Constitution duly established and set March 4, 1789 for launching the new government under the Constitution.

Ⅳ. The Formation of the National Government

On April 30, 1789 George Washington solemnly took his oath as President swearing to "preserve, protect, and defend the Constitution of the United States". After he took office, he began to organize the executive office by appointing Thomas Jefferson as Secretary of State, Alexander Hamilton as Secretary of the Treasury, Henry Knox as Secretary of War, Edmund Randolph as Attorney General. Of all these men, Hamilton was to have the most immediate influence on legislation.

For Hamilton government was primarily a matter for the rich and well-born, whose interests were inextricably tied to the nation. His program was designed to bind the wealthy classes to the creation of a strong and energetic government in favor of the prior development of commerce and industry. His financial measures were: 1) to pay the entire national debt, both foreign and domestic, at its face value by the federal government;

2) to assume state debts left over from the Revolutionary War by the federal government; 3) to establish a national bank with capital supplied partly by the government and partly by private investors; and 4) to raise federal funds by protective tariffs on imports and by *excise taxes*[14].

Thomas Jefferson personally and philosophically opposed Hamilton.[15] He feared Hamilton's program would degrade liberal and humane principles. He believed that mankind was basically rational, capable to learn to participate in self-government. For Jefferson government could be entrusted to people because they were ultimately "the most honest and safe, although not the most wise depositary of the public interests". Jefferson placed greatest faith in the independent-minded freeholding farmers and thought of himself as the spokesman for the 90 percent of Americans who earned their living in agriculture. In a word, he wanted to build a strong and democratic government in favor of the prior development of agriculture.

Jefferson opposed Hamilton's financial measures, arguing that payment of the domestic debt in full would benefit speculators who had purchased government bonds from indebted farmers and veterans far below face value; assumption of state debts would be unfair to those states, chiefly in the South, that had paid off their debts; imposition of tariffs on imports would raise prices for the consumers and the excise taxes would hurt western farmers who converted much of their grain to liquor.

The rivalry between Jefferson and Hamilton deeply distressed Washington, but his efforts to reconcile their differences failed. Although Jefferson served as Secretary of State under Washington, the President found himself more closely attuned in both foreign and domestic policies to Hamilton's administrative realism. Washington was also disturbed at the spread of factionalism and partisanship in American politics. As early as 1792, *the conflict personified by the Hamilton-Jefferson rivalry crystallized into Federalist versus Democratic Republican parties*[16], which competed with each other in the influence of the formation of the new nation.

During his administration, Washington largely succeeded in the fulfillment of Hamilton's goals. The National Bank was set up; a sound credit system was laid down; most of the debts were paid off; development of commerce and industry was motivated. But his forceful and activist policies also encouraged the rise of strong opposition among the people which culminated in *the Whisky Rebellion*[17]. In 1794, farmers in western Pennsylvania led by various democrats rioted against the tax law and defied the federal agents from collecting taxes. With the advice of Hamilton, Washington called out a militia army of 13 000 men to put down the insurrection. The Whisky Rebellion was a serious challenge to federal law. Its speedy suppression at once strengthened federal authority and aroused strong opposition to Federalists and started its march towards decline.

During and beyond Washington's administration, the dominating factor in international relations was the French Revolution which began in 1789. French leaders assumed that the old 1778 wartime alliance between France and the United States would continue in force at least to the extent of economic assistance.

Hamilton objected, however, arguing that America should stay out of war between England and France and that the best course was neutrality; and Jefferson argued that the United States should honour its treaties with France and should accept as a minister the representative of the new French revolutionary government. Unfortunately, the French Minister, Edmond Genet, violated every rule of foreign diplomacy by commissioning American ships to sail as privateers under French flags and by trying to arrange for an expedition of western frontiersmen to attack Spanish New Orleans. Washington issued a formal declaration of neutrality in April 1793, and when Genet continued to abuse his position, *Washington asked for his recall*[18].

England in the meantime stopped American ships and searched them for goods in transit to France. The Congress debated which methods should be used to punish England, and American mobs mistreated British seamen and tarred and feathered pro-British Americans. In 1795 Washington sent John Jay as his special representative to England for negotiations. He secured a treaty by which Great Britain promised to surrender its Northwest posts and made some slight trade concessions. Though Jay's Treaty was unpopular with most Americans, it helped avoid a war with England that the nation might have found both costly and dangerous.

After Washington left office, John Adams assumed Presidency. He was confronted with division within his own Federalist party, sustained and often violent opposition from the Republicans, and the growing menace of Revolutionary France. Indeed, the French problem colored both foreign and domestic concerns, for it brought the United States to the brink of war and encouraged repressive measures at home.

The French retaliated against American favoritism toward England in trade by breaking off diplomatic relations and despoiling American shipping. By June 1797 French privateers had captured over 300 American ships and confiscated their cargoes. Seeking to avoid war, Adams sent a special mission to France to secure compensation for American losses and to negotiate a new trade treaty. However, the French Foreign Minister, Talleyrand demanded a personal bribe of $250 000 and a $12 million loan for France through three agents (designated *XYZ*[19] in the American report of the incident) before he would even receive the mission officially. When news of these demands reached the American Congress, Federalists were outraged with the French insult to American honour. The United States adopted a policy of "armed neutrality" and during 1798 and 1799 engaged in an undeclared but limited, naval war with France.

Yet Adams still entertained hopes for peace and in late 1799 sent a second commission to Paris. This time Talleyrand received the commission, for he was now secretly negotiating with Spain to reacquire the North American territory of Louisiana and feared the potential danger of continuing Franco-American hostility. The result of the Convention of 1800 removed the immediate threat of full-scale conflict. Adams' judicious conduct prevented an unnecessary war with France but cost him dearly in political popularity and party solidarity.

Faced with the growing opposition from the Republicans, *Adams took measures to curb freedom of press and speech and limit liberty of aliens*[20]. The Federalists who dominated Congress used the war fever to pass *the repressive Alien and Sedition Acts*[21], which sought to injure the Republican party by intimidating Republican editors and potential Republican voters. Under the Sedition Act, the courts convicted ten Democratic Republican publishers for printing statements critical of the President or the Congress. Obviously the law endangered freedom of press and speech and turned federal courts into machines for political persecution.

This intolerable situation turned public opinion to the support of the Republicans. James Madison and Thomas Jefferson responded by drafting the Virginia and Kentucky Resolutions, which declared the Alien and Sedition Acts null and void as violations of the Federal Bill of Rights. Under the strong opposition from the people, the Alien and Sedition Acts eventually expired without fanfare.

By 1800 the popularity of the Federalists had slipped badly. In the election campaign of 1800 Jefferson was elected President, effecting a peaceful transfer of power from the Federalist party to the Democratic Republican party.

Notes

1. ... should it be a strong union or a loose confederation?

……它应该是一个强大的联邦还是一个松散的邦联？ 前者建立有力的中央政府，统一领导联邦；后者只建立一个松散的邦联政府，没有一个有力的中央机构，实行统一领导，各州保持自治。

2. critical period

困难时期或危急时期 在邦联时期，国会没有一个统一的中央领导机构负责解决各州间出现或发生的种种问题、矛盾和困难，甚至发展到危及国家的安全、独立和发展，故称困难时期或危急时期。

3. The Articles of Confederation

《邦联条例》 独立后立即订立此条例建立一个松散的邦联国家,各州保持自治,以防中央政府出现暴政。

4. from dissension over the status of western land claims

来自对西部土地所有权争论的意见分歧 已占有西部土地的州称这些土地的所有权归它们,但未占有西部土地的州则坚持西部土地应归属国会所有。

5. The Articles created a de jure government in place of a de facto government.

按《邦联条例》建立一个法律上的政府,替代一个事实的政府。

de jure(拉丁语)是 by law,意为“法律上”。

de facto(拉丁语)是 in fact,意为“事实上”。

6. the Northwest Ordinance of 1787

1787 年西北土地法令 按此法令,位于俄亥俄和密西西比河之间的土地要测量划分为不少于三块、不多于五块的土地,结果划分为五块土地建立了五个州,即俄亥俄州、伊利诺伊州、印第安纳州、密歇根州和威斯康星州,从而解决了西北土地所有权归属问题的争论。

7. Shay's Rebellion

“谢氏叛乱” 这是美国独立后第一次农民组织起来反对邦联政府的斗争,他们驱散法庭,打开监狱,释放债人,游行抗议州议会政府,反对高债务、高税收、通货膨胀和破产,最后被政府平息。

8. This realization prompted the calling of a Constitutional Convention to form a more perfect union.

鉴于这种认识,他们立即召集制宪会议,建立一个更为完善的联邦。

9. the “Great Compromise”

“大妥协” 康涅狄格州代表提出国会由参、众两院组成,前者由各州选两名参议员组成,后者由各州按人口比例选举产生的众议员组成,但人口最少的州至少有一名代表,这提案既照顾了大州的利益也照顾了小州的利益,故被称为“大妥协”。

10. but controversy arose over the status of slaves for taxation and representation

当争论奴隶的人头税和代表制问题时,奴隶问题便产生了 当时在美国，奴隶被看作私人财产，北方人认为他们应该缴纳人头税，但不能赋予代表权，而南方奴隶主则认为他们应赋予代表权，但不能缴纳人头税，争论结果达成妥协，3/5 的奴隶既要纳人头税也赋予代表权。

11. According to the principle of separation of powers the U. S. government was set up with separate legislative, executive and judicial branches.

按照权力分立的原则，美国中央和州政府分别建立行政、立法和司法三个部门。它们既有各自的权力又相互制约和平衡，以防某个部门独揽大权。

12. The ratification debate in the country raged furiously and cut across economic, sectional and class divisions.

签署宪法的辩论在全国引起了极大的反响，产生了经济、地区和阶级的分裂。

13. The champions of the Constitution were called Federalists.

宪法的拥护者被称为联邦拥护者或联邦党。与之相对，反对宪法者则被称反联邦制度者或民主共和党人(Anti-Federalists or the Democratic Republicans)。

14. excise taxes

货物税　中央政府向国内货物的征税。

15. Thomas Jefferson personally and philosophically opposed Hamilton.

托马斯·杰弗逊，就个人而言和从哲学上，都反对哈密尔敦。

16. the conflict personified by the Hamilton-Jefferson rivalry orytallized into Federalist versus Democratic Republican parties

以哈密尔敦和杰弗逊为代表的敌对冲突具体地表现为联邦党和民主共和党的对抗

17. the Whisky Rebellion

威士忌叛乱　在民主党人的领导下，宾夕法尼亚州西部农民起来反抗货物税法和抵制邦联税务官员收集税款的斗争。

18. Washington asked for his recall

华盛顿请求把他(法驻美大使)召回国。　华盛顿认为法驻美大使凌辱华盛顿的权威，违反国际法，侵犯、危害了美国的利益，独立和安全。

19. XYZ

XYZ 事件　在约翰·亚当斯执政期间，美法关系紧张，他派了一个特别使团赴法谈判，以求解决矛盾，但法国外长三个代理人(美国在该事件的报告里用 XYZ 代表)要求给外长个人 $ 250 000 的贿赂和给法国 $ 12 000 000 的贷款，故称 XYZ 事件。该事件恶化了美法关系。

20. Adams took measures to curb freedom of press and speech and limit the liberty of aliens

亚当斯采取措施抑制出版、言论自由，并限制外侨的自由

21. the repressive Alien and Sedition Acts

镇压性的外侨法和叛乱法　根据外侨法，外侨在美国侨居取得美国国籍的年限由 5 年延长至 14 年，从而限制了外侨对民主共和党的支持；叛乱法旨在伤害民主共和党，恐吓民主共和党人的报纸及杂志的编辑、记者对总统和国会的批评和揭露，为此，一些民主共和党人被依法判处有罪，入狱坐牢。这激起了民主共和党对联邦主义者更加强烈的反抗。

Exercises

Ⅰ. Fill in each blank with the right word or expression from the test:

1. The long delay of the ratification of the Articles of Confederation resulted from dissension over the status of ________.
2. According to the Northwest Ordinance of 1787 ________, ________, ________, ________ and ________ were formed out of the western territory.
3. All delegates present at the Constitutional Convention represented the ________ class that would gain the most from a strong central government.
4. The Great Compromise provided for a two-house congress composed of the ________ with ________, and the ________ with ________.
5. At the Constitutional Convention, the slavery issue was settled by counting ________ of the slaves in determining both ________ and ________.
6. According to the principle of separation of power, the U. S. government was set up with separate ________, ________ and ________ branches.

7. In the process of forming the new government, there emerged two political factions, ________ headed by ________ who represented the interests of ________, and ________ headed by ________ who represented the interests of ________.

8. The Whisky Rebellion was a riot against ________ and ________.

9. During and after Washington's administration, the dominating factor in international relations was ________.

10. In 1797 when John Adams was sworn into the White House, he was confronted with the problems of ________, ________ and ________.

11. President John Adams urged the passage of ________ and ________ Acts with an aim to injure the Democratic Republican Party by intimidating the Republican editors and voters into submission.

Ⅱ. Questions for discussion:

1. Why were the years between 1781 and 1789 called the critical period?
2. Why was the ratification of the Articles of Confederation delayed until 1781?
3. State the importance of the Northwest Ordinance of 1787.
4. On what issues did the delegates at the Constitutional Convention debate? How were they settled?
5. Why did the ratification debate on the U. S. constitution cut across economic, sectional and class lines? How was it settled?
6. How do you understand the division of power of the U.S. government?
7. What do you think about George Washington?
8. What was Hamilton's philosophical thought in the building of the national government? What were his financial measures?
9. In what ways did Jefferson oppose Hamilton?
10. State the different characteristics of the Federalists and the Democratic Republicans.
11. Why did President Adams push through the Alien and Sedition Acts?
12. What was Washington's foreign policy? Why was the Cabinet divided on the issue?

Chapter 9
Adolescent America and Westward Expansion

Jeffersonian Era

Text

Thomas Jefferson viewed his election to the Presidency as the "Revolution of 1800", but no radical change occurred in governmental structure. He favored greater self-government and placed emphasis on concern over individuals and business. "*The aim of legitimate government*," *Jefferson asserted*, "*is to secure the greatest degree of happiness possible to the general mass of those associated with it*."[1]

Jefferson acted to strengthen the position of the average citizen. He pardoned and released victims of the Sedition Act; ended the excise tax on whisky; abolished or reduced internal taxes; emphasized governmental thrift and economy; and paid off over 30 per cent of the national debt. More significantly, he adopted a new land act which provided for the sale of the minimum tract of 160 acres at a price of $2 an acre. This act stimulated both westward expansion and individual land ownership.

But Jeffersonian administration preserved most Federalist programs, strengthened governmental power and authority, and promoted such national programs as interstate canals and roads. However, *the Federal judiciary remained a Federalist stronghold*[2].

The Chief Justice John Marshall had made a series of decisions, through which the Supreme Court established a set of principles: 1) the Supreme Court possessed the power to nullify laws in conflict with the Constitution; 2) the Supreme Court alone had the right to interpret the Constitution; and 3) the "law of the land"—*the Constitution—took precedence over all other laws*[3]. Thereby the Supreme Court established itself by Constitution as the final judge.

Ⅰ. *The Louisiana Purchase*[4] (1803)

The Republicans, led by Jefferson, prided themselves on championing governmental economy, states' rights, and strict constitutional interpretation. But above all, they turned the Louisiana Purchase of 1803, an ominous threat to national interests, into an astonishing opportunity. Soon after Jefferson assumed the Presidency news reached him that Napoleon had forced Spain to transfer Louisiana to France. Jefferson feared French designs on America and, especially, the economic stranglehold on American commerce on the Mississippi River. He, therefore, instructed Robert Livingston and James Monroe to seek guarantees of American rights of commerce in New Orleans and to negotiate for the purchase of New Orleans alone at $7.5 million. As Napoleon was now at war with England and he did not want to have American as enemy, he suddenly decided to sell all of Louisiana to America at $15 million. Livingston and Monroe boldly agreed to pay the offer. Jefferson worried that the purchase violated the Constitution but nevertheless submitted the treaty to the Senate for ratification. The Senate quickly ratified the treaty, and the House readily appropriated funds. Jefferson later justified the purchase in terms of placing the nation's paramount interests above the Constitution. Most Americans rejoiced over this unexpected but splendid bargain which doubled the size of America's territory and made possible further westward expansion by pushing American frontier far beyond the Middle West. This bargain also put the Mississippi River system under the complete control of the United States. Cheap water transportation stimulated fast development of agriculture, industry and cities in the Middle West.

Ⅱ. *The Lewis and Clark Expedition*[5]

Another noteworthy event that took place during Jefferson's administration was the Lewis and Clark expedition to the Pacific Coast. In 1804 a party led by Lewis and Clark started from St. Louis up the Missouri River into North Dakota. During 1805 the expedition moved through Montana and

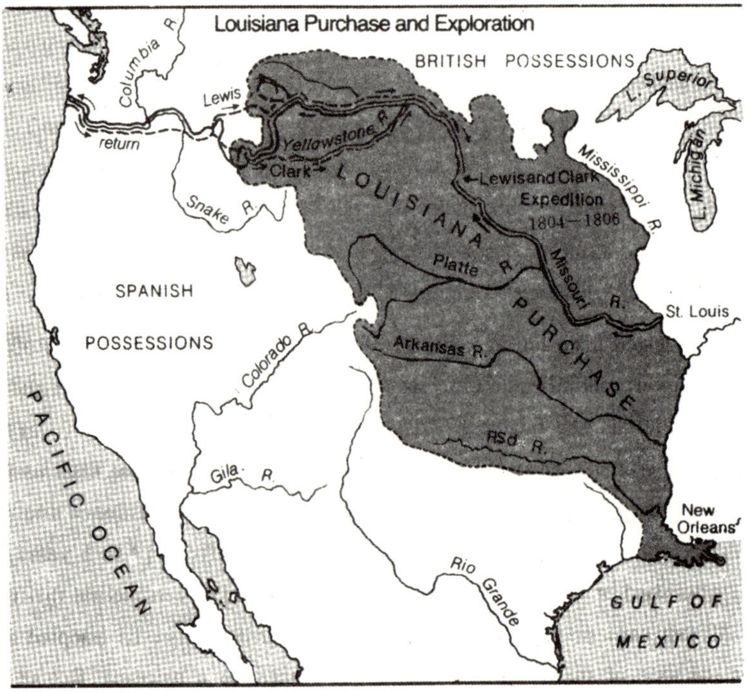

Idaho and crossed the Rocky Mountains. Then they drifted down the Columbia River to the Pacific Coast. This expedition lasted over two years. Its success gave the United States new claims to the Oregon Country by virtue of discovery and settlement, provided much information on the Missouri and Columbia valleys. Soon traders and fur-trappers swarmed into this area through Louisiana territory.

Ⅲ. *The Embargo Act of 1807 and Non-Intercourse Act of 1809*[6]

During Jefferson's administration, the dominating factor in international relations was the resumption of European war. He sought neutrality between Britain and France, but neither of them made it an easy position. Initially European war stimulated American trade but it moved swiftly toward a stalemate which both Britain and France attempted to end by way of commercial warfare.

Thereafter both nations interfered with American trade and seized American vessels and cargoes. In addition, the British *continued the practice of boarding American vessels and impressing into their service any soldier suspected of being an English deserter*[7]. Jefferson sought to use peaceful means to settle the issue, but had no success. He therefore persuaded Congress in late 1807 to pass the Embargo Act, which prohibited all exports from the United States to any European country.

This measure brought economic pressures to bear on Britain, but damaged American commerce and raised political protest. American shippers had to give up their profitable war trade; planters and farmers lost their European markets. New England merchants, including many Federalists, denounced the Embargo Act as unconstitutional, defiantly engaged in illicit trade through Canada, and threatened to secede from the Union. Faced with the strong opposition a Non-Intercourse Act was substituted, permitting American trade with all foreign countries except England and France.

Ⅳ. The War of 1812

After Jefferson left the White House in 1809, the central stage of American politics was no longer in the hands of the veteran revolutionary founders of America. Instead, a new generation of self-conscious and militant Americans known as "*War Hawks*"[8] increasingly secured the seats of power. These new leaders became more acquisitive and aggressive and propelled the United States into a war with Great Britain.

Historians agreed that the demand for war centered in the Mississippi Valley and the South Atlantic states. Factors simulating war fever included problems with the Indians and suspicion that the British in Canada encouraged and armed them; the land hunger of the frontiersmen which inspired dreams of conquering Canada from Britain and Florida from Spain, agrarian discontent with the economic depression brought on by the British trade restrictions; and perhaps, a more important intense American spirit of personal and national honor which *demanded resort to arms to revenge the seizure and impressment of seamen*[9]. In summarizing the causes of the war, Andrew Jackson mentioned neutral right, impressment, national vindication, Indian pacification, and the desire for territorial conquest.

By the spring of 1812 the war fever had grown so strong that President James Madison asked Congress for a declaration of war against Great Britain. The South and the West supported the war while New England states steadfastly opposed it.

The Americans were lucky in that the British had Napoleon as their major enemy at the time. In 1812 America had only a small navy and an army of 7 000 ill-trained and poorly supplied men.

The Americans began the war with an attempt to invade Canada, but it failed. Two other attempts in the same direction were also rebuffed. But American warships sank some British ships and won a great victory on Lake Erie. This victory encouraged the Americans, though it was not a decisive one.

By 1814 a major crisis had emerged. British blockade of the American coastline was becoming much more effective and Napoleon had been defeated. After Napoleon's defeat, the British concentrated their forces and planned three attacks on America, in the South and the North and directly at the American capital, Washington D.C.

The British first landed at the Chesapeake Bay and marched against Washington D.C. They burned the Capitol, the White House, and other government buildings. From there the British moved to Fort McHenry, which guarded the city of Baltimore. The British ships bombarded the fort a whole night but Americans held their ground and the U.S. flag kept waving over the fort. Francis Scott Key, being detained on a British ship, watched the whole scene and wrote with deep emotion *a poem entitled "The Star-Spangled Banner" in commemoration of the victorious defense of Fort McHenry*[10]. The poem was officially acknowledged as the national anthem in 1931.

After the setback, London came to realize that a massive military effort would be necessary before victory could be achieved. Meanwhile the British people were heavily taxed and were losing enthusiasm for a distant war against the United States. Thus a peace talk was arranged at Ghent, Belgium on December 24, 1814, which recognized that neither side had won the war.

Ⅴ. Immediate Effect of the War of 1812

The War of 1812 was, in a sense, a second war of independence, for before that time the United States had not yet been accorded equality in the family of nations. After the war the United States was recognized as an independent nation internationally. Most of the serious difficulties that the young republic had faced since the Revolution now disappeared. National union and patriotism were greatly strengthened and stimulated. Now a prospect of peace, prosperity and social progress opened before the nation.

Following the war and the election of James Monroe to the Presidency in 1816, America enjoyed the "*Era of Good Feelings*"[11]. The period was marked by three features: the tremendous economic development both in industry and in agriculture; disappearance of party struggle and the international peace.

During the war, northern industry had grown very fast and the West increasingly produced foodstuffs in abundance. The United States seemed now to have become self-sufficient and self-independent from Europe. In the meantime the Federalists had slipped badly and was disbanded in 1820. Thus ended the twenty-five-year struggle between Federalists and Republicans. A series of international agreements with England and Spain were reached. As a result, international conflicts diminished and American sovereignty and independence were consolidated.

Yet the term "Era of Good Feelings" was misleading. The first national depression in American history—*the Panic of 1819 took place*[12]. It was the result of the quick over-expansion that followed the War of 1812. This panic was soon followed by the sectional struggle of the admission of the state of Missouri. In 1819 Missouri asked to be admitted to the Union as a slave slate. The South favored the admission, but the

North opposed it because it would give the South control in the Senate which now held an equal number of slave and free states. The issue was settled by *the Missouri Compromise of 1820*[13] by which Missouri was admitted into the Union as a slave state while Maine was admitted into the Union as a free state. In addition, an imaginary line was drawn across the Louisiana territory at 36°30′. The further spread of slavery was prohibited north of the line. The Missouri Compromise eased the tension between north and south for a few years. Of course. the Compromise did not settle permanently the issue of slavery, nor did it please either side. John Quincy Adams called this struggle, "a title page to a great tragic volume", and Thomas Jefferson called it "a firebell in the night", a further dampening effect on the Era of Good Feelings.

Ⅵ. *The Monroe Doctrine*[14] (1823)

However the most notable event during Monroe's administration was the declaration of the Monroe Doctrine in 1823. By the 1820s America was increasingly becoming concerned over affairs in the Western Hemisphere. Most of Spain's colonies in the Americas had revolted and established themselves as independent republics. The U. S. government supported the independence movement then sweeping over Americas and recognized the new nations. They feared that *the Holy Alliance*[15] would restore direct control in the old Spanish colonies. Meanwhile the Russians had been moving south from Alaska and now were claiming all the coastal area north of the 51 parallel. On December 2, 1823, Monroe sent to Congress his annual message stating his foreign policy dealing with such situation. This policy was known as the Monroe Doctrine. The Doctrine covered four major points: 1) the Western Hemisphere was no longer open to colonization by any European power; 2) the U. S. would not interfere with the existing colonies of any European power; 3) the U.S. would not interfere with European affairs; 4) any attempt to reassert control over former colonies or to establish new ones was to be considered as a threat or an unfriendly act against the U.S.

The Monroe Doctrine laid down the basis of American foreign policy. For a long time thereafter the United States did not allow the European powers to interfere with American affairs and refused to be involved in European disputes. This kind of isolation was advantageous to American cause, offering a better chance for internal development and more flexibility in foreign affairs, and the realization of the slogan "America for Americans", was made possible.

Ⅶ. Westward Expansion

The Jeffersonian Era (1800—1828) was a very important stage for the growth of young America. *Nationalism grew along with individualism*.[16] After the War of 1812, America's independence was consolidated and the authority of the Federal government established. Individualism urged equal chances for life, rights and liberty. Competition and equality characterized the growth of the Era. And the territorial expansion in turn provided much room for the development of these values. Industry and agriculture developed very fast. Canals, highways and railways were being constructed. Factories and cities sprang up wherever frontiersmen came and settled. All these factors combined facilitated further westward expansion.

Westward expansion marked every phase of American history, but it had special significance as the United States rounded out its contiguous continental expansion. Between 1830 and 1860 westward expansion became inextricably interwoven with concepts of *manifest destiny*[17] and with ideas of sectional interests which colored territorial discussion with the slavery issue.

The lands that Americans most coveted were naturally those to which they had the least claims but which would complete their conquest of the continent—the Spanish-Mexican borderlands. In the 1830s and 1840s this territory felt the full impact of the aggressive nationalism and land-hungry individualism of Americans. Movement into Texas, California, and other borderlands by Americans who had every intention of retaining their U. S. citizenship established de facto American colonies and, thereby, strengthened U.S. claims to the territory.

Ⅷ. Settlement of the Oregon Territory (1846)

American interest in Oregon began in 1787, when a Boston ship, Columbia, made one of the greatest pioneer trading voyages in history. After the Louisiana Purchase of 1803, Oregon became one of the frontiers of the United States, and more and more Americans moved into this territory. By the 1820s, it was jointly settled by England and the United States, but Americans extended their settlement very fast, and in 1843 a government was set up to rule themselves. By 1846 there were 10 000 Americans in Oregon. Being a strong expansionist, President James K. Polk decided to arrange for the substantial occupation of the Oregon territory. In 1846, England was forced to sign the Oregon Treaty, extending the U.S.-Canadian boundary at the 49 parallel to the Pacific.

Ⅸ. *The Annexation of Texas*[18] (1845)

After gaining independence from Spain in 1821, Mexico allowed Americans to settle in Texas. By 1830 over 20 000 Americans had settled in Texas, and Mexican officials had become alarmed by the troublesome demands of Americans there for greater self-government. In 1830 the Mexicans forbade further immigration, ordered customs duties collected along the Texas-Americans border, and sent troops to occupy Texas and to enforce obedience. Then in 1835 General Santa Anna who assumed dictatorial powers in Mexico, abolished the federal constitution and sent a military governor to rule Texas. Deprived of both constitutional liberties and local rights, the Texas-Americans declared independence from Mexico on March 2, 1836, but the Mexican government refused to recognize it officially.

On March 3, 1837, President Andrew Jackson gave official U. S. recognition to the new Republic of Texas, but Texans who hoped for immediate annexation were disappointed. For eight years Northerners

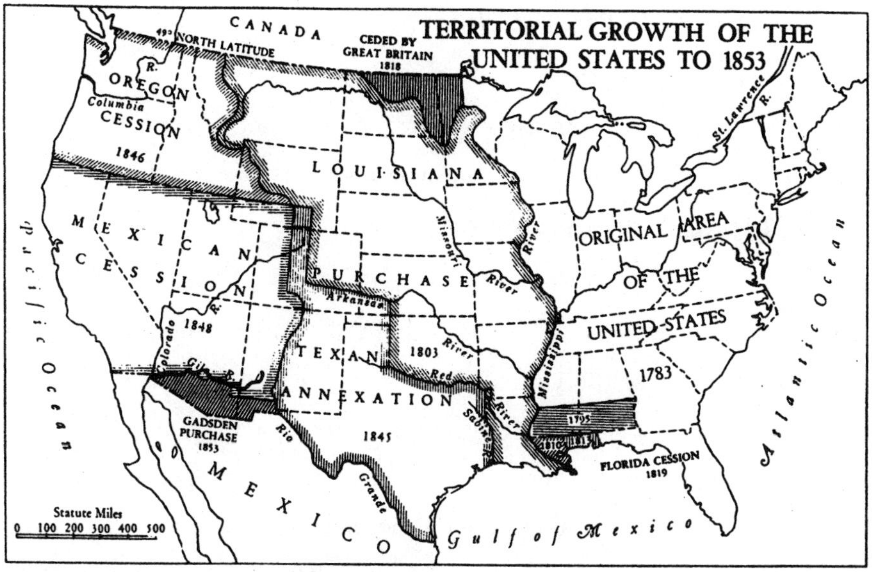

blocked annexation of the vast slave territory of Texas, fearing that it might be carved into as many as six or eight slave states and, thereby, permitted the South to dominate the congress. Only after the election of James K. Polk in 1844 to the presidency on a strong expansionist platform did the annexation treaty win congressional approval.

Ⅹ. The Mexican War (1846—1847)

Mexico had earlier threatened to declare war if the U. S. annexed Texas. It now withdrew its minister and severed official relations with the American government. President Polk in turn ordered U. S. forces into the disputed territory between the Nueces River and the Rio Grande, and Congress responded with a formal declaration of war on Mexico. American troops during 1846 and 1847 not only won decisive victories in Mexico, but also moved into New Mexico and California. By the Treaty of Guadeloupe Hidalgo, signed on February 2, 1848, Mexico ceded all claims to Texas, New Mexico and California to the United States in return for a payment of $15 million. By this treaty Mexico was robbed half of its total territory. This was known as the *Mexican Cession*[19].

Ⅺ. The Gadsden Purchase (1853)

The Gadsden Purchase of 1853 added territory in what is today Southern Arizona and the New Mexico panhandle. Thus, the United States completed its contiguous continental expansion.

Ⅻ. The Alaska Purchase (1867)

The Alaska Purchase was made in 1867. It was as much a bargain as the Louisiana Purchase. Alaska was admitted into the Union in 1959. It is the largest state of the United States and is rich in mineral resources.

A century of expansion following 1776 increased the U.S. territory to ten times its size at the time of its founding through invasion, purchase, treaty, etc. During the same period, the population had increased from about 7 million to 33 million. Many of them were new immigrants from Europe. History had seldom seen such a large scale of territorial expansion going along with such a large scale of immigration within such a short period of time.

The expansion involved a heroic struggle against the wilderness, which shaped the American nation with special character and values.[20] In the meantime the westward expansion resulted in different sections with different political influence and economic strength. As a result sectional conflicts intensified, disputes over important issues rose one after another. All these would inevitably lead to a new hot fight between different groups and sections.

Notes

1. "The aim of legitimate government," Jefferson asserted, "is to ensure the great degree of happiness possible to the general mass of those associated with it."

"一个正统政府的目的，"杰弗逊宣称，"是尽可能为与该政府相依为命的广大群众谋取最大的幸福。"

be associated with ... 与……相关联

2. the Federal judiciary remained a Federalist stronghold

联邦政府的司法部仍然是联邦党人的一个大本营

3. the Constitution—took precedence over all other laws

宪法的权力大于其他一切法律

take/have precedence over/of 优先于……;地位在……之上

4. the Louisiana Purchase

购买路易斯安那 路易斯安那原为西班牙领地，后转让给法国，再后由美国购买。

5. the Lewis and Clark Expedition

刘易斯与克拉克远征探险 他们率领的远征探险队于1804年从圣路易斯城出发，沿密苏里河逆流而上，越过落基山脉，沿蛇河顺流而下，经哥伦比亚河到达太平洋沿岸,后大致沿着原路返回圣路易斯城，历时两年多。这次远征是美国国内首次横越大陆西抵太平洋沿岸的活动。

6. the Embargo Act of 1807 and Non-Intercourse Act of 1809

1807年的禁运法令和1809年的不交往法令 禁运法令禁止美国向欧洲国家运送一切出口物资。按不交往法令，美国允许与欧洲所有国家，除英国与法国之外的贸易往来。

7. continued the practice of boarding American vessels and impressing into their service any soldier suspected of being an English deserter

继续强行登上美国船只俘虏并强迫被怀疑是英国逃兵的美国兵为他们服役

impress ... into the service of ... 强迫……为……服役

8. War Hawks

好战分子 指美国第二代人中的激进派，他们急于以战争手段从英、法手中夺取更多的土地。

9. demanded resort to arms to revenge the seizure and impressment of seamen

要求诉诸武力，就海员被俘和被强迫服役问题，向英、法报复

10. a poem entitled "The Star-Spangled Banner" in commemoration of the victorious defence of Fort McHenry.

一首题为"星条旗"的诗纪念马亨利堡胜利保卫战。 这首诗于1931

年被正式确认为美国国歌的歌词。

11."Era of Good Feelings"

"好感时代" 它有三个特征:一是工农业的惊人发展,二是党派斗争的消失,三是国际和平的实现。

12.the Panic of 1819 took place

1819年大恐慌爆发 源于1812年战后的发展过于迅猛。

13.the Missouri Compromise of 1820

1820年的密苏里和解 根据该和解,密苏里作为奴隶州加入联邦,而缅因则作为自由州加入联邦,因而南、北方仍在国会保持同等席位,另在路易斯安那北纬36°30′画一虚线,奴隶不准进入此线以北。

14.the Monroe Doctrine

门罗主义 1823年,门罗总统向国会做的年度报告阐明了国际形势,提出了以外交政策解决俄国向太平洋沿岸南下的威胁及西班牙在美洲殖民地的争端。

15.the Holy Alliance

神圣同盟 1815—1816年俄罗斯帝国、奥地利帝国、普鲁士王国三国签订,同盟目的是为了镇压欧洲各国的民主革命运动。

16.Nationalism grew along with individualism.

民族主义精神和个人主义精神同时发展。

17.manifest destiny

命定说 19世纪美国民主党所持的一种信念,他们认为美国被赋予向西扩张直至横跨北美大陆的天命。这种思想促进了西部扩张、移民和定居的迅速发展。

18.the Annexation of Texas

吞并得克萨斯州 1837年得州被吞并之后,曾被北方人阻止加入联邦达8年之久,因为他们害怕得州可分割为6—8个奴隶州,加入联邦会对他们不利。

19.the Mexican Cession

墨西哥割让 按瓜达鹿白—希达哥条约,墨西哥把得克萨斯、新墨西哥及加利福尼亚割让给美国,故称墨西哥割让。

20.The expansion involved a heroic struggle against the wilderness, which shaped the American nation with special character and values.

西部扩张是一场向荒野的英勇宣战，它塑造了美国民族的特殊性格和价值观。

Exercises

Ⅰ. Fill in each blank with the right word or expression from the text:

1. The westward expansion was completed through ________, ________ and ________.
2. Through the Mexican War, the United States annexed ________, ________ and ________.
3. The basic causes for the announcement of the Monroe Doctrine were ________ and ________.
4. The "Era of Good Feelings" was marked by ________, ________ and ________.
5. The War of 1812 was known as the Second American War of Independence, because ________.
6. The most important contributions made by Thomas Jefferson to the development of his country were ________ and ________.
7. Historians agreed that the immediate cause for the War of 1812 was the struggle for the control of ________ land ________.
8. The national anthem, "The Star-Spangled Banner", was written by ________.
9. The westward expansion was a heroic struggle against the wilderness, which shaped the American nation with ________, and resulted in different sections with ________.
10. The belief that the Americans were the race chosen by God to expand to the West, and even North America was known as ________.

Ⅱ. Questions for discussion:

1. What were Thomas Jefferson's main liberal ideas?
2. What effects did Jefferson achieve during his administration?

3. What was the importance of the Louisiana Purchase and that of the Lewis and Clark Expedition in America's development?
4. What were the causes of the War of 1812?
5. What is meant by the "Era of Good Feelings" in American history?
6. What were the main points of the Monroe Doctrine? Why was it significant in American history?
7. Give a brief account of the Mexican War and the Mexican Cession.
8. How did America finish its westward expansion?
9. What important spirits and values grew in strength during the westward expansion?
10. How did nationalism grow side by side with democracy and individualism?

Chapter 10

Sectional Conflicts[1]

Text

Between 1820 and 1860 the United States witnessed the completion of the westward expansion, and the rapid growth of the nation's economy and a revolution in industry, agriculture and transportation. Nationalism grew in momentum along with factionalism; slavery hardened the sectional lines; anti-slavery movement hastened the growth of sectional conflicts.

Ⅰ. Three Different Sections

Three different sections—North, South and West had developed differently in politics, economy and social systems since the 1820s. The nation began with its political base in the northeast and the middle-Atlantic states, but that base gradually shifted to the middle-Atlantic, South and Southwest. Then as the Northwest gained strength and stability, it began to exercise its political muscle.

Between 1820 and 1860 the North sprang to life, bringing with it all the power and wealth. It was traditionally a shipping area for foreign trade. But with the revolution in industry, agriculture and transportation, New England and the middle-Atlantic states became the important center in manufacturing, shipping, trade, commerce. Textiles, lumber, clothing, machinery, leather and woolen goods were the chief products in this area. The fast economic development of the area had laid down the solid foundation for the growth of the nation. In order to protect and help the healthy growth of national industry, the North favored protective tariffs and opposed slavery.

The South was known as "*King Cotton*"[2] though there were rice, tobacco, indigo and so on. After the cotton gin was invented in 1793, the South increasingly tied itself to cotton plantation. With the full development of the Gulf plains, cotton production nearly doubled during the 1850s. Cotton furnished raw materials not only for northern textile mills but also for more than half the nation's exports. Since cotton was the chief source of wealth, the South favored slavery and opposed protective tariffs.

An important stimulus to western prosperity was the great improvement in transportation facilities. After the West was linked with the East by canals and railroads, Chicago quickly grew into a very important railway, shipping and industrial center and Detroit the automobile-manufacturing center of the United States. Most frontiersmen and farmers at first produced for self-sufficiency. Then after the introduction of reapers and other new machines and techniques, agriculture flourished, producing most of the nation's corn and more than half the nation's wheat for eastern markets and exports. Like the South with its dependence on raw materials for exports, the West opposed protective tariffs but it needed free labor and opposed slavery.

Ⅱ. *Party Spirit Mounts*[3]

In the year 1816 when Monroe was elected President he found the country in a complaisant mood, everywhere he saw abundant signs of national unity and prosperity. Economy boomed and political factionalism was at a low ebb. But the election of 1824 not only marked the end of the "Era of Good Feelings" but the end of a brief period of political unity.

In the election campaign, the Democratic Republican Party quickly disintegrated as a national political organization with four competing candidates—John Quincy Adams, Henry Clay, William H. Crawford and Andrew Jackson, each attracting different sections and interests. None of them polled a majority in the Electoral College. Thanks to Clay's backing, Adams was chosen by the House and Clay was made the Secretary of State. They called for a vigorous federal action and pursued a more radical program for national economic growth. Hardly had they put into operation their program effectively than they met with hostile forces both in and out of Cabinet and Congress. Andrew Jackson and Van Buren rallied against Adam' administration. After a bitter contest in the election of 1828, Andrew Jackson won the Presidency and the present Democratic Party was founded. After Jackson took office, America ushered in the "*Age of the Common Man*"[4]. Two-party system was considered inevitable and constructive. Jackson pledged to be faithful to traditional Jeffersonian Republicanism. Having in mind the concept "Equal Rights for All, Special Privileges for None", he held that the federal government was one of limited power, and emphasized strict interpretation of the Constitution, and state sovereignty. He opposed the protective tariff, the rechartering of the bank and slavery.

Ⅲ. *The Nullification Struggle*[5]

The protective tariff was an important policy concerning "bread and butter" of the people. It was also an issue that helped determine jobs, economic opportunities and regional development. The North favored the protective tariff while the South and the West opposed it. When the protective tariff was passed in 1828, the South opposed it, arguing that if the federal government had exceeded its delegated powers, then the state could interpose state authority to nullify the federal law and prevent federal enforcement. When in 1832 Congress passed another high tariff measure, the South pronounced the Tariffs of 1828 and 1832 "null and void", prohibited officials from collecting duties within the state and threatened to secede from the Union if the federal government attempted to enforce compliance.

President Jackson wished to enforce the laws by force. Congress met to consider both a "force bill" and a compromise that would gradually reduce tariff duties so that by 1842 no tariff would exceed twenty per cent. Both measures were accepted and open conflict was avoided, but the principle of Union was not yet fully established.

Ⅳ. The Bank War

During the nullification crisis the United States held the 1832 presidential campaign and election. The chief issue was whether *to recharter the Second Bank of the United States*[6]. It focussed on the struggle between men who would use the Second Bank to control state banks and financial monopolies and men who distrusted the federal Bank but favored state banks and financial democracy. When the Second Bank was passed by Congress, Jackson vetoed the Bill, arguing that the bank was undemocratic and unconstitutional and it was a monopoly for the wealthy. As Jackson had wide popularity, Congress failed to achieve a two-thirds votes *to override the veto*[7].

Jackson's open militancy during the Bank War and his direct use of Presidential power led to the formation of *the "Whig Party"*[8] headed by Adams and Clay which advocated protection of industry and limitation of the power of the executive branch of government.

Ⅴ. The Slavery Issue

Negro slaves were first brought into Virginia in 1619. Within two hundred years or more slavery spread to all the thirteen colonies, but it took the strongest hold in the South. By 1860 there were roughly three and a half million black slaves in the South. To Northerners slavery system was the "peculiar institution" to be responsible for the backwardness of the South; to Southerners slavery became an integral part of its basic economy. The new territorial expansion pushed the slavery issue into American politics with fresh intensity. Southern slave-holders wanted the extension of slavery into any new territory as they wished while Northern abolitionists vigorously opposed it. *This struggle focused on control of power in Congress.*[9] Whether new territory was admitted into the Union as a free state or a slave state would determine whether the North or the South would dominate the U.S. political system.

Ⅵ. The Abolitionist Movement[10]

During the 1830s and 1840s appeared the anti-slavery or abolitionist movement. This movement aimed at abolishing inhuman slavery and demanding individual liberty and equality. In 1831 William Lloyd Garrison began publishing a weekly newspaper, *The Liberator* demanding that Americans consciously confront the existence and evils of slavery, bringing to light the most repulsive aspects of black slavery and denouncing slave-holders as torturers and traffickers in human life. This newspaper played a very important part in the abolitionist movement.

One phase of the abolitionist movement involved helping slaves escape to freedom in the north or into Canada. Known as the "*Underground Railroad*"[11] was an elaborate network of secret routes firmly established in the 1830s in all parts of the north. It was estimated that from 1830 to 1860. It helped at least 60 000 slaves to freedom. Harriet Tubman was the most famous Negro woman leader of the movement who helped over 300 slaves north to freedom.

Ⅶ. The Compromise of 1850

By 1849 there were thirty-one states in the Union, but almost one half of the country was still made up of the new territories. Whether this territory was open or closed to slavery would determine whether the North or South would control Congress. Thus, Southerners were outraged when California (in 1849) and New Mexico (in 1850) each adopted a free-state constitution and sought admission as non-slave states into the Union. Militant Southern leaders vowed to split the Union before seeing slavery prohibited, Abolitionists fueled the fire by demanding that slavery be abolished in Washington D. C. Texas and New Mexico moved to the verge of a private war concerning boundary questions. Mississippi called for a convention of southern states to determine their future course, while Massachusetts Democrats and Free Soilers declared opposition to slavery "in every form and color". The nation seemed off the brink of disunion and facing the threat of a civil war.

In January 1850, the old Whig Henry Clay proposed a compromise to settle the disputed problems. As approved by the Congress, this Compromise of 1850 provided for: 1) the admission of California as a free state, which upset the balance between North and South in the Senate; 2) settlement of the boundary dispute between Texas and New Mexico by satisfying the claims of Texas to a portion of Mexico by a payment of $10 million; 3) organization of the New Mexico and Utah territories with the slavery issue in each to be determined by *popular sovereignty*[12]; 4) the abolition of the slave trade in the District of Columbia; and 5) the adoption of *the Fugitive Slave Act*[13], which gave the federal government almost unlimited powers to assure the return of runaway slaves. The Compromise of 1850 passed and the nation breathed a sigh of relief.

For three years the Compromise seemed to settle all problems. However, the tension grew beneath the surface. The new Fugitive Slave Act deeply offended many northerners, who refused to have any part in catching slaves. Instead, they continued to help fugitives to escape, and made the Underground Railroad more efficient and more daring than it had been before.

Ⅶ. *The Kansas-Nebraska Act*[14]

The 1852 saw the publication of Harriet Beecher Stowe's *Uncle Tom's Cabin*, which caused an immediate sensation. More than 300 000 copies were sold the first year, and eight power presses ran day and night to keep up with the demand. The novel showed that cruelty was inseparable from the institution of slavery and that free and slave societies were fundamentally irreconcilable. The novel fueled northern conviction that slavery was wrong in every form or place. Whereas Southern leaders still demanded that slavery be extended into western frontier lands and be protected everywhere.

An inevitable clash occurred in 1854 when Senator Stephen Douglas of Illinois proposed organization of Kansas-Nebraska territory on the basis of popular sovereignty. This proposal was passed by Congress. The passage of this act nullified the Compromise of 1820 and created a new sectional crisis. "Bleeding Kansas" was the result. Slave-holders poured into Kansas to make it a slave state, while Northerners moved in to make the territory free. Neither side gave way and it was here in 1856 that shooting first started, foreshadowing the Civil War of five years later.

Ⅸ. The Formation of the Republican Party

The immediate result of the Kansas-Nebraska Act was the death of the Whig Party; and in its stead arose a powerful new organization, the Republican Party, that advocated the repeal of the Missouri Compromise and prohibition of slavery in all the new territories. The new party failed in the 1856 presidential election, but it held on. Abraham Lincoln, its leader, remarked: "'*A house divided against itself cannot stand.' I believe this government cannot endure permanently half-slave and half-free.*"[15] For this firm abolitionist stand Lincoln soon became known to the whole nation.

Ⅹ. John Brown

Sectional strife again became acute. In 1859 the Kansas abolitionist John Brown decided to raise a private army to defeat the evil of slavery. To acquire arms Brown and his followers attacked the federal arsenal at Harper's Ferry, West Virginia. He was captured and imprisoned; after being tried for conspiracy and treason he was condemned and hanged. *To many Northerners he became Saint John, a martyr to the cause of freedom. To Southerners he became the devil trying to destroy the southern way of life.*[16]

Ⅺ. The Election of 1860

By 1860 the Union seemed split beyond healing. The Democratic Party was badly disintegrated over the issue of slavery. Southern Democrats nominated John Breckingridge of Kentucky for president and declared in favor of slavery. Northern Democrats nominated Senator Douglas who was anti-slavery but in favor of popular sovereignty. This open break in the Democratic ranks gave Republicans the chance to victory in the election of 1860. As the presidential candidate of the Republican Party, Lincoln opposed the extension of slavery into the new territories but promised not to interfere with slavery in the states where it already existed. He proposed free land through a Homestead Act, as well as a higher tariff. In the election Lincoln won a clear majority. The Union split and the Civil War began.

Notes

1. sectional conflicts

地区冲突　自1820年以后，由于政治、经济、社会制度的不同发展，美国可分为北部、南部和西部三个地区，它们之间在保护关税、中央银行和奴隶问题上经常发生冲突。

2. "King Cotton"

"棉花王国"　南部主要依靠奴隶发展种植园经济，因气候和土壤适宜，以种植棉花为主，大量生产供应北部市场和出口，成为南部经济的支柱，故有"棉花王国"之称。

3. party spirit mounts

党派精神发展　在1824年的总统选举中，民主共和党迅速分裂，出现了四个竞选对手，各自代表不同地区的利益，结果无一人获得多数票获选总统，最后由众、参两院分别选举产生正、副总统。

4. "Age of the Common Man"

"平民时代"　自1829年至1837年，安德鲁·杰克逊总统的两届任期被称为"平民时代"。他出身平民，由平民发展为总统。他来自南部，自称代表平民利益，所以他的支持者称之为"平民时代"。

5. the Nullification Struggle

取消(保护关税的)斗争　北部拥护保护关税，以发展工业；南部和西部则反对之。因为物价上涨，影响人民生活，当国会通过1828和1832年保护关税法之后，南、北、西部之间展开了取消和反取消保护关税的激烈斗争，结果三方达成妥协，逐年减少关税，到1842年关税不超过20%。

6. to recharter the Second Bank of the United States

重新特许建立美国第二银行　北部要重新特许建立美国第二银行，南、西部则反对。国会于1816年特许建立第二银行，为期20年，到1836年期满。但在1832年的总统选举中，南部、西部和北部三方便围绕是否重新特许建立第二银行的问题展开了激烈斗争，当国会通过重新特许建立第二银行的议案时，杰克逊加以否决，参、众两院未能以2/3的多数票使总统的否决无效。

7. to override the veto

使否决无效　要使总统的否决无效，参、众两院必须再次拥有2/3以上的多数票才能使总统的否决无效。

8. the Whig Party

辉格党　该党是以亚当斯为首的仿效英国的辉格党而建立起来的，借以保护北方工业，限制总统和行政部门的权力。

9. This struggle focused on control of power in Congress.

这种斗争集中在国会权力的争夺上。

10. the abolitionist movement

废奴运动　亦称反对奴隶运动。

11. the "Underground Railroad"

"地下铁道"　废奴运动者在全国范围内建立了一个秘密组织，帮助南部奴隶逃往北部，甚至加拿大，该组织也被称为"地下铁道"。

12. popular sovereignty

人民主权论　该论点在1850年和解的第三点内容里提及。按该论点，新墨西哥和犹他两个地方有权决定它们是否建立奴隶制度。

13. the Fugitive Slave Act

《逃亡奴隶法》　按该法，所有逃亡的奴隶都要被遣返至他们原来的奴隶家园。

14. The Kansas-Nebraska Act

《堪萨斯—内布拉斯加法》　该法废除了1820年密苏里和解，允许奴隶进入密苏里36°30′虚线以北，为此，北方人和南方奴隶主都涌进堪萨斯争夺地盘，从而发生了堪萨斯流血事件，这是内战的前兆。

15. "'A house divided against itself cannot stand.' I believe this govetnment cannot endure permanently half-slave and half-free."

"'分裂之家不能持久。'我相信我们的政府不能永远忍受一半奴役一半自由的状况。"　由于这种坚定的反奴隶主义立场，林肯不久闻名全国。

16. To many Northerners he became Saint John, a martyr to the cause of freedom. To Southerners he became the devil trying to destroy

the southern way of life.

对于北方人来说，他成为圣约翰，一个献身自由事业的烈士；对南方人来说，他则成为一个企图摧毁南方生活方式的魔鬼。

Exercises

Ⅰ. Fill in each blank with the right word or expression from the text:

1. The Democratic Party was formed in ________ (year) while the Republican Party in ________ (year).
2. Negro slaves were first brought to America in ________ (year).
3. The author of *Uncle Tom's Cabin* was ________, this novel showed that ________ and that ________.
4. Three sections: ________, ________ and ________ had developed differently in politics, economy and social systems since the 1820s.
5. The three different sections often had conflicts and struggles over the issues of ________, ________ and ________.
6. In 1831 William Lloyd Garrison published a weekly newspaper called ________, which demanded that ________, brought to light the ________ and denounced ________.

Ⅱ. Questions for discussion:

1. Define the differences between the North, South and West.
2. On what important issues did the three sections often have different attitudes? Why?
3. Define the political changes when Andrew Jackson was elected President.
4. How did slavery begin in America?
5. Who were the chief abolitionists? Who was John Brown?
6. Give a brief account of the Compromise of 1850.
7. Cite one or two examples to explain why the slavery issue became the most sensitive and prominent issue that led to the outbreak of the Civil War.
8. For what reasons was the present-day Republican Party founded?

Chapter 11

The Civil War and Its Aftermath[1]

Text

Ⅰ. The Secession Crisis

After Lincoln was elected President, South Carolina held a convention which voted unanimously on December 20, 1860, for secession, declaring independence from the Union. Within six weeks six other southern states also declared independence. In February 1861 the seceding states met in Montgomery, Alabama, and organized themselves as *the Confederate States of America*[2] (also called the Confederacy) with Jefferson Davis as President. They publicly declared that the "Union is hereby dissolved".

When Lincoln was sworn in as President on March 4, 1861, he faced an extremely critical situation. Should the Union be dissolved or should it be preserved? How was the Union to be preserved, through negotiation or by war? The whole nation anxiously waited the decision of the new President. In his inaugural address he made his last attempt to avoid war by expressing kind feeling for the South, but he solemnly declared that he would "preserve, protect and defend" the Union.

The Civil War broke out on April 12, 1861 when the Confederate states bombarded Fort Sumter in the Charleston harbor, South Carolina.

Ⅱ. Comparison of Strength

In terms of strength, the North enjoyed great superiority. The North was far ahead in economic advantages. Four-fifths of the nation's manufacturing was located in the North, two-thirds of its railroad truck, three-quarters of the wealth produced; whereas the South mainly grew cotton and depended too much on it. The North had 23 states with a population of 22 million, while the South had only 11 states with a population of 9 million, including 3.5 million blacks. The North controlled the navy and a large part of the merchant marine, which enabled it to carry on a fairly effective blockade of the southern coastline.

On the other hand, the South had also some advantages. It fought a defensive war and so needed fewer men and resources than did the North. The South had strong military leadership and its soldiers were skilled in shooting and horse-back riding. The Davis government thought that Great Britain and France would undoubtedly come to the aid of the South, because of their economic dependence on southern cotton.

Ⅲ. *Emancipation Proclamation*[3]

When the war began President Lincoln hesitated to emancipate the blacks at once for fear that military service would raise the status of the blacks in society and enrage his opponents from within. He initially saw his task not in terms of winning an all-out war, but rather of destroying the Confederate government and restoring the South to the Union by capturing Richmond, the Capital of the Confederate States of America. However, after the failures of the war in the first two years in the east, Lincoln *saw the need of giving the Union army a new morale boost*[4], enlarging the army and keeping neutrality of the European countries, especially Britain and France in the war. On September 22, 1862, he issued the famous Emancipation Proclamation which went into effect in January, 1863. This Proclamation did not apply to slaves in *border states*[5] or to slaves in the states under the control of the federal government, but to the slaves in the Confederate states. This action liberated four million Negro slaves and won popular support among the people. It stopped Britain and France from supplying the South with manufactured goods and ammunitions. And in January, 1865, Congress adopted the Thirteenth Amendment to the Constitution. which prohibited slavery in the United States.

Ⅳ. Military Contest in the War

The Civil War turned half of America's lands into battle-fields, and resulted in the death of over 600 000 Union and Confederate soldiers.

The war was fought on four fronts: the East, the Mississippi West, the trans-Mississippi West and the Atlantic Ocean.

In the East, the Union strategy was to capture Richmond and restore the South to the Union. Along the Mississippi and its tributaries, the Union army attempted to stop all commerce and isolated the lower South. Along the Atlantic coast, the Union navy was to blockade the coastal line and prevent the European countries from supplying the South with manufactured goods.

The first major battle of the Civil War was fought at Bull Run for the control of Richmond. However, General Robert E. Lee of Army of Northern Virginia took advantage of the natural barriers formed by broad rivers and defeated the Union troops again and again, causing heavy, losses to the Union army. Taking advantages of the defeat of the Union army, General Lee struck northward into Pennsylvania, but his march was intercepted at Gettysburg in July 1863 by a strong Union force. After a three-day battle, the Confederates failed to break the Union lines and fell back to the Potomac with heavy losses. *To many historians the Battle at Gettysburg was considered the turning point of the war*.[6]

In the West, the Union army under General Ulysses S. Grant made remarkable gains. He moved down the Mississippi and captured 30 000 Confederate troops at Vicksburg on. July 4, 1863. In the meantime a navy under Farragut captured New Orleans and moved up the Mississippi to meet General Grant. Thus the Union army gained complete control of the Mississippi River, separated the trans-Mississippi West from the rest of the southern states, stopped all commerce from Europe.

In 1864 General Grant was appointed Supreme Commander of the Union army. He ordered General Sherman to fight his way to the sea, sweeping through Mississippi, Alabama, Georgia and Carolinas with an aim to lay siege to Richmond from the south. Meanwhile the Union troops under General Grant moved south conducting an all-round campaign against

Lee's forces, *putting Lee's forces under pincer attacks*[7]. After several bloody combats, Richmond fell. Now Lee saw his doom was certain, so he surrendered to Grant at Appomattox Court House, Virginia, on April 9, 1865. On May 26, 1865, the rest of the Confederate army finally surrendered, and the Civil War was over.

Ⅴ. Lincoln's Assassination

Lincoln was a great leader in the war and a great hero of the American people. Without his wise leadership, firmness, far-sightedness, warmth and generosity, Americans perhaps wouldn't have reunited the nation. In 1864 he was elected President for a second term. In his inaugural address he pledged to strive for a new Union based on human liberty and justice, but the hopes of his fellow Americans were crushed on the night of April 14, 1865, at Ford's Theatre in Washington, when a crazed actor, John Wilkes Booth, shot the President to death. His assassination shocked the nation and left behind was the prospect that the nation might be reunited "*with malice toward none; with charity for all; with firmness in the right, as God gives us to see the right*[8]. Let us strive on to finish the work we are in; to bind up the nation's wounds, to care for him who shall have borne the battle, and for his widow, and his orphan—to do all which may achieve and cherish a just, and a lasting peace, among ourselves, and with all nations."Though Abraham Lincoln did not see the reunion of the United States he would have probably been satisfied with his hope that "the dead shall not have died in vain, that this nation, under God, shall have a new birth of freedom, and that the Government of the people, by the people, for the people shall not perish from the earth."

Ⅵ. Effect of the Civil War

The American Civil War was a great revolutionary war. It ended in the victory of the capitalist system and put an end to slavery and the feudal slavery-plantation system which had been an obstacle on the path of the development of capitalism. It marked the triumph of nationalism over factionalism. Supreme authority of the federal government was immensely strengthened, which ensured the rapid development of capitalism.

After the formal abolition of slavery by the Thirteenth Amendment to the U.S. Constitution, Congress passed the Fourteenth and Fifteenth Amendments to the Constitution which provided equal rights and equal votes for the blacks. Despite the laws the slavery issue was only superficially solved. Late in the 1960s violent struggles for Negro rights renewed.

Ⅶ. Opposing Views on Reconstruction

President Lincoln knew that the end of secession and the abolition of slavery would not restore unity. As to how to reconstruct the nation, Lincoln proposed three principles for an ideal government: "Government of the people, by the people, for the people." Two days after Lee's surrender, Lincoln delivered his last public address, unfolding a generous reconstruction policy. *Former Confederate stales could be readmitted to the Union as soon as ten percent of the voters had taken an oath of allegiance*.[9] In the light of this policy, Virginia, Tennessee, Arkansas and Louisiana had set up their new governments and ratified the Thirteenth Amendment to the Constitution. Yet Congress rejected their seats in the Senate and the House of Representatives. The radical Republicans who controlled Congress adopted severe measures to punish all the seceded states. According to their program, ten southern states were divided into five military districts, each under a commanding officer. The officer was to oversee the formation of the new government. Voters were to be registered without distinction of race or color, but *ex-Confederates were disqualified*[10]. State constitutions were drawn to embody black suffrage. In 1868 Congress passed the Fourteenth Amendment and in 1870 the Fifteenth Amendment which provided that "The rights of citizens of the United States to vote shall not be denied or abridged by the United States or any state on account of race, color, or previous condition of servitude".

The policies pursued by the radical Republicans met with Johnson's strong opposition. In order to prevent Johnson from interfering with their reconstruction program, Congress passed "*The Tenure of Office Act*"[11] in 1867, which prohibited the President from dismissing important officials without the consent of the Senate. Johnson vetoed the law and removed from office the secretary of War, Edwin M. Stanton. a radical Republican. The House moved quickly to impeach Johnson. When the impeachment trial was held in the Senate, it was proved that Johnson was technically within his rights in removing the Cabinet member and what's more, it was pointed out that a dangerous precedent would be set if Congress were to remove a President because he disagreed with the majority of its members. The attempted impeachment failed, and Johnson continued in office until his term expired.

Under the Congressional Reconstruction Act, the new governments of seven states were headed by governors from the North, and in three others blacks gained complete control. In alarm, the Southern Whites, finding no legal way to stop the course of events, turned to illegal means, and some reacted with a campaign of terror. By 1867 there arose a popular terrorist movement, *the Ku Klux Klan*[12], which effectively prevented the enfranchised blacks from voting by means of whipping, lynching, tar-and-feathering, etc.

As time passed, it became more and more obvious that the problems of the South were not being solved by harsh laws which deprived almost all of the ex-Confederates of their rights to vote and participation in the new governments. In May 1872, Congress passed *the General Amnesty Act*[13], restoring full political privileges to all but 500 Confederate sympathizers. In 1876, President Hayes removed the Northern troops from the South. Thereby the radical Republican reconstruction ended in 1877 with a span of 12 years (1865—1877).

Gradually the Southern Whites set up their supremacy in the South. They passed state laws to minimize black suffrage by imposing poll tax or property and education qualification. *With the pursuance of Jim Crow Segregation laws, the Negroes were separated from the whites in public places and services*.[14] The "emancipated" slaves were forced to be *sharecroppers*[15] who worked for the white landlords for a share of the crop. However, sharecropping was different from the feudal slavery-plantation system. It was the budding of capitalism, a form of exploitation of man by man in the capitalist relations of production. Blacks were no longer the private property of slave-holders, they became either sharecroppers or wage-earners under the capitalist system.

The Civil War and Reconstruction consolidated and expanded the power of the rising industrialist order in the North. The war may have disturbed "normal" industrial growth, but war demands compounded the profits and capital of the industrialists, which in turn provided solid foundation for rapid industialization in post-war years. The late 19th century triumph of industrial capitalism had many causes, but restoration of union and elimination of slavery freed Americans to turn to business enterprise on a grand scale which soon outstripped all rivals.

Notes

1. the Civil War and its aftermath

内战及其后果　内战是在北方新兴的资产阶级和南方的封建奴隶主阶级之间展开的，前者要推翻封建奴隶制度，建立资本主义制度，后者要维护封建奴隶制度，并要把它扩展到全国各地，战争结果是前者胜利，封建奴隶制度被消灭，美国走上了资本主义发展的道路。

2. the Confederate States of America

美国南部邦联　由南部 11 个州从联邦分裂出来之后于 1861 年建立的，并公开宣布联邦从此解散。

3. the Emancipation Proclamation

《解放宣言》　这是林肯总统发布的黑人解放宣言，是美国历史上第一次宣告黑人被奴役、被压迫、低人一等的日子已经结束，并获得与白人平等地位的法律保障。

4. saw the need of giving the Union army a new morale boost

看到重振联邦部队士气的必要　因为联邦军在内战的头两年里损失惨

重，影响了部队的作战士气。

give a morale boost to ... 振作……的士气

5. border states

边界州 在内战中，特拉华、马里兰、弗吉尼亚、肯特基和密苏里5个州保持中立，自然形成了南、北战争的边界线。

6. To many historians the Battle at Gettysburg was considered the turning point of the war.

依很多历史学家的看法，盖茨堡战役是内战的转折点。 因为南部邦联主力部队已被消灭，无法重振士气；而北部联邦虽然损失惨重，但能很快重振士气，调整武装力量，补充兵力、作战设备和战略物资等，以继续作战。

7. putting Lee's forces under pincer attacks

把李将军的兵力置于两面夹击之中 经过几场浴血战斗，里士满失陷，李将军投降，不久邦联全军投降，内战于1865年结束。

8. "with malice toward none; with charity for all; with firmness in the right, as God gives us to see the right"

"对任何人不存恶意；对每个人仁慈；坚持正义，因为上帝要我们识别正义" 这是林肯第二任就职演说的结束语。

9. Former Confederate states could be readmitted to the Union as soon as ten percent of the voters had taken an oath of allegiance.

以前的邦联各州一旦有10%的选民宣誓忠于联邦，就可以重新加入联邦。 这是林肯总统重建南部各州的宽容、团结政策和方针。

10. ex-Confederates were disqualified

退役的邦联官兵被剥夺了选民条件 这是国会激进派对重建南部各州所采取的激进政策和方针，以对抗林肯总统的宽容、团结的方针和政策。

11. the Tenure of Office Act

《任职法案》 该法案禁止总统事先未征得参议院同意就解除重要的政府官员职务，但安德鲁·约翰逊总统否决了该法案，解除了国防部长，一位激进派的职务，激发了总统与国会激进派之间的严重矛盾和斗争。

12. the Ku Klux Klan

三K党 这是一股右翼势力。其掀起一场恐怖运动，用鞭打、私刑、涂柏油、粘羽毛的刑罚，恫吓有公民权的黑人参加选举，以维护白人的统治地位。

13. the General Amnesty Act

《大赦法案》 该法案恢复所有退役的邦联官兵，除了五百名邦联同情者之外的政治权利。

14. With the pursuance of Jim Crow Segregation laws, the Negroes were separated from the whites in public places and services.

因种族隔离法的推行，黑人被迫在公共和服务场所与白人隔离开。

Jim Crow 黑人

segregate ... from ... 把……与……隔离开

15. sharecroppers

用谷物交租的佃农

sharecropping 用谷物交租的制度。这是资本主义制度的萌芽，黑奴不再是奴隶主的私有财产，而成为佃农或雇佣劳动者。

Exercises

Ⅰ. Fill in each blank with the right word or expression from the text:

1. In comparison of strength on the eve of the Civil War, the North had ________ states with a population of ________, while the South had only ________ states with a population of ________, including ________ blacks.
2. At the outset of the Civil War, President Lincoln's strategic plan was to ________ by ________.
3. The basic causes for the Emancipation Proclamation were ________, ________ and ________.
4. The Civil War was fought on four fronts: ________, ________, ________ and ________.
5. To many historians the Battle at ________ was considered the turning point of the Civil War.
6. The Civil War broke out in ________ (year) when the Confederates

bombarded ________ and it ended in ________ (year) when the Confederate army surrendered completely.

7. The Civil War ended in the ________ of the ________ and an end to ________ in the ________.

8. President Lincoln's generous reconstruction policy was that ________.

9. In the process of reconstructing the South, there appeared a terrorist movement known as ________.

Ⅱ. Questions for discussion:

1. Which were the Confederate states? Which were the neutral states when the Civil War began?
2. Why was Fort Sumter famous in American history?
3. What were the basic causes of the Civil War?
4. Compare the strength of the North with that of the South at the outset of the war.
5. By what considerations did President Lincoln issue the Emancipation Proclamation?
6. What is the significance of the Civil War?
7. What were the two opposing views on the post-war reconstruction of the South?
8. What was the result of the post-war reconstruction of the South?

Chapter 12

The Era of Economic Expansion and Reform

Text

Between the two great wars—the Civil War and the First World War was a period of "*Gilded Age*"[1] which marked the transition of the United States from a primarily agricultural nation into a highly industrialized nation. Free competition gradually gave way to monopoly. The once seemingly boundless frontier vanished. Large cities, factories and farms mushroomed all over the country. Railroads, highways and water routes wove the nation into a giant organic shipping system, giving forth much vigor and vitality. The rapid growth of industry and agriculture outstripped all leading European countries, such as Britain, France and Germany. In 1860 the United States was a second rate industrial country, but by 1890 the United States had stepped into the first place and the value of its manufactured goods almost equaled the total value of all the three former leading countries. With the rapid growth of economy came corresponding difficulties. Big corporations sought to extend a wholesome and exclusive control over markets and production. Workers and farmers cried out against big business and monopolistic exploitation. These new conditions caused changes in the U. S. policy in search of social reform, foreign markets and new sources of raw materials.

Ⅰ. The Rapid Growth of Industry and Agriculture

After the Civil War the slavery-plantation system was destroyed; new socio-economic structure was established; slaves were liberated and provided abundant supply of free labour for industrial development. Protective tariff was largely established which protected the development of America's industry against foreign competition.

The rapid development of science and technology was the key to U.S.

industrialization. Before 1860, 36 000 patents were granted, and in the first quarter of the 20th century the number of patents reached nearly one million.

As early as 1844, Samuel F. B. Morse had perfected electrical telegraphy, and before long distant parts of the continent were linked by a network of telegraph communication. In 1876, Alexander Granham Bell made a telephone apparatus which quickened the social and economic life of the nation. The growth of business was sped up by the invention of the typewriter, the adding machine and the cash register. The rotary press and paper-folding machinery made it possible to print 240 000 eight-page newspapers in an hour. Edison's electric bulb lit millions of factories and homes. His talking machine was perfected and his motion picture was developed. Wilbur and Orville Wright made the first plane in 1903 which began the era of aviation. All these and other numerous items of scientific discoveries and inventions resulted in a new level of productivity in almost every field.

In this new industrial order the city was the nerve center[2], bringing to a focus all the dynamic economic forces: vast accumulation of capital, business and financial institutions, railroads, factories, and armies of manual and clerical workers. Villages grew into towns and towns into cities almost overnight. No single city had as many as a million inhabitants in 1860, but thirty years later New York had a million and a half, and Chicago and Philadelphia each had over one million. Meanwhile Philadelphia and Baltimore doubled in population. Kansas City and Detroit grew fourfold, Chicago tenfold, and some others increased fifty times or more in population.

The making of iron and steel was the nation's basic industry. Previously it was concentrated near deposits in the eastern states. As new ore deposits were discovered, the iron industry moved westward. The Mesabi iron range at the head of Lake Superior became one of the largest ore producers in the world. Around the Great Lakes quickly appeared the industrial cities:

Chicago, Detroit, Pittsburgh and Buffalo.

Along with the growth of iron industry grew the desire to speed up railway construction. *Gold discoveries in California gave it further stimulus.*[3] To promote railway construction Congress passed a law in 1862 and another in 1864 that authorized the Union Pacific and Central Pacific railway companies to build a transcontinental railway. Congress also offered the companies extensive tracts of land along the tracks at low prices. In 1869 the first transcontinental railway was completed at Promontory, Utah. Four more transcontinental railways were built within the next quarter of a century. By the early 1900, America possessed one-third of the world's railway tracks. These railway lines benefited greatly the rapid development of the national economy and the colonization of the West.

Similar growth occurred in agriculture, which had also become big business. Between 1860 and 1890, the production of such basic commodities as wheat, corn, cotton outstripped all previous figures in the United States. The revolution in agriculture involved a shift from hand labor to machine farming and from subsistence to commercial agriculture. Between 1860 and 1910 the number of farms in the United States trebled, increasing from two million to six million while the area farmed more than doubled (from 160 million to 352 million hectares). This was largely due to policies, railway construction and the use of machinery and technology. Public land policies, such as *the Homestead Act*[4], made free lands available for farmers while railroads not only connected farms with urban markets, but stimulated development of regional granaries, stockyards and new towns. Railroad companies became the principal landowners and colonizers in the new West. They controlled the settlers' lives by determining the price of everything the farmer bought and sold.

Machinery was the basic element of the agricultural industrialization. With the use of the threshing machine, the automatic wire binder, the reaper-thresher or combine, the automatic planter, manure spreader, hay drier and hundreds of other inventions, the efficiency of the farm worker increased by over eighty per cent and provided for dramatic leaps in crop production. Between 1840 and 1894 production in major crops increased by over five hundred percent, while the average time of human labor needed to produce a bushel of corn decreased by over 67%, to produce a bushel of wheat by almost 95%. This new machinery not only made larger farms possible but necessary since the yield from a small farm would not pay for the machinery to work it.

Scarcely less important than machinery in the agricultural revolution was science. In 1862 Congress passed *the Morill Land-Grant College Act*[5] which allotted public land to each state for the establishment of agricultural and industrial colleges. These were to serve both as educational institutions and as centers for research in scientific farming. Congress also appropriated funds for the creation of agricultural experiment stations for research purposes throughout the country. By the beginning of the 19th century, scientists throughout the land were at work on a variety of agricultural projects. Better strains of seed such as the rust-and-drought-resistant winter wheat from Russia and Kaffir corn from Africa were introduced; hog cholera and hoof-and-mouth disease were conquered: new fruits and vegetables were developed. The great black scientist George Washington Carver found hundreds of new uses for the peanut, sweet potato and soybean. These achievements released a torrent of production that resulted in surpluses. Farmers benefited at first, but soon suffered as farm prices fell faster than general prices. This caused farmers' dissatisfaction and resistance.

Ⅱ. The Appearance of Monopoly Business

Most American businesses before the Civil War were small, owner-operated, and highly competitive. After the war, however, businessmen sought to raise profits by cutting costs, increasing production, and limiting competition through combination and consolidation.

John D. Rockefeller pioneered this development in the oil industry. After becoming in 1867 the largest refiner of oil in Cleveland, he organized the Standard Oil Company with a capital of $ 1 million. He soon established a virtual monopoly in Ohio and then he applied the same methods to other states until by 1900 the Standard Oil Company controlled ninety per cent of oil refining in the United States. Competitors who joined Rockefeller's trust made huge profits, while those who did not join were driven out of business by price-cutting wars and special advantages in transportation and marketing which he enjoyed.

Andrew Carnegie followed Rockefeller's lead. He came to America from Scotland at the age of 12. He progressed from a bobbin boy to an industrialist. By 1865 he organized companies making iron, rails and locomotives. Then he bought out his steel-producing competitors and in 1892 formed the Carnegie Steel Company with assets of $ 25 million and control of raw materials and a fleet of steamers on the Great Lakes. His company produced one-fourth of all the unfinished steel in America. By 1900 he had increased his capital to over $ 160 million.

While Rockefeller and Carnegie began as producers, J. P. Morgan acquired power through the capital he invested in control of industry. He first organized and formed *the Northern Securities Company*[6] between 1894 and 1898. Then he turned to the steel industry by initiating new combinations. After repeated failures, he purchased Carnegie Steel for a half-billion dollars and formed in 1901 the United States Steel Corporation, which controlled three-fifths of the steel industry and was capitalized at $ 1.5 billion. His use of finance capitalism led to more supercorporations in the early years of the 20th century.

During the same period, large corporations such as the McCormick Harvester Company, the American Tobacco Company, the American Sugar Refining Company expanded and incorporated until they dominated their respective fields of industry.

Ⅲ. Foreign Adventures

The tremendous economic growth of the United States stimulated search for industrial markets and sources of raw materials. This contributed to the disruption of the old balance of world power caused by the rise of a powerful and aggressive Germany in Europe and Japan in Asia. Moreover, between 1870 and 1914 both old and new powers engaged in imperialistic competition. Into this world of rivalry the United States entered at the beginning of the 20th century as a new world power.

Ⅳ. War with Spain

The United States had long been covetous of Cuba, then controlled by Spain, America's offer of 100 million dollars in exchange for Cuba was refused. Not discouraged by the failure, American monopolists succeeded in controlling much of Cuba economy through large investment and trade.

America's chance finally came in 1895 when a war of independence in Cuba broke out against the Spanish. After keeping neutral for three years, America found a pretext to declare war on Spain in 1898. To prevent Spain from reinforcing its troops in Cuba, the U.S. navy attacked the Philippines, also controlled by Spain. Spain was no match for America and lost all its fleets both in Cuba and in the Philippines.

By the treaty signed in December 1898, Cuba was transferred to the control of the United States. In addition, Spain ceded Puerto Rico and Guam to America and America purchased the Philippines on payment of 20 million dollars.

Ⅴ. The Panama Canal Zone

A canal that joined the Atlantic and Pacific Oceans through the Isthmus of Panama seemed to be of vital importance to America's strategic defense. Before America, a French company had shared the right to cut such a canal, then it was bought by America. When the Colombian Senate refused the transfer, Americans engineered a "revolution" of Panama against Colombia. America recognized the new government and obtained a treaty for constructing the Panama Canal in 1903. After ten years' construction the canal was completed in 1914. Together with the canal, America secured a strip of land along both banks of the canal, called the Panama Zone.

Ⅵ. Aggression against China

In the Far East, the United States chose China as its main target. Its aggression against China dates back to the Opium War. In 1844, taking advantage of China's defeat in the war, the United States forced the Ching government to sign the Wanghsia Treaty which gave the United States advantages in the spheres of trade and privilege of settlement and consular jurisdiction in China.

After America occupied the Philippines, it became more covetous of China. Since several European countries had acquired spheres of influence in China, the U. S. government put forward *the "Open Door" policy*[7] which demanded that all imperialist powers should enjoy equal opportunities (including equal tariffs, harbor duties and railway rates) in the areas they controlled.

In 1900 America joined the Eight-Power Alliance in their aggressive war against China on the pretext of suppressing the Boxers Movement. They forced the Ching government to sign another unequal treaty and to pay the United States 25 million dollars as indemnity.

Ⅶ. *The Rise of Big Labor*[8]

With the rapid growth of economy and monopoly capitalism, class differences widened and class contradictions intensified. A handful of industrialists, financiers and bankers became millionaires and multimillionaires who fattened on the exploitation of the working people. But the broad masses of laborers often worked long hours for subsistence wages under bad working conditions. As there was greater need of labor force, the use of child labor, women, immigrants at the machines became commonplace. It was surprising to note that in some factories children under age sixteen constituted one-third to one-half of the labor force. By 1850 five per cent of the entire slave population worked in factories. About four-fifths of them were owned by those using their labor, and the rest were rented by month or year to factory owners by their masters.

Immigrants also lived at the bottom of society. Between 1870 and 1900 almost fourteen million immigrants arrived in America and most of them settled in cities. Usually of peasant backgrounds, illiterate and poor, they suffered economic exploitation, social discrimination and illegal treatment.

Against all these social evils arose a chorus of angry voices from laborers, farmers, city-dwellers, writers, journalists and even middle-class who sought social reform.

The first significant national labor movement was *the Knights of Labor*[9] founded in 1867. It was class-oriented, organizing all skilled and unskilled workers, including blacks and women, for the general betterment of their lot. By 1886 its membership reached 700 000. After the bloody Haymarket Square bombing in 1886, it came to a quick decline.

However, unionization movement continued. In 1886, the crafts union united as *the American Federation of Labor*[10] under the leadership of Samuel Gompers. They viewed strikes and boycotts as legitimate means for collective bargaining. They struggled for higher wages and better working conditions. The AFL membership grew into over two million in 1914 despite employer opposition.

In 1894 workers at the Pullman Sleeping Car Company struck after receiving their fifth pay-cut in one year. In cooperation the American Railway Union led by Eugene V. Debs refused to handle Pullman cars until the company agreed to arbitrate the dispute. When the railroads General Managers Association ordered workers fired for boycotting Pullman cars, the Railway Union stopped almost all traffic to the west of Chicago. The strike was put down by the federal troops sent by President Cleveland in which twelve people were killed, hundreds arrested, and thousands of dollars in property destroyed. Meanwhile an injunction was issued to prohibit interference with the railroads.

A group of AFL industrial unions wanted to organize the workers in the mass-production industries, chiefly the semi-skilled and unskilled, who had been neglected by the AFL. They separated from the AFL and established a new organization, *the Congress of Industrial Organizations*[11] headed by John L. Lewis in 1935. The CIO developed rapidly and grew into a full competitor with the AFL.

In 1955, the AFL and CIO reached agreement to merge into a single organization, the AFL-CIO (the American Federation of Labor and Congress of Industrial Organizations), and it is the nation's largest labor organization today.

From 1870 to 1890 prices of most farm products moved irregularly downward, and the value of American farm products increased only $500 million. In the same period, however, the value of manufactures increased by $6 000 million.

This economic imbalance prompted formation of the Grange in 1867 with a total membership of over three-quarters of a million. They sought unity among farmers, organized political and business discussions. Soon many Granges set up their own marketing systems, stores, loan agencies, processing plants and factories. In a number of midwestern states they elected members to legislature and had a vital influence in legislation.

Depression in the late eighties and the early nineties led to the formation of Farmers' Alliance. By 1890 they had two million members. In addition to an extensive educational and economic program, the Alliance also made vigorous demands for political reform. Before long the Alliance gave birth to *the Populist Party*[12] made up of farmers and many other minority groups. They called for a program of political reform: government ownership of railroads, the abolition of national banks, prohibition of alien landownership, reduction of tariff, a national system of loans for farmers, an eight-hour day for labor, and an increase in the supply of currency by the free and unlimited coinage of silver. Though not all their demands were achieved, many Populist ideas were made into laws. The Populist movement had a glorious page in American history.

Ⅷ. *Literature of Exposure*[13]

The years between 1902 and 1908 marked the era of greatest reformist activity. Many progressive writers, journalists joined the workers' and peasants' movement. As early as in 1873 Mark Twain published *The Gilded Age*, exposing the various social evils then prevalent in America. Before long Upton Sinclair published *The Jungle*, exposing unsanitary conditions in the great Chicago meat-packing houses and the grip of the beef trust on the nation's meat supply, Theodore Dreiser wrote *The Financier* and *The Titan* to lay bare the machinations of big business. Frank Norris *The Pit* cried out the protest of farmers. *The Shame of the Cities* by Lincoln Steffens bared political corruption. This "literature of exposure" had a vital effect in rousing the people to action.

Ⅸ. Social Reform during the Gilded Age

Spurred by the progressive ideas and attitudes toward big business and people's struggle against monopolistic exploitation, thoughtful political leaders took some practical measures to reform the society.

Firstly the reformers sought to reform the government itself. Once Mark Twain remarked that there was "no distinctly American criminal class except Congress". During this period, though all the Presidents, except Cleveland, were Republicans, the federal government seldom rested in the hands of a single party. Democrats usually dominated the House of Representatives, while Republicans dominated the Senate. Not only did Republicans and Democrats compete primarily for the spoils of office, but within each party factional bosses built political machines which in exchange for favors to business interests received graft on a shameful scale. Both corrupt and incompetent, the government often suffered division and deadlock. Following the assassination of President Garfield in 1881 by a disappointed office-seeker, Congress approved the first *Civil Service Act*[14], establishing a merit system in government service.

Between 1900 and 1920, a reform spirit pervaded almost every aspect of

American life. Progressive political thought emphasized the goal of the "common good". Government should be made more responsive and responsible to the people. Before 1900 almost all state and local candidates were nominated by conventions dominated by machine politics. By 1916, laws providing for direct popular primaries were enacted. State reformers sought to secure better representation in the Senate and in 1913 won direct election of Senators with the ratification of the Seventeenth Amendment. With the Eighteenth Amendment, they secured prohibition of intoxicating liquors within the United States. Moreover, women after almost seventy years of struggle finally won the right to vote with the Nineteenth Amendment in 1919. However, black Americans were still confined to racism. *Jim Crow Segregation laws disfranchised the blacks.*[15] Not until the 1950s and 1960s did they make substantial advance toward equality.

Secondly, the reformers fought against monopoly. In order to check monopolistic practices, Congress passed the Interstate Commerce Act in 1887 and the Sherman Anti-trust Act in 1890. The Interstate Commerce Act provided that railroad companies must charge only "just" and "reasonable" rates and established a Commission to investigate complaints. The Sherman Anti-trust Act outlawed monopolistic combination in restraint of trade. Yet these laws had not been enforced earnestly because the Supreme Court always favored business ownership. It was not until Theodore Roosevelt was reelected President did Congress enact the Hepburn Act which empowered the Interstate Commerce Commission to establish fair rates. By the Clayton Anti-trust Act and the Federal Trade Commission Act, the federal government strengthened to suppress monopolistic business practices. "Unfair methods of competition" were prohibited; interlocking directorates, price discrimination among purchasers and ownership by one corporation of stock in similar enterprises were condemned. However, anti-trust struggle by no means ended.

Thirdly, the reformers took measures to reform the banking and currency system. *The Federal Reserve Act*[16] was passed in 1913. It imposed upon the existing banks a new organization that divided the country into twelve districts with a Federal Reserve Bank in each, all supervised by the Federal Reserve Board. These banks were to serve as depositories for the cash reserve of the various private banks that joined the system. To assure greater flexibility in the money supply, provision was made for issuing federal reserve notes to meet business demands.

In 1913 passed the Underwood Tariff which not only substantially reduced duties for the first time since the Civil War, but also provided for a *graduated income tax*[17] on individual and corporate income.

Farmers and labor also benefited from the reforms. These social-justice measures include long-term credit at low interest rates for farmers, an eight-hour working day for railroad employees, the first federal child-labor law and a workmen's compensation system for federal employees.

Indeed, the social reform had achieved progress. Some measures were significant while many were only stop-gap measures. The U.S. Constitution had been designed to limit the powers of the federal government in order to preserve liberties for the states and protect private ownership. Problems caused by the contradictions between the socialized production and the private ownership of the means of production can never be solved by moderate means under capitalist system.

Notes

1. "Gilded Age"

"镀金时代" 它指的是1860年至1898年间，其标志着美国由农业国发展为高度发达的工业国，财阀金融、垄断企业已经出现。

2. in this new industrial order the city was the nerve center

在这新的工业秩序中，城市起着核心作用 这是指把各种积极的经济力量汇集于一体，如大量的资金积累，企业金融机制，铁路、工厂，脑力和体力劳动大军。

3. Gold discoveries in California gave it further stimulus.

加利福尼亚州金矿的发现进一步促进了铁路建设。 加州于1848年发现了金矿，随后便迅速掀起了淘金热，从而促进了西部铁路建设和经济发展。

4. the Homestead Act

《宅地法案》 依此法案，美国政府分给定居移民耕种的土地，从而加速了西部的发展、定居和土地私有化。

5. the Morill Land-Grant College Act

《莫里尔公地兴学法案》 按此法案，美国政府为各州留有公地兴办工、农学院，为工业、农业培养人才。

6. the Northern Securities Company

北方债券公司 美国最早建立的金融债券公司。

7. the "Open Door" policy

"门户开放"政策 美国对中国的侵略政策。按此政策，美国和其他帝国主义列强一样在中国控制一些地区，享有同等的机会(包括关税、港口税和铁路税率)。

8. the rise of big labor

劳动大军的兴起

9. the Knights of Labor

劳工骑士团 第一个全国性的工人组织，由技术工和半技术工组成，争取提高工资待遇和生活水平。

10. the American Federation of Labor

美国劳工联合会 由行业工会组成，争取改善工资待遇和工作条件。

11. the Congress of Industrial Organizations

产业联合会 由半技术工人和不熟练的工人组成。

12. the Populist Party

民粹党 由农民联盟发展而来，主要成员是农民和其他少数民族团体，他们争取政治改革，废除中央银行，减少关税，实现8小时工作制等。对美国历史发展颇有影响。

13. literature of exposure

暴露文学 以马克·吐温为代表的暴露文学作家出现在1902年和1908年之间社会改革很活跃的时期，他们的作品暴露了社会的各种黑暗面。

14. the Civil Service Act

《文官任职法案》 按此法案，美国政府建立了政绩档案体系，考核政府官员是否贤能，防止腐败、无能。

15. Jim Crow Segregation laws disfranchised the blacks.

种族隔离法剥夺了黑人的公民权。

16. the Federal Reserve Act

联邦储备银行条例　按此条例，全国划分为12个区，每区设一个中央储备银行，协调下属私人银行的资金周转，既有政府参与协调金融事务，又保证私人银行的利益。

17. graduated income tax

分级所得课税或累进所得税率

Exercises

Ⅰ. Fill in each blank with the right word or expression from the text:

1. The Panama Canal connects ________ with ________.
2. Through the American-Spanish War in 1898, the United States acquired ________, ________ and ________.
3. The U. S. policy that demanded equal opportunities with other imperialist powers in China was ________.
4. The important reform of the banking and currency system during the Gilded Age was the establishment of ________ by the ________ which imposed upon the existing banks a new organization that divided ________ with ________ in each, all supervised by ________.
5. In 1869 the first transcontinental railway, ________, was completed at ________.
6. The Gilded Age marked ________.
7. After the United States entered into imperialism, it pursued the policy in search of ________, ________ and ________.
8. During the Gilded Age, appeared around the five Great Lakes four important cities: ________, ________, ________ and ________.

Ⅱ. Questions for discussion:

1. Why were the years between the Civil War and World War Ⅰ called

the Gilded Age?

2. Describe the basic causes of the rapid growth of American industry.

3. Mention some important industrial cities in the Middle West.

4. What were the important factors that contributed to the rapid development of agriculture?

5. Describe some of America's early monopoly businesses.

6. Why did America begin to make foreign adventures in the late 19th century?

7. What were the U.S. policies in Latin America in this period?

8. Why and how did the U.S. government pursue the "Open Door" policy against China in this period?

9. How did workers and peasants fight against trusts and monopoly? What were they fighting for?

10. Name some important progressive writers and mention the role they played in the anti-trust movement.

11. What important steps did reformers take to reform the society?

12. What do you think of the social reform in that period?

Chapter 13
America During and after World War Ⅰ

Text

Ⅰ. Outbreak of World War Ⅰ and America's Neutrality

In the late 19th century, the whole world had been partitioned by the imperialist powers. When the United States, a new rising imperialist power, gained evident balance of power in Asia and the U.S. supremacy in the Western Hemisphere, Germany, a newly-developed imperialist power, sought repartition of Europe but Great Britain and France firmly opposed it. Thus appeared two military blocs in Europe: *the Allies made up of Great Britain, France, Russia and their supporters and the Central Powers made up of Germany, Austria-Hungary, Turkey, Italy and others*[1]. They competed with each other for control of the Balkans, the Near East and Africa.

The crisis came when a Serbian patriot assassinated the Austrian heir to the throne on June 27, 1914. With the support of Germany the Austrians decided to teach Serbia her lesson, while Russia backed Serbia and France and England entered into war on the side of Russia. Within five weeks all Europe was locked in the greatest war of modern times.

When the war broke out, the U. S. President Wilson immediately declared the U. S. neutrality with an aim to continue trade with the warring nations so as to keep its prosperity in industry and agriculture. In January, 1915, Wilson offered good services as a mediator for peace, but was rebuffed by both sides. He also insisted that the warring nations respect the right of neutrals to freedom of seas and trade. However, the British successfully blocked Axis ports, while the Germans launched devastating submarine attacks against all shipping to Allied countries. Wilson protested both nations but reserved his chief complaints for the total destructiveness of submarine warfare on human lives and prosperity. For a time Germany curtailed attacks in response, but by January, 1917, its military situation had become so desperate that unrestricted submarine warfare was resumed. Within a few weeks eight American vessels were sent to the bottom, and the nation was aroused by the revelation of Germany's plot to seek an alliance with Mexico and Japan against the United States which seriously threatened America's national security. Traditionally, the United States had close ties and sympathy with the Allied countries and feared for German policy and ruthless acts of German militarists against the world people. If Germany would win the war, the United States would have lost all its friends in Europe and Germany would have become its dangerous enemy in Europe as well as in the world. All these seemed to justify the U.S. declaration of war against Germany.

Ⅱ. America's Entrance into the War

In April 1917, after eight American vessels had been sunk by German submarines, the United States declared war on Germany. Its intervention broke the military deadlock in Europe. Large quantities of war materials were shipped to the Allied countries in 1917 and 1918. This destroyed any chance that Germany could starve the Allies into submission. Even more importantly, the arrival in Europe during 1819 of over one and three-quarter million American soldiers gave the Allies superiority in numbers and fire power. After a little more than six months of heavy fighting, the German submarine blockade was broken, their defense line cracked. In the face of combined attacks Germany surrendered in November 1918, and appealed to Wilson for a negotiated peace settlement.

***Ⅲ. America and the Treaty of Versailles*[2]**

The peace conference was arranged in Paris in January, 1919. As Wilson believed that American involvement in the world would thrust him into the position of world leader, he announced in January 1918 a "*Fourteen Points*"[3] program to insure world peace. The keystone of this peace would be a general assembly of nations affording mutual guarantees of political independence and territorial integrity to its members. The program also called for freedom of seas and trade, an end to secret treaties, reduction of armaments, fair adjustment of colonial disputes and self-determination for subject nationalities. The latter meant specially German withdrawal from Russian territory, restoration of Belgium independence, establishment of an independent Poland and self-government of Austria-Hungary and that of Balkan Turkey. These objectives encountered dissent at home and abroad.

In January 1919, leaders of the Allied countries met at Versailles to draw up a peace treaty for Germany. At the Conference, Wilson wanted the Allies to establish *the League of Nations*[4] with America as the world leader and accept the concept of the Fourteen Points. Meanwhile other diplomats saw the peace meeting as an opportunity to revenge on Germany and enact many of the secret treaties that had been already formulated. The Fourteen Points were whittled away one after another. Despite the U.S. refusal of the proposal to carve up the territory of Germany and the clause that Germany should pay harsh reparations for starting the war, the Treaty of Versailles in the end was a victors' treaty. All diplomats blamed Germany for its crimes of starting the war. Its territory was carved up, heavy reparations were imposed. What were more unacceptable to Wilson, all League members had to place their military force at the disposal of the League.

By the time the Treaty of Versailles reached the U.S. Senate in July 1919, isolation renewed and the opposition from the Republicans was already powerful. Opponents of the League concentrated their attack on U.S. commitments to the League. Twice the Treaty of Versailles failed of ratification. Ultimately the United States had to sign separate treaties with Axis countries and refused to join the League of Nations. It was ironical to Wilson that he proposed the establishment of the League of Nations and ended with his refusal to join the League.

Ⅳ. America in the 1920s

After the war, the United States *took steps to return itself to "normalcy"*[5]. The United States sought not isolation from world affairs but rather a lower U. S. profile through reduction of political-military commitments. Thus, while the United States did not become a member of the League of Nations, it took part unofficially in forty League conferences and cooperated with such non-political agencies as the League Health Organization and the International Labor Organization. Moreover, during 1921—1922 Secretary of State Charles Evans Hughes led *the Washington Disarmament Conference*[6] and reached a series of interlocking treaties by which the United States, Great Britain, Japan, and other countries agreed to limit construction of capital ships to the ratio of 5 : 5 : 3 which for a time curtailed a potentially disastrous naval rivalry in the Far East but guaranteed U.S. naval supremacy in this area. Besides, the United States signed separate treaties with Germany, Austria and Hungary, which claimed for the United States all the rights and advantages but none of the responsibilities of the Paris peace settlement. Though at the Paris Conference the United States rejected Japan's demand that Germany hand over China's Shandong province to Japan, it further continued its "Open Door" policy and backed Japan's aggression against China by keeping trade with and supply of arms and ammunitions to Japan.

The 1920s witnessed a tremendous economic expansion, and the total production increased by 46%. By the mid-1920s, the United States enjoyed a total wealth almost as great as that of all of Europe and the world's highest living standard. This was largely accomplished through the nation's policies, the use of machinery and new techniques of mass production. Between 1921 and 1933, the Presidents Harding, Coolidge and Hoover had the view that the "business of the United States is business", therefore, government should assist business. They passed the high protective tariff acts of 1922 and 1930 guaranteeing to American manufactures in one field after another a monopoly of domestic market. Besides, they enacted a series of laws to encourage investment in industrial development by reducing income taxes, excess profit taxes, corporation taxes and so on. They even subordinated federal business to private management.

The scientist, Frederik W. Taylor, was the founding father of "scientific management".[7] By applying the resulting data, by breaking the process of manufacturing into separate parts, and by specializing the functions of the worker and the machine involved in each part, he substantially increased the rate of production. Henry Ford introduced this moving assembly line with an endless-chain overhead conveyer for the production of the popular Model T automobiles. As a result the labor required for assembly of an automobile chassis was reduced from $12\frac{1}{2}$ to $1\frac{1}{2}$ man hours. Ford doubled his wages to $5 a day and cut labor force by 90%. Yet his profits also doubled from $30 million after taxes in 1914 to $60 million in 1916. Ford's assembly line later became standard in many other industrial branches, which contributed greatly to the tremendous economic expansion in the 1920s and 1930s. New America seemed to have stepped into a new era.

Prices were stable, annual real earnings increased by 26% and workers in industry made substantial advances. Yet most American families did not reach the standard living level. In 1929, when it was estimated that a family needed an income of $2 500 a year to maintain a decent standard of living, 71% of American families had not reached that level. The average factory worker received less than $1 500 a year and farmer less than $700. Though large quantity of wealth was created by the broad masses of workers and peasants through the use of machinery and new techniques, it went into the hands of the wealthy few. Of course, this unfair distribution of wealth was inevitable under the capitalist system.

Ⅴ. *The Lost Generation*[8]

The Russian October Revolution[9] exerted great impact in the whole world as well as in the United States. Under the influence of the revolution, the U.S. Communist Party was founded in 1919. The U.S. government feared the growth and threat of the Communist movement and Red Scare became popular. Between 1919 and 1920 thousands of aliens were suspected of radicalism, many were arrested and put into prison, and some 500 members of the Communist Party were deported. This Red Scare wave led the way to a quota system for immigrants. In 1924 *the National Origins Act*[10] was pushed through which restricted immigration to 150 000 total immigrants a year, to be distributed among peoples of various nationalities in proportion to the number of their respective countries already arrived in the United States in 1920. This restriction virtually closed immigration from Southern and Eastern Europe and forbade all immigration from the Orient. The Ku Klux Klan revived and sought to enforce perpetuation of a native, white, protestant "100 percent America" through intimidation of Catholics, Negroes, and Jews. Fearing that Darwin's concepts would destroy belief in a personal God and encourage immorality *led to campaigns for state laws forbidding the teaching of the revolutionary concepts and to the sensational trial of Scopes in Tennessee*[11]. Prohibitionists' desires to protect citizenry from temptation of vice brought passage of the Eighteenth Amendment and the Volstead Act, which prohibited manufacture, sale of alcoholic liquors. Instead of ending drunkenness, the prohibition experiment encouraged a nationwide wave of boot-legging and gangsterism that weakened respect for law generally.

In the face of the deteriorating morality, many young people, especially writers and intellectuals, became tragically disillusioned. They were generally known as the "lost generation". Criticism became the dominant note in American literature in this period. The most famous among the "lost generation" were Ernest Hemingway, Sinclair Lewis, F. Scott Fitzgerald, Eugene O'Neill. In Ernest Hemingway's *Farewell to Arms* and *The Sun Also Rises*, one finds the American idealist tragically disillusioned by the horrors of war and his lost innocence. In F. Scott

Fitzgerald's *This Side of Paradise* and *The Great Gatsby*, one discovers the beautiful and the damned who having realized the dream of success now find it meaningless. In Sinclair Lewis' *Babbit* and *Main Street*, one sees small town business hypocrisy, provincialism, and materialism leading to a stifling conformity. In Eugene O' Neill's *The Hairy Ape* and *Desire under the Elms*, one views life through Freudian eyes to behold its emotional and psychological frustrations.

Ⅵ. *The Great Depression*[12]

During and after World War Ⅰ, America enjoyed a period of economic growth and prosperity, but soon depression ensued. The core of the problem had been the immense disparity between the high productive power and the American's ability to consume. Because of the workers' low wages the growth of social productivity far surpassed the growth of demand. After the war, Europe restored production and reduced imports from America. At the same time European countries limited large importation from America by raising import tariffs in retaliation against U. S. protective tariffs. As a result, the world market was swinging shut to American goods, causing reduction of the U.S. foreign trade by two-thirds.

In the face of a shrinking market and falling prices, the wealthy and middle classes refused to make new investment and put their money in frantic speculation in stocks or real estate. Thus the normal process of production and circulation was upset, and the economic crisis inevitably got worse.

The Great Depression actually began with the stock market crash in 1929. As the economic situation deteriorated, stockholders sold their shares in a frantic way. Savings in the banks were withdrawn into speculation. Factories curtailed their production sharply. By 1930 the country was in the midst of a full-scale economic depression. Banks failed, millions of investors and savers lost their life savings, business houses closed their doors, and factories were shut down. As a result, one-third of the potential labor force was out of work, unemployment grew by leaps and bounds from about one million in 1929 to between thirteen and seventeen million in 1933; the total value of industrial output dropped from about seventy billion dollars to more than thirty-one billion dollars. It was estimated that the national income declined 54 percent, salaries 40 percent, stock values 78 persent and farm income 59 percent. The whole country was in a state of poverty and panic.

Ⅷ. *President Roosevelt's "New Deal"*[13]

Franklin D. Roosevelt took office on March 4, 1933, at the depths of the Great Depression. He assured the American people that "the only thing we have to fear is fear itself". Being determined and confident the President felt no fear and intended to lead his people in waging a war against the depression with all the powers in hand. Soon after he took office he proposed a series of policies or bills. After congressional approval, these policies or bills, generally known as the "New Deal", were put into practice gradually.

The general objectives of the New Deal were "relief, recovery, and reform". The most immediate need in March 1933, was to halt the nation-wide financial panic that threatened to bring the complete collapse of the banking system. Roosevelt closed all banks for four days, while Congress passed the Emergency Banking Act which provided federal inspection of all banks in the Federal Reserve System and authorized the Reconstruction Finance Corporation to make loans to the banks in shaky conditions. Within a week three-fourths of the banks had reopened and public confidence was restored. Subsequently the Federal Deposit Insurance Corporation was created to guarantee the savings of Americans even when banks failed. In addition, millions of farm and home mortgages were refinanced on better terms by the Farm Credit Administration and the Home Owners' Loan Corporation. These measures did much to insure the well-being of America's middle-class citizens.

Relief for the hungry unemployed was also an immediate need. While Roosevelt believed that direct relief through provision of money or food was the responsibility of state governments, he assisted the states by making outright grants of billions of dollars from federal banks. Moreover, through agencies such as *the Civilian Conservation Corps and the Works Progress Administration*[14], millions of Americans acquired work relief on projects ranging from road maintenance to theatrical productions. Even more important was the Public Works Administration, which embarked on a massive construction program in highways, hospitals, dams and public buildings. The PWA projects not only created jobs, but also stimulated private businesses that supplied construction materials.

Relief and recovery for America's farmers seemed more difficult to achieve. The Agricultural Administration Act gave initial priority to cash relief, paying farmers to plow under crops and slaughter livestock in order to raise the prices of farm products through scarcity. However, *the long-range goal of the New Deal was to establish "parity" with the farmers' income level through provisions for marketing agreements, commodity loans, export subsidies, government agreements, soil conservation, and acreage restriction*[15]. Though the cash income increased much, it was still far behind the level of 1929. Farmers in the South and West benefited little from these measures, many were still left impoverished and desolate.

Generally speaking, workers' conditions were better off and progress was made in labor organization during the New Deal. Though the American Federation of Labor was slow to take in the unorganized, a new trade union, the Congress of Industrial Organization appeared, making successful progress in organizing the basic industries like automobiles and steel. By 1929 there were only four million organized workers, but by 1939 organized workers had reached eleven million. This greatly strengthened the workers' position in bargaining with the employers.

The New Deal had made some important achievements. It enlarged government interference in monopolistic production and marketing, promoted large-scale public projects, strengthened workers' organization and their bargaining position. Social welfare was promoted, adjustment was made between production and consumption, and above all, people's confidence was restored.

However, the New Deal was capitalistic in nature. It did not solve the relationship between the productive force and the ownership of means of production, and make any change in the state organ under the bourgeois dictatorship.

Notes

1. the Allies made up of Great Britain, France, Russia and their supporters and the Central Powers made up of Germany, Austria-Hungary, Turkey, Italy and others

协约国由大不列颠、法国、俄国和其他拥护国组成,同盟国由德国、奥匈帝国、土耳其、意大利和其他国家组成 这两大军事集团为了争夺巴尔干半岛、近东和非洲爆发了第一次世界大战,历时五年,协约国胜利,同盟国失败。

2. the Treaty of Versailles

《凡尔赛和约》 于1919年6月28日签订,主要内容有:德国将阿尔萨斯、洛林交还法国,其他许多边界地区割让给丹、比、捷、南、波等国;萨尔区交国际联盟保管15年;德国的殖民地由英、美、日等国瓜分;德国向美、英、法等战胜国交付巨额赔款;德国承认奥地利独立;限制德国军备等。以威尔逊总统为首的美国代表团虽曾在条约上签字,但因参议院没有批准,美国未能参加国际联盟。

3. "Fourteen Points"

"十四点计划" 这是美国总统威尔逊于1918年1月8日向协约国宣布的,其要点是建立国际联盟,并以美国为领导,但没有被其他协约国国家接受。

4. the League of Nations

国际联盟 存在于1920年至1946年,是现今联合国的前身。

5. took steps to return itself to "normalcy"

采取步骤使其自身恢复正常化 恢复国际关系正常化。

6. the Washington Disarmament Conference

华盛顿裁军会议　第一次世界大战后，美国虽然没有参加国际联盟，但组织、领导了这次国际会议，达成协议，把美、英、日、法、意建造主力舰的吨位限制为 5∶5∶3∶1.75∶1.75 的比例，保证美国海军在远东占有优势。

7. The scientist, Frederik W. Taylor, was the founding father of "scientific management".

科学家，腓特烈·W. 泰勒，是"科学管理"的创始人。　所谓科学管理即工业生产流水线作业。

8. the "lost generation"

"迷惘的一代"　在第一次世界大战后，面对日益衰败的社会道德，很多美国青年，尤其以海明威为代表的青年作家、知识分子对时局感到极度悲观失望，故出现了"迷惘的一代"。

9. the Russian October Revolution

俄国十月革命　以列宁为首的布尔什维克党号召无产阶级举行起义，推翻沙皇专制统治，建立了世界上第一个社会主义国家，震撼了全世界。在它的影响下，美国于 1919 年建立了共产党。

10. the National Origins Act

《民族祖籍法案》　把每年的移民限制在 150 000 人，其比例按 1920 年各国已经到达美国的移民人数分配，这实质上关闭了欧洲东南部国家的移民，并禁止了远东的移民。

11. led to campaigns for ... and to the sensational trial of Scopes in Tennessee

引起各州制定法律禁止革命理论宣传的浪潮和轰动全国的田纳西州对苏格白司的审判

12. the Great Depression

经济大萧条　从 1929 年开始的经济大萧条始于美国，后来影响扩展到全世界，其根本原因是美国高度发展的生产力和美国人民低消费能力之间的矛盾。

13. "New Deal"

"新政"　罗斯福总统上任之后，提出了一揽子政策和法令，经国会批准，用以应对经济大萧条，其主要目标是“救济、恢复和改革”，即救济失业贫困的人民、恢复工业和农业生产及经济建设，并进行社会改革。

14. the Civilian Conservation Corps and the Works Progress Administration

民工保护团和工程开发局

民工保护团为失业工人提供维修公路等工作机会，提高其就业率。

工程开发局则组织失业工人进行公共工程的开发和建设，如对田纳西河区进行开发利用，从而解决大量工人的失业问题，并开始了许多公共福利事业建设。美国有“福利社会”之称，便有其一份功劳。

15. the long-range goal of the New Deal was ... and acreage restriction

“新政”的长远目标是通过市场协议、商品贷款、出口补贴、政府收购、水土保养和减少耕地等措施和农民建立对等价值的收入平衡

Exercises

Ⅰ. Fill in each blank with the right word or expression from the text:

1. In the late 19th century, there emerged two military blocs: ________ and ________, competing with each other for control of ________, ________ and ________.
2. At the outset of World War Ⅰ, the U. S. government adopted the policy of ________, because they wanted to ________.
3. The keystone of the “Fourteen Points” was ________.
4. The failure of congressional ratification of the Treaty of Versailles was mainly due to ________.
5. In the post-war years, the United States gained naval supremacy over Japan in the Far East through limiting the construction of capital ships to a ratio of ________ between ________, ________ and ________.
6. Soon after F. D. Roosevelt came to office, he proposed a series of policies or bills passed by Congress to deal with the Great Depression generally known as ________, whose objectives were ________, ________ and ________.

Ⅱ. Questions for discussion:

1. State the reasons why the United States entered into World War Ⅰ.

2. Make a comment on President Wilson's "Fourteen Points" and America's refusal to join the League of Nations.
3. What do you know about the "lost generation" in the 1920s?
4. What was the background of the Great Depression?
5. What is the main content of President Roosevelt's "New Deal"?
6. What is your comment on the "New Deal"?

Chapter 14
America During and after World War Ⅱ

Text

Ⅰ. On the Eve of World War Ⅱ

During the 1920s the United States gradually built up the foundations for a peaceful and stable international order through disarmament limitations, peace treaties and *the Good Neighbor policy*[1], but the foundations crumbled in the 1930s, as the economic collapse of the Great Depression intensified nationalistic policies throughout the world. World relations quickly deteriorated. In 1931 Japan invaded China and set up the puppet state of "Manchukuo" in 1932. The next year Japan announced intention to establish "New Order" in the Far East and in 1934 Japanese militarists seized control of the Japanese government and prepared for the military conquest of Asia. Under desperate conditions caused by heavy war reparation after World War Ⅰ, Benito Mussolini and his fascist government rose to power in Italy and seeking to build an empire in Africa, invaded Ethiopia in 1935. Although the League of Nations denounced Italy as an "aggressor" and voted economic sanction, it failed to stop the invasion. In 1935, led by Adolf Hitler Nazi Germany began to rearm itself in defiance of the Treaty of Versailles and reoccupied the Rhineland in 1936. In the same year Francisco Franco began a fascist rebellion against Spain's republican government. Both the isolation of the U. S. and the indecision and ineffectiveness of Britain and France encouraged the fast fascist aggressive expansion in Europe.

World relations continued to deteriorate. In 1937, Japan launched its second aggressive war against China. In 1938, Germany annexed Austria and threatened Czechoslovakia. In *the infamous Munich Conference*[2] Britain and France sought to appease Hitler, who took their offerings and then contemptuously seized all Czechoslovakia. Subsequently Italy invaded Albania and Germany set its eyes on Poland. With Germany's obvious intent upon the conquest of Europe, France and England declared war on Germany on September 3, 1939. Thus began World War Ⅱ.

After the fall of Poland, Hitler moved his armies into Denmark and on to Norway and within a little more than a month the resources of most of Scandinavia were in German control. On May 10 Germany turned westward and struck at Holland, Belgium and France. Within a little more than a month, the three countries fell to Germany's blitzkrieg attacks. Now Britain was alone and suffered continual bombing by Germany.

Ⅱ. America Abandons Neutrality

In the 1930s, when fascist forces were fast growing, *many Americans favored isolationism and opposed the involvement in a new world war*[3]. In 1935, 1936 and 1937, a series of Neutrality Acts was passed that forbade arms sales and loans to all belligerent nations no matter whether aggressors or victims and prohibited Americans from travelling on ships of belligerents. But German attack on Poland was a challenge to America's isolationism and a great debate was aroused over the Neutrality Acts. Roosevelt moved energetically for the repeal of the acts and Congress passed "*the cash-and-carry*" *legislation*[4] which made American resources available to the Allies. The fall of France convinced most Americans of Germany's possible conquest of Europe and the danger of America's isolated position in the face of the Axis military coalition in Europe. By this realization Roosevelt by executive action ordered the U. S. naval convoying of British merchant ships and traded fifty overage destroyers to England in exchange for naval bases on British islands in the Caribbean and Western Atlantic. He also called upon Congress to approve $1 billion defense appropriation and the first peacetime conscription law in American history. In March 1941, Congress, urged by president Roosevelt, passed *the Lend-Lease Act*[5] which gave the President authority to transfer war materials directly to any country whose defense was considered vital to that of the United States.

Thus when in June 1941 Hitler launched German troops into Soviet Russia, Roosevelt extended lend-lease aid to the beleaguered nation.

In the Far East, tension mounted quickly. Japan had formally joined the Axis after the war broke out, and now, taking advantage of British and American involvement in the European war was pushing boldly ahead with her "New Order" in the Orient. In June 1941 when the German army crossed the Russian border and forced their way towards Moscow and Leningrad, Japan poured its troops into French Indo-China and prepared air bases along the border of Thailand. In December it began its ferocious attacks at American outposts in Hawaii, Guam, Midway, Wake and the Philippines. An allround war had started in the world.

Ⅲ. America's Entrance into the War

In December 1941 the Japanese made a surprise attack on Pearl Harbor. Germany and Italy made subsequent declarations of war on the United States and thus a global war was initiated.

During the winter between 1941—1942 conditions seemed bleak indeed. Germany not only held captive the greater part of Europe but also threatened to cut England's western supply line, to bring a complete collapse to Russia, and to drive through North Africa and the Middle East to link up with Japan somewhere in India. Japan had meanwhile conquered northern and coastal China, Burma, the Philippines, the Pacific islands such as Guam and Midway, as well as Malaysia.

Although Japan had attacked the United States, America directed its chief offensive against Germany. After the intervention of the U. S., situation gradually turned favorable for the Allies. In October 1942 the British stopped Germany's drive towards the Suez Canal at El Alamein, while in winter of 1942—1943 Russia stopped Germany at the Battle of Stalingrad to begin recovery of its lost territory. *In 1943 Anglo-American forces not only cleared Africa of German forces, but also invaded Scilly and Italy.*[6] Henceforth Germany was subjected to nation-wide bombing which eventually brought her transportation facilities to a standstill.

Meanwhile Americans developed an island-hopping strategy against Japan which isolated the latter's Pacific outposts and drove closer and closer to Japanese homelands.

Then in June 1944 Anglo-American forces invaded German-occupied France with a beachhead in Normandy. By November most of France and Belgium had been recovered, and the Allies posed for thrusts into Germany itself. Russian troops entered Poland, Yugoslavia, Hungary, and the eastern fringe of Germany. In the Pacific the United States captured the Marshalls, Marianas, and Carolines, and crushed the Japanese fleet at Leyte Gulf in October, 1944. The U. S. air forces, on the other hand, had begun devastating bombing on Japan. The end of global war was in sight.

In early 1945 Anglo-American forces commanded by General Dwight D. Eisenhower drove to the Rhine and then to the Elbe Rivers in Germany. Meanwhile Russia pressed onto Berlin and Prague. On May 7, 1945, Germany surrendered unconditionally. That was *the V-E Day*[7].

Three months later, Russia in accordance with an early agreement declared war against Japan and drove into Northeast China. With the help of the Red Army, the Chinese forces defeated the Japanese forces in China. On August 6 American aircraft dropped the first atom bomb in Hiroshima and the second in Nagasaki on August 9, killing almost 300 000 people in both cities. On August 14, 1945, Japan surrendered unconditionally and World War Ⅱ came to an end. That was *the V-J Day*[8].

During the war, more than fifteen million Americans served in the armed forces with over one million casualties of whom one-third were listed as killed or missing in action. However, for most Americans the war was a battle for production. The gross national product almost doubled between 1939 and 1945 while the production of munitions increased over 600 per cent. During the war the United States produced over 296 000 airplanes, 86 000 tanks and 75 000 naval and merchant ships. By 1944 the nation turned out twice the war materials of its enemies combined. American industrial and agricultural production worth of almost $50 billion was sent to the Allied countries under Lend-Lease program. In its war effort between 1941 and 1945 the U.S. government spent over $321 billion—twice as much as the total for the preceding 150 years.

Ⅳ. Big Labor During the War

The war accelerated the growth of the big government, big business, big agriculture, and big labor in the United States. As expenditure increased from $9 billion in 1940 to $98 billion in 1945, big government through big federal agencies such as *the War Production Board*[9] purchased about one-half of the nation's economic output and controlled wages, prices, allocation of new materials, plant resources, and distribution of commodities. Government leaders cared more about efficiency in production than they feared the threat of monopoly. Almost one-third of all war orders went to only ten corporations, while over one-half million small businesses disappeared. Big farmers also benefited for the same reason of efficiency in production. Although the farm population decreased by 17 per cent, farm production increased by 23 per cent and farm income jumped from $2.3 billion in 1940 to $9.5 billion in 1945. During the same period the AFL and CIO merged into a big organization, *the AFL-CIO*[10] comprising a membership of 15 million while employment itself increased from 46 to 63 million persons. Not only did woman workers increase by over 30 percent, but also they found employment in heavy industry jobs reserved for men. Although prices rose by 29 percent, real wages in manufacturing increased over 50 percent. It was obvious that more and more Americans crossed the poverty line to join the middle class, and America had become the most powerful nation in the world by making huge profits to fatten its country through exports of large quantities of war materials to the world.

Ⅴ. Strategy During the War

Europe was the central stage for contention of the world by the imperialist powers. During the war, the United States used both economic powers to effect a beneficial change and a reshaping of European order. However, Great Britain wanted to retain its empire, and Russia wanted to create spheres of influence in Eastern Europe and elsewhere. In 1942 hard-pressed Russia wanted Anglo-American forces to relieve German pressure by establishing a western front in France. But it was refused by the United States, instead, they initiated the North African Campaign that saved British interests in the Suez and the Middle East. However, England was displeased by America's refusal to launch an attack through the Balkans that could have not only preserved Britain's imperial life-line but also given Anglo-American voices equal weight with Russia in disposition of Eastern Europe. American leaders seemed to sympathize with Russian desire *to create an East European "buffer zone" between itself and Germany*[11]. *At the Yalta Conference*[12] in February 1945, agreement was reached for "free elections" in Eastern Europe, but Russia used her military control of the region to create pro-Soviet governments and to link their economies with Russia. This distressed the United States so much that it did not permit Russia to participate in either the reorganization of Italy or that of Japan. These were just a few of the problems that confronted and divided the United States, Great Britain and Russia during the war itself.

After the war America's chief hopes for a new world order lay in the creation of an international organization under its control. In April 1945, representatives from forty-six nations met in San Francisco to draft a charter for *the United Nations Organization*[13]. After bitter wrangling between American and Russian delegates, a charter was written that provided for world confederation and cooperation. Initiative and authority was vested in the Security Council, composed of representatives from the United States, Great Britain, France, Russia, China and other six nations to be elected by the General Assembly, those mentioned being the five permanent member states.

Ⅵ. *The Civil-Rights Movement*[14] in the 1960s

The 1960s witnessed an upsurge of the "civil-rights movement" in the United States. Though Lincoln proclaimed the emancipation of the black slaves in 1863, rarely had they achieved any substantial gains. The blacks were still suffering discrimination in voting, education, housing and employment. They lived in a segregated society extending to railroads, street cars, parks, schools, hospitals and even cemeteries. In some states the blacks had to pay a poll tax as a requirement for voting in elections. The costly Vietnam War afflicted millions of Americans, especially the blacks, which in turn resulted in economic recess, sharp unemployment and social disorder. All these seemed to justify the nation-wide civil-rights movement in the 1960s.

The struggle against racial discrimination went through many changes. In 1960 black and white students held "sit-ins" to demand an end to segregation. In 1961 "freedom riders" protested against segregation in interstate bus transportation. In 1963 Martin Luther King Jr. began a campaign to end discrimination in shops, restaurants and employment, but it was harassed by the police. Public discontent grew. In the same year Luther King and other black leaders staged an impressively dramatic but peaceful "March on Washington" that drew 250 000 demonstrators demanding federal action to provide "jobs and freedom". In 1965 Los Angeles witnessed big riots which resulted in the death of 35 persons and the destruction of hundreds of buildings. As the civil-rights crusade forged ahead, racists' fear and hatred grew and violent retaliations were conducted and Martin Luther King fell a victim to racial discrimination.

The civil-rights crusade helped push forward desegregation in America. Bus segregation was banned; schools were open to black students; poll tax and literacy tests in elections were abolished; housing was improved; fair jobs and chances were provided. Yet real equality was still far from being achieved and the civil-rights movement has been and is still going on.

Ⅶ. *The Counterculture*[16] from the mid-1950s to the late 1960s

Counterculture was a culture that ran counter to the traditional American culture. It was a widespread revolt against the accepted values and institutions of middle-class American society. The counterculture represented the right side of the American youth movement in the 1960s.

In the mid-1950s, groups of Bohemians began to practise free love, take drugs, repudiate the straight world and detest everything in the world. They preferred long hair, mini-dress or close-fitting clothes to show off the body. They advocated freedom of sex and cohabitation.

What influenced the young were popular music and folk music first and then rock. Large-scale enthusiasm for folk music began in 1958 when the Kingston Trio recorded a song "Tom Dooley" that sold two million records. The folk music vogue was an early stage in the politicalization of youth, a forerunner of the counterculture.

The Beatles contributed most to the counterculture. Beatlemania began on October 13, 1963 when the quartet played at the London Palladium. On February 9, 1964, they appeared on the U.S. television. They sang poignant and evocative songs about drugs, race, sex, life and memory which won adoration in the United States. These Beatles became millionaires overnight.

Beatlemania coincided with the rise of drug addiction. The forerunners were two scientific researchers at Harvard University who studied the effects of hallucinogenic drugs, notably a compound "LSD" or "acid".

Hippies appeared around 1965, seeking to build alternatives to the straight world. They lived together in "tribes" or "families" by selling drugs, begging, cashing checks from home. Their belief was "be nice to others, even when provoked, and they will be nice to you". The most famous communities were the East Village in New York and the Hashbury in San Francisco. LSD became an important part of the hippie culture. This culture took root in varying degrees in many urban centers and college communities. Its influence was great, even elementary children were affected. They dismayed their mothers by coming home chanting:

Marijuana, Marijuana,

LSD, LSD,

College kids are taking it,

High school kids are taking it,

Why can't we? Why can't we?

...

Under the counterculture influence, miniskirts appeared; bikinis were seen on American beaches in sizable numbers and soon became standard among girls and young women. Male clothing changed too. Fur coats for man appeared. Young men began to flower themselves. They never smelt better. They became almost as gorgeous as women.

Rock music fed the counterculture. The greatest event in counterculture history was the Woodstock Rock Festival in New York. Since then large numbers of large rock festivals had been organized on similar patterns throughout the country. It was a terrific confusion.

The hippie era did not last long, perhaps from 1965 to 1969. After 1969 the counterculture gradually declined because of public opinion and social hostilities and other reasons.

Nonetheless, the hippie culture left its mark. Drugs, rock music, man's fashion still exist. This undercurrent is still undermining American traditional culture.

Notes

1. the Good Neighbor policy

睦邻友好政策　指美国对南美洲邻国所采取的友好政策。

2. the infamous Munich Conference

臭名昭著的慕尼黑会议　在慕尼黑会议上，英国的外交大臣张伯伦和法国的外交大臣达拉第没有谴责以德国希特勒和意大利墨索里尼为首的法西斯分子的侵略行为，而是步步退让，更加助长了他们的侵略气焰和野心，从而导致了第二次世界大战的爆发，这是英、法采取绥靖政策的结果，故有

“臭名昭著的慕尼黑会议”之称。

3. many Americans favored isolation and opposed the involvement in a new world war

很多美国人民拥护孤立主义，并反对卷入一场新的世界大战

4. the “cash-and-carry” legislation

“现购自运”法规　美国政府准许美国商人与交战国进行除军队之外的交易，但要求后者现金购物、自行运送的法律规定。

5. the Lend-Lease Act

《租借法案》　该法案授权美国总统直接向盟国转运军需品和战略物资，如飞机、弹药等，美国也通过该法案向苏联提供援助。这是美国参战后所采取的主要外交政策。

6. In 1943 Anglo-American forces not only cleared Africa of German forces, but also invaded Scilly and Italy.

1943 年，英美联军不仅把德军从非洲清除出去，而且占领了锡利群岛和意大利。

clear ... of ...　把……从……清除出去

7. the V-E Day

“欧洲胜利日”　1945 年 5 月 8 日是同盟国结束在欧洲对联盟国作战的胜利日。

8. the V-J Day

“同盟国对日作战胜利日”　指日本于 1945 年 8 月 14 日宣布无条件投降之日。其 1945 年 9 月 2 日正式签字投降。

9. the War Production Board

战时生产局　该局收购全国一半左右的经济产品，而且控制工资、价格及物资商品分配等。

10. the AFL-ClO

美国劳工产业联合会　1955 年，原来的美国劳工联合会和产业联合会合并成美国现在最大的劳工组织。

11. to create an East European “buffer zone” between itself and Germany

在其与德国之间建立一个东欧“缓冲地带”

12. the Yalta Conference

雅尔塔会议　于1945年2月11日，由苏、美、英三国首脑在雅尔塔举行。会议签署了《雅尔塔协定》。协定主要内容的一项为：在德国投降及欧洲战争结束后两三个月内，苏联将参加同盟国方面的对日作战。

13. the United Nations Organization

联合国组织　其前身是国际联盟(the League of Nations)。

14. the civil-rights movement

民权运动　指争取人民基本权利，如人生、财产、自由等基本权利的运动。

15. the counterculture

反主流文化　这是一种反对美国传统文化的文化，反对美国中产阶级公认的价值和制度，它代表20世纪60年代美国青年运动的右翼。

Exercises

Ⅰ. Fill in each blank with the right word or expression from the text:

1. In the United States, the largest labor organization at present is ________.
2. In the 1960s, the most prominent black leader of the civil-rights movement was ________.
3. The counterculture was a widespread revolt against the ________.
4. The V-E Day means ________ and the V-J Day means ________.
5. At the beginning of World War Ⅱ, the U.S. government pursued a policy of ________.
6. In the infamous Munich Conference, both Britain and France adopted the policy of ________ that ________.
7. The main purpose for U.S. entrance into World War Ⅱ was ________.

Ⅱ. Questions for discussion:

1. State the main causes of the outbreak of World War Ⅱ.
2. What was the policy of the U.S. at the beginning of World War Ⅱ? Why did the U.S. government take such a policy?
3. What strategic measures did America take after the repeal of the

Neutrality Act?

4. What is your comment on the role of the U.S. in winning the victory of World War Ⅱ?

5. What was America's strategic goal during and after World War Ⅱ?

6. How did the United States become the largest imperialist power after World War Ⅱ?

7. What do you know about McCarthyism?

8. Give a brief account of the causes and purposes of the civil-rights movement in the 1960s.

9. What is meant by counterculture? What is your comment on counterculture?

Chapter 15
The Cold War and U.S. Foreign Policy

Text

After World War Ⅱ, the U.S. government pursued a policy of "containment" against the communist movement headed by the Soviet Union and this resulted in the Cold War.[1] The United States and the Soviet Union emerged from the war as rivals for world leadership, economic power and political supremacy. Both competed vigorously for control of the post-war power vacuum that touched off confrontations throughout the world. Along with the easing of world tension, *the policy of "containment" was shifted to the policy of detente in the late twentieth century*[2]. At the Malta Conference held in 1989, both the U.S. President George Bush and the Soviet President Mikhail Gorbarchev declared that the Cold War between the East and the West was over and that U.S.-Soviet relations had entered a new era of mutual accommodation and cooperation.

Ⅰ. The Policy of Containment

The brief period of Soviet-American alliance in their struggle against the Axis headed by Adolf Hitler came to an end immediately following the close of World War Ⅱ. In an important speech on February 9, 1946, Stalin declared that communism and capitalism were incompatible and true peace was impossible until capitalism had given way to communism. In response, Churchill asserted that the Soviet Union was an expansionist state, *an iron curtain had descended from Stettin in the Baltic to Trieste in the Adriatic across the continent*[3]. He contended that while the Soviet Union might not want war, it desired the fruits of war and the infinite expansion of their power and doctrines. What should the West do to meet the Soviet challenge? Churchill said, "I'm convinced that there is nothing they admire so much as strength and there is nothing for which they have less respect than for weakness, especially military weakness. " Now that Germany and Japan had been defeated, the Soviet Union loomed as a major threat to the West.

George Kennan, an ambassador and expert on the Soviet Union, published an article on the *Foreign Affairs 25* in July, 1947 with the name *The Sources of Soviet Conduct*, saying that "the political action of the Kremlin is a fluid stream which moves constantly, wherever it is permitted to move, toward a given goal. Its main concern is to make sure that it has filled every nook and cranny available to it in the basin of world power", and "the main element of any United States policy toward the Soviet Union must be that of a long term, patient but firm and vigilant containment of Russian expansive tendencies". President Truman took Kennan's views seriously and decided to meet the Soviet challenge with a policy of containment.

After the Soviet Union had gained supremacy in the Eastern Europe, especially in the Balkans, the U. S. government feared that if Greece collapsed, the crumbling of Turkey and Japan before the Soviet power would be only a question of time. President Truman made to Congress a speech declaring, "One of the primary objectives of the foreign policy of the United States is the creation of conditions in which we and other nations will be able to work out a way of life from coercion ... We shall not realize our objectives, however, unless we are willing to help peoples to maintain their free institutions and their national integrity against aggressive movements that seek to impose upon them totalitarian regimes". He concluded in his speech "it must be the policy of the United States *to support free peoples who are resisting attempted subjugation by armed minorities or by outside pressures*[4]". With this goal in view, Congress urged by Truman appropriated $ 400 million for economic assistance and military aid to Greece and Turkey. *This was the Truman Doctrine which inaugurated the policy of containment*.[5] It was what the journalists called the Cold War.

World War Ⅱ had wrought havoc with economies of Western Europe. A severe winter in 1946—1947 dealt Europe another heavy blow. These conditions, in the view of the U.S. government, could easily be exploited by the Soviet Union and eventually lead to communist take-over in some of the Western European countries. Speaking at the Harvard Commencement on June 5, 1947, the Secretary of State, George Marshall said, "Our policy is not directed against any country or doctrine, but against hunger, poverty, desperation and chaos. Its purposes should be the revival of working economy in the world so as to permit the emergence of political and social condition in which free institutions can exist." Accordingly, he formulated a plan that could offer direct economic aid to the ailing nations of Europe. This was *the Marshall Plan*[6], officially called the European Recovery Program(ERP) with an aid of over $13 billion in four years. This recovery program strengthened an area which was vital to the United States strategically, economically and culturally and an area which was likely to stop the advance of the Soviet power.

Alarmed by the expansion and consolidation of Soviet influence in Eastern Europe and the Balkans, the United States with other countries in Western Europe and North America signed the North Atlantic Pact in Washington D. C. and established in April, 1949 *the North Atlantic Treaty Organization* (*NATO*)[7] composed of the United States, Britain, France, Denmark, Iceland, Belgium, Italy, the Netherlands, Luxembourg, Portugal, Norway, Canada, West Germany into a military alliance against Soviet power. Thus far the United States had completed its strategic building of containing communism in Europe.

In the Far East, the United States had been covetous of China. After its occupation of Japan after World War Ⅱ, the United States doubled its efforts to aid Chiang Kai-shek in his resistance against the Chinese People's Liberation Army in the Chinese Liberation War. The United States failed and its aid availed nothing. Chiang Kai-shek and his followers were driven out of the mainland and escaped to Taiwan province.

The People's Republic of China was founded on October 1, 1949.

After the victory of the Chinese Revolution, Truman's foreign policy was attacked by conservatives for the failure of containing communism in Asia. John Foster Dulles condemned containment as negative, futile, and immoral and asserted that containment was a treadmill policy that would go nowhere. But when he became the Secretary of State under the Eisenhower Administration after the 1952 general election, he still pursued the policy of containment and even pushed it to a new extreme—*the doctrine of instant and massive retaliation*[8]. Not reconciled to its failure, the United States tried to plot a return by launching the Korean War. In defense of the national security and North Korea's sovereignty, the Chinese People's Volunteer Army crossed the Yalu River and drove the aggressors back to the south of the 38th Parallel. An armistice was signed in July, 1953 and peace was restored in North Korea. Massive retaliation ended with massive failure. Eisenhower could not but admit that the United States fought the wrong war in the wrong place and in the wrong time.

After the defeat in the Korean War, the U. S. troops occupied China's territory Taiwan and enforced a strict blockade on China with its fleets riding roughshod along the Chinese coast and the Taiwan Strait in a vain attempt to force the Chinese people into submission.

In the meantime the United States entered into Vietnam after French withdrawal. This resulted in the Vietnam War that lasted about twenty years, the longest war in American history. It left more Americans dead—fifty-seven thousand than any war except the Civil War and the two world wars, and cost more money than any war except World War Ⅱ. Direct war cost amounted to $150 billion. The ultimate cost was impossible to determine; estimates ranged from $350 to $676 billion.

In 1954 the United States created *the South-East Asia Treaty Organization*[9] for military alliance with Britain, France, Australia, New Zealand, the Philippines, Pakistan and Thailand. In 1955 *the Central*

Treaty Organization[10] allied the United States, Turkey, Iraq, Pakistan, Iran and Britain in the defense of the Middle East status quo. By this point the United States had set up a military alliance for forty-four nations around the world against the communist movement and the struggle for national independence and sovereignty of the third world countries. After long years of competition, the communist movement has gained momentum and more and more third world countries have won their independence and sovereignty. On the contrary, the United States has lost many colonies and is faced with new and forcible challenges throughout the world.

Ⅱ. A Shift of Policy from Containment to Detente

After the policy of containment and the doctrine of massive retaliation failed, the U.S. government made adjustment in its diplomatic strategy based on Henry Kissinger's ideas. Kissinger criticized the policy of containment as a short-sighted strategy by relying on long-range, powerful nuclear weapons, and massive retaliation as an all-or-nothing strategy that allowed Moscow to nibble away the status quo bit by bit and impose a series of piecemeal defeats on the West.

John F. Kennedy, the youngest American President who had ever entered the White House, had an acute sense of the limitations of American power. He called on the American people in 1961 to "face the fact that *the United States is neither omnipotent nor omniscient*[11]—that we are only six per cent of the world population—that we cannot impose our will upon the other ninety-four per cent of mankind—and therefore there cannot be an American solution to every world problem". He shared the views of Henry Kissinger and was strongly opposed to the doctrine of massive retaliation. He argued in his book, *The Strategy for Peace*, that the greatest danger of the United States did not come from direct nuclear attack, but from "sputnik diplomacy, limited brush-fire wars, indirect non-overt aggression ..." In such a situation, he declared, "Massive retaliation had not worked in the past and would not work in the future. We have been driving ourselves into a corner where the only choice is all-or-nothing at all, world devastation or submission." Therefore he advocated a more diversified military capability, that would make it possible for the United States to fight limited wars with nonnuclear weapons and to use strategic nuclear weapons only as the ultimate sanction. This was known as the "*flexible response*"[12].

The Cuban missile crisis was an example of flexible response. When Kennedy found evidence that the Soviet Union had sent medium-range ballistic missiles to Cuba, he ordered a naval blockade of the island and urged the Soviet Union to remove the missiles. Khrushchev backed down. The missiles were withdrawn. Kennedy's flexible response to the crisis had paid off.

Meanwhile John F. Kennedy proposed the organizations of *the Peace Corps and the Alliance for Progress*[13] in an attempt to exert peaceful evolution in the underdeveloped countries of the world. The Peace Corps recruited specially trained young Americans to work in underdeveloped countries and teach their people the benefits of technology while instilling them with the doctrine of so-called democracy. The Alliance for Progress was to raise the living standard of the people in Latin American countries. This policy worked somewhere and it had been followed by his successors and neocolonialism is today stealthily moving forward somewhere in the world.

In January, 1969, Richard Nixon came to the White House and Henry Kissinger became his Special Advisor on National Security. Both initiated an age of detente. "The central thesis", Nixon said in his report to Congress on February 18, 1970, was that "the United States will participate in the defense and development of allies and friends, but cannot—and will not—conceive all the plans, design all the programs, execute all the decisions and undertake all the defense of the free nations of the world". Henry Kissinger was strongly opposed to the Cold War, the policy of containment and nuclear "massive retaliation" to Soviet attack, advocating a "flexible response", combining the use of tactical nuclear weapons as well as conventional forces. He thought that "the concept of war in today's world has changed. The means and purpose with which wars are staged, have changed". He stressed "co-existence with the Soviet Union. As mankind has lost its balance, the government of the world should restore this balance through negotiations. It is better to start conventional war than to go to all-out war right away. The longer time between the conventional war and the all-out war the more room there is for peaceful negotiations to achieve world peace". *His ideas laid down the cornerstone of the U. S. foreign policy, the triangular policy—the triangle of the United States, Europe and Japan and the triangle of the United States, China and the Soviet Union.*[14] This policy changed the U.S. diplomatic tradition, advocating the establishment of a balance of power around the world.

Nixon's boldest step was to reverse the U. S. policy toward the People's Republic of China. Soon after he came to office, he instructed Kissinger to begin privately exploring the possibility for a rapprochement with the Chinese people. On July 15, 1971, it was announced that Henry Kissinger and Premier Zhou Enlai had held talks in Beijing from July 9 to 11, and that Nixon had accepted an invitation to visit China at an appropriate date before May 1972. Nixon visited China in February, 1972 and issued *the Shanghai Communique*[15] in which the United States acknowledged that Taiwan was a part of China and reaffirmed its interests in a peaceful settlement of the Taiwan question by the Chinese themselves. This was a heroic turning point in postwar U.S. diplomacy.

For Nixon and Kissinger the next goal was the maintenance and extension of detente between the United States and the Soviet Union, moving from an era of confrontation to an era of negotiation in the U.S.-Soviet relationship. In May, 1972, Nixon and Brezhnev met in Moscow and signed a number of documents, including *the Strategic Arms Limitation Talks (SALT I)*[16], which limited the development of antiballistic missiles (ABMs) and put a ceiling on the number of permissible offensive weapons. This event symbolized the end of the Cold War.

When Jimmy Carter came to the presidency, he decided to push forward the complete normalization between the United States and the People's Republic of China in an attempt to resist Soviet expansive moves around the world. On December 16, 1978, the two nations issued a joint communique, declaring that from January 1, 1979, they accorded mutual recognition and opened their embassies in Beijing and Washington D.C. Normalization was realized; however there were still disputes between the two countries, especially over the question of Taiwan.

In relation with the Soviet Union, President Carter at first held hope for Soviet-American detente, but when Soviet troops invaded Afghanistan on December 27, 1979 and threatened Western access to the Persian Gulf area, Carter announced a new Persian Gulf strategy that "an attempt by any outside force to gain control of the Persian Gulf region will be regarded as an assault on the vital interests of the United States of America, and such an assault will be repelled by any means necessary, including military force". As a result, the SALT Ⅱ agreement was removed from Senate consideration, grain and high technology exports to the Soviet Union were suspended, the United States boycotted the 1980 Moscow Summer Olympics and its military expenditures increased significantly, and the Cold War seemed to return stealthily.

When Ronald Reagan was sworn in the White House in 1981, he was openly opposed to the policy of detente. In his address to Congress on February 6, 1983, he declared, "We must stand by all our democratic allies. And we must not break faith with those who are risking their lives on every continent, from Afghanistan to Nicaragua, to defy Soviet-supported aggression and secure rights which have been ours from birth." On March 14, 1986, Reagan further elaborated this policy as "Freedom, Regional Security and Global Peace", by which he emphasized that the United States had to offset Soviet influence around the world by using military, diplomatic, economic and propaganda means in a bid not only to contain Soviet expansion abroad, but also to roll back the Soviet sphere of influence to its homeland. This was known as *the Rollback Strategy*[17] pursued by Ronald Reagan. By this policy, the Pentagon budget was to be increased by an annual rise of 7 percent for expanding U. S. armed forces, so as to restore military superiority over the Soviet Union.

Reagan was not friendly enough with the Chinese people. He had close ties with Taiwan and tried to keep China at a certain distance by continuing to support Taiwan separatists. He refused to terminate arms sales to Taiwan on the pretext that the Taiwan Relation Act of 1979 committed the United States to sell to Taiwan arms necessary to maintain a so-called "sufficient self-defense capability". However, he played "Chinese Card" as a trick to limit Soviet expansion and *promised in the U. S. -China Communique of August 17, 1982, to reduce gradually its sales of arms to Taiwan, leading over a period of time to a final resolution*[18]. This accord alleviated but did not dispose of the crisis between the United States and China.

Despite his hardline policy, Reagan could not turn back the general international trend—from confrontation and tension to dialogue and detente, and from a bipolar to a multipolar pattern development.[19]

Ⅲ. Drastic Changes in Eastern Europe and the Soviet Union and the U. S. Policy

World situation continued to change drastically. As the Soviet Union had been competing with the United States for control of world power, it had met with a given situation: increased economic difficulties, ever-increasing strike activities, sharp national contradictions, as well as rapid changes in Eastern Europe. Faced with severe challenges at home and abroad, President Mikhail Gorbachev published in November 1987, his pamphlet entitled "*Reform and New Thinking*"[20] and started economic and political reform in the Soviet Union, which exerted great impact on Eastern countries or even the whole of Europe, creating an immediate sensation throughout the world.

The year of 1989 witnessed a series of turmoil, riots, chaos, and political struggles in the Eastern countries and the Soviet Union as well. In Poland, the United Labor Union came to power; in Hungary, the Socialist Workers' Party split and gave rise to the multi-party system and practice of free market economy of the country. Turmoil within the Socialist Democratic Germany, downfall of the Berlin Wall and flux of large numbers of people from East Germany to West Germany finally led to the unification of Germany. With the rushes of violent storms, the communist regimes crumbled one after another in Czechoslovakia, Bulgaria, Romania and other countries. Drastic changes in the Eastern Europe in 1989 caught worldwide attention.

Faced with these new challenges, President George Bush proposed talks with President Mikhail Gorbachev in Malta in 1989 to discuss the current situation and other issues. At the summit, both sides declared that the Cold War between the East and West was over and that U.S.-Soviet relations had entered a new era of mutual accommodation and cooperation. In the light of this situation, Washington formulated a bold strategy known as "*Beyond Containment*"[21] with an aim at the Soviet Union and Eastern Europe in the belief that the historic opportunity to bring about peaceful evolution in Eastern Europe, for which it had waited for more than 40 years, had come at long last.

As world situation continued to change toward detente, both President Bush and President Gorbachev held in Washington in June, 1990, their second summit meeting which resulted in eleven agreements on chemical weapons reduction, bilateral trade, cultural exchanges, environmental protection and scientific research. Four statements, including two on cutting strategic arms and conventional forces in Europe, were also signed. Both Presidents pronounced their summit a success, just as Bush said at a joint news conference with Gorbachev at the end of their meeting that they made great progress in their mutual efforts towards building a more peaceful and stable world. One day after the outbreak of the Gulf War, foreign ministers of both countries held an emergency meeting to exchange views and issued a joint statement condemning the Iraqi invasion of Kuwait. This was the first time the two countries cooperated in a regional conflicts since the end of World War Ⅱ.

On July 31, 1991, Soviet President Mikhail Gorbachev and U.S. President George Bush held a summit in Moscow in which they signed *the Strategic Arms Reduction Treaty* (*START*)[22]. The treaty laid down stringent conditions for checking and verifying the destruction of about one third of the superpowers' strategic nuclear arsenals. Under this treaty, to be carried out over seven years, the Soviet long-range nuclear bombers would be cut by 35 percent overall and the Unites States by 28 percent, the Soviet Union would cut its 10 800 warheads to 8 000, while the 12 000 U.S. warheads would be reduced to 10 400. However, the treaty did not prevent the two superpowers from improving the quality of their weapons and stopping arms competition.

At the summit, Bush pledged U.S. assistance to improve food distribution, transportation, oil exploration, conversion of military plants, economic education and an aid of U.S. $20 million to the Soviet Union. What's more, Bush awarded Gorbachev the most-favored-nation trade status.

Both Presidents agreed that the summit was a success, a major step toward mutual security and world peace, and recognized that they set the basic tone for the U.S.-Soviet relations in the 1990s—stressing arms control talks and political cooperation and regional conflicts.

At the summit, Bush reaffirmed U.S. support for Gorbachev's bold economic and political reform, but he warned against any expectation of direct financial help to the Soviets. "A shortage of foreign capital is not what plunged your economy into crisis, nor can your economic ills be cured by simple infusion of cash," the U.S. President said, "and aid will depend on the Soviet democratic and market reforms."

The U. S. financial aid and support did not help much in Gorbachev's political and economic reform programme. Things got worse and deteriorated quickly in the Soviet Union. Independent movement swept all over the Baltic countries; political and economic reforms caused great discontent and strong opposition from among the people; strikes and chaos emerged one after another, and all these culminated in the "*August 19 Coup*"[23] in which Gorbachev was put under arrest in the Black Sea resort where he was having a vacation. With the help of Boris Yeltsin, Gorbachev was freed and resumed his office. After the coup, the Central Committee of the Soviet Communist Party was disbanded, the whole Party disintegrated, a nation-wide anti-communist movement raged throughout the country. Thousands of communists were arrested and put into prison, and many were killed. Communism collapsed and the Soviet Union was split overnight on August 24, 1991, into fifteen independent republics. With the disintegration of the Soviet Union, Gorbachev lost his power and influence as a president while that of Boris Yeltsin, Russian President, has been greatly enhanced and consolidated, and he has played the role as head of *the Confederation of the Independent Republics*[24].

After Bill Clinton was sworn in the White House in 1993, he pledged to fulfil commitments to the treaties and agreements reached between the United States and the former Soviet Union, to further promote overall accommodation and cooperation with Russia and other independent republics, to ensure gradual reduction of armed forces, limitation and destruction of ballistic missiles, warheads and chemical weapons, to promote science and space programs, to give financial aid and support to Russia and other independent republics with an aim at bringing them into line with the Western democracy and free market system. However, cooperation often coincides with strife and difficulty whenever and wherever their interests run counter to each other.

In his policy toward China, Bill Clinton reaffirmed that the United States will follow the "one China" policy and observe the three Sino-U. S. joint communiques by strictly placing U. S.-Taiwan tie within the limits of their unofficial nature and refusing visits by Taiwan's top leaders or agree to their *so-called "transit diplomacy" and "holiday diplomacy"*[25]. *He decided to extend China's most-favored-nation trade status and delink it from human rights issue*.[26] The goal of the U. S. policy is to maintain a cooperative relationship with a "strong, stable, prosperous and open" China. However, there remain obstacles here and there and from time to time to the progress of the Sino-U. S. relationship because of the different social systems, different cultures and ideas between the two countries.

The United States and its allies showed great concern over the dramatic changes taken place in Eastern Europe and the Soviet Union. In order to build up a new order in Europe, heads of state or government of 32 European nations together with those from the United States and Canada, who gathered in Paris from November 19 to 21, 1990 at a summit meeting of the Conference on Security and Cooperation in Europe, signed at the end of the meeting the Charter of Paris for a new Europe, a document which defines guidelines for the future of Europe and the new institutions designed to implement these principles.

Prior to the meeting, the 22 countries of both the NATO and *the Warsaw Pact*[27] also signed a Treaty on Conventional Forces in Europe (CFE) which placed ceilings on the numbers of tanks, artillery, armoured combat vehicles, helicopters and aircraft to be held by the NATO and the Warsaw Pact countries. According to this treaty, each bloc was limited to possession of, no more than 20 000 battle tanks, 30 000 armoured personnel carriers, 20 000 artillery pieces, 5 800 combat aircraft and 2 000 helicopters in Europe.

The results of the meeting indicated that the old order characterized by the division of Europe into two blocs and the dominance of European affairs by the two superpowers, the United States and the Soviet Union, had ended, while a new era of realignment of major European forces and competition has begun.

Since the collapse of the Soviet Union and the Warsaw Pact, most of the conventional forces, tanks, artillery, armoured combat vehicles, helicopters, aircraft, missiles and warheads had been withdrawn from Warsaw Pact countries and part of the weapons had been destroyed. Direct military confrontation between the two military blocs, the NATO and the Warsaw Pact, had disappeared. The Warsaw Pact was dead while the NATO was not only alive but also enlarging and expanding eastward, gradually taking in Eastern European countries(including the independent republics of the former Soviet Union) one by one as NATO members.

Notes

1. After World War Ⅱ, the U.S. government pursued a policy of "containment" against the communist movement headed by the Soviet Union and this resulted in the Cold War.

"二战"结束后，美国政府推行一条遏制政策，对抗以苏联为首的共产主义运动，其结果产生了冷战。

2. the policy of containment was shifted to the policy of detente in the late twentieth century

在20世纪晚期遏制政策向缓和政策转变

3. an iron curtain had descended from Stettin in the Baltic to Trieste in the Adriatic

波罗的海的斯德丁（波兰西北城市之一）到亚德里亚海的里亚斯德港（意大利北部海港），一幅横贯欧洲大陆的铁幕已经降落下来　这形成了欧洲大陆冷战中以苏联为首的社会主义阵营和以美国为首的帝国主义阵营相对抗的局面。

4. to support free peoples who are resisting attempted subjugation by armed minorities or by outside pressures

支持自由的人民（主要指希腊和土耳其的人民）反抗武装的少数派（主要指希腊和土耳其国内共产党武装的少数派）或外来的压力（苏联）

5. This was the Truman Doctrine which inaugurated the policy of containment.

这就是杜鲁门主义首创了遏制政策。

6. the Marshall Plan

马歇尔计划 即欧洲复兴方案。由美国国务卿马歇尔倡议制订，故名马歇尔计划。依照其方案，美国在四年里提供逾130亿美元援助战后布满创伤的西欧各国复兴经济建设，以防苏联共产主义乘虚而入。

7. the North Atlantic Treaty Organization(NATO)

北大西洋公约组织(简称北约组织) 于1949年4月4日成立，总部几经迁址，最后设在布鲁塞尔，其目的是“联合一切力量，进行集体防御及维持和平与安全”，以抵御以苏联为首的共产主义可能的扩张和侵犯。

8. the doctrine of instant and massive retaliation

快速大规模报复的理论 主张立即采用具有大规模杀伤力的弹道核武器进行报复。

9. the South-East Asia Treaty Organization(SEATO)

东南亚条约组织 这是美国遏制政策在东南亚的产物，以遏制所谓远东的共产主义运动和民主、民族独立解放运动的发展，其矛头直指中国，还包括当时的越南民主共和国和朝鲜。

10. the Central Treaty Organization(CTO)

中央条约组织 其目的主要是维持中东的现状，即维持美国在中东的有利地位。

11. the United States is neither omnipotent nor omniscient

美国既不是全能的，也不是无所不知的

12. the “flexible response”

灵活反应 这是肯尼迪提出的战略思想，鼓吹使用常规军事力量打有限的战争，将战略核武器作为最后制裁。

13. the Peace Corps and the Alliance for Progress

和平工作团和(美洲)进步联盟 这两个组织均为肯尼迪倡议建立的：前者为发展中国家提供技术服务，如教育、技术培训，传播所谓的美国民主思想等；后者帮助拉丁美洲从事社会和经济发展工作。

14. His ideas laid down the cornerstone of the U.S. foreign policy, the triangle policy—the triangle of the United States, Europe and Japan and the triangle of the United States, China and the Soviet Union.

他的思想奠定了美国的外交政策——三边政策的基石，即美国、欧洲、日本和美国、苏联、中国的三边政策。

15. the Shanghai Communique

《上海公报》 发表于1972年，其中包括美国承认台湾是中国的一部分，重申美国对中国自己和平解决台湾问题的关切。

16. the Strategic Arms Limitation Talks(SALT Ⅰ)

战略武器限制谈判 主要限制反弹道导弹，并规定最多许可进攻武器的数量。

17. the Rollback Strategy

推回战略 这是里根对苏联采取的强硬政策，不仅要遏制苏联的对外扩张，而且要把他的势力范围推回到苏联本土，故称推回战略。

18. promised in the U.S.-China Communique of August 17, 1982, to ... to the final resolution

在1982年8月17日的中美联合公报里，答应逐渐减少对台湾的武器出售，经过一个时期之后终止出售

19. Despite his hardline policy, Reagan could not turn back the ... to a multipolar pattern development.

尽管里根的政策强硬，但他不能阻止国际总趋势的发展——从对抗和紧张转向对话和缓和，从两极向多极化发展。

20. "Reform and New Thinking"

《改革和新思维》 发表于1987年，是戈尔巴乔夫抛出的对苏联进行经济和政治改革的总纲领，是苏联和东欧社会主义国家演变的信号和开始，对苏联、东欧社会主义国家、整个欧洲，乃至全世界产生重大影响，引起了全世界的关注。

21. "beyond containment"

"超越遏制"政策 面对苏联与东欧的巨变，布什总统建议在马耳他与戈尔巴乔夫总统举行峰会，讨论苏联和东欧的形势与美苏关系。在会上双方宣布东西方之间的冷战已经结束，美苏已经进入一个相互谅解和相互合作的

新时代,为此华盛顿制订了“超越遏制”战略,这标志着缓和时代的开始。

22. the Strategic Arms Reduction Treaty(START)

削减战略武器条约

23. the “August 19 Coup”

“8·19政变” 1991年8月19日,当戈尔巴乔夫在黑海疗养所休假时,被反对派就地软禁,逼他下台,但政变未遂。

24. the Confederation of the Independent Republics

独联体 苏联瓦解后成立了15个独立共和国,由他们组成的松散邦联,称独联体。

25. so-called “transit diplomacy” and “holiday diplomacy”

所谓的“弹性外交”和“度假外交”

26. He decided to extend China's most-favored-nation trade status and delink it from human rights issue.

他(克林顿)决定延长中国的最优惠国待遇,并把它与人权问题脱钩。

27. the Warsaw Pact

华沙公约组织 成立于1955年,是以苏联为首的社会主义国家(除中国与朝鲜)的军事同盟,与北大西洋公约组织相抗衡,随着苏联和其他社会主义国家的演变,华沙公约于1991年解散。

Exercises

Ⅰ. Fill in each blank with the right word or expression from the text:

1. After World War Ⅱ, the U.S. government pursued the policy of ________ against the communist movement headed by ________.
2. Along with the easing of world tension in the late twentieth century, the U.S. government has shifted the policy of ________ to the policy of ________.
3. By the Truman Doctrine, Congress appropriated $400 million for economic aid and military assistance to ________ and ________.
4. In the Eisenhower Administration, the Secretary of State, John Foster Dulles, pushed the policy of containment to the extreme—the policy of

________.

5. After the defeat in the Korean War, the U.S. troops occupied ________ and entered into ________.
6. The SEATO aimed at ________.
7. As a change to U.S. diplomatic tradition, Henry Kissinger's ideas laid down the cornerstone of the U.S. foreign policy, ________—________, ________________.
8. The Shanghai Communique of 1972 reached by the United States and China acknowledged that ________ and ________. And in a joint communique of 1978, both governments accorded ________ and opened ________, as a result the Sino-U.S. relationship was restored.
9. The full name of SALT Ⅰ is ________, which symbolized ________.
10. By playing the"Chinese Card"as a trick to limit Soviet expansion. Ronald Reagan could not but promise in the U.S.-China Communique of August 17, 1982, to reduce gradually ________.
11. Faced with severe challenges at home and abroad, President Mikhail Gorbachev published in 1987 his pamphlet entitled "________", which started ________ in the Soviet Union.
12. At the Malta Summit Meeting in 1989, both President Bush and President Mikhail Gorbachev declared that ________ and that ________.
13. The full name of START is ________, which laid down stringent conditions for ________.

Ⅱ. Questions for discussion:

1. Why did the Cold War emerge after World War Ⅱ?
2. Why did the U.S. government pursue the policy of containment against the Soviet Union?
3. What was the Truman Doctrine? What was the Marshall Plan?
4. What is the NATO? Why was it established after World War Ⅱ?
5. What was the U.S. policy toward the Chinese Liberation War?
6. What did the United States do to contain the communist movement and the third world independent movement in the Far East after World

War Ⅱ?

7. What was meant by the U.S. policy of "flexible response"?

8. What foreign policy did Henry Kissinger's ideas lay down for the U.S. government in the international affairs?

9. What was President Nixon's foreign policy towards the People's Republic of China?

10. What drastic changes occurred in Eastern Europe in the late 1980s?

11. What changes took place in the Soviet Union after Mikhail Gorbachev came to office? What was his policy?

12. What policy did the U.S. government take towards the upheavals of the Eastern European countries and the Soviet Union?

13. What was the "August 19 Coup" in 1991 in the Soviet Union?

14. What was meant by the U.S. policy of "beyond containment" towards the Soviet Union?

15. What important changes have taken place in Eastern Europe since the 1980s?

17. How do you comment on the development of Sino-U.S. relationship?

Appendix

Ⅰ. The U.S. National Flag and Anthem

National flag: with 13 alternating stripes (seven red and six white) and a dark blue rectangular canton containing 50 white stars in the upper hoist.

National Anthem: *The Star-Spangled Banner*

(i)

Oh, say can you see by the dawn's early light
What so proudly hailed at the twilight's last gleaming?
Whose broad strips and bright stars thru the perilous fight.
O'er the ramparts we watched were so gallantly streaming?
And the rocket's red glare, the bombs bursting in air,
Gave proof through the night that our flag was still there.
Oh, say does that star-spangled banner yet wave
O'er the land of the free and the home of the brave?

(ii)

On the shore, dimly seen through the mists of the deep,
Where the foe's haughty host in dread silence reposes,
What is that which the breeze, o'er the towering steep,
As it fitfully blows, half conceals, half discloses?
Now it catches the gleam of the morning's first beam,
In full glory reflected now shines in the stream:
'Tis the star-spangled banner! Oh long may it wave
O'er the land of the free and the home of the brave!

(iii)

And where is the band who so vauntingly swore
That the havoc of war and the battle's confusion
A home and a country should leave us no more!
Their blood has washed out their foul footsteps' pollution.

No refuge could save the hireling and slave
From the terror of flight, or the gloom of the grape:
And the star-spangled banner in triumph doth wave
O'er the hind of the free and the home of the brave!

(iv)

Oh! Thus be it ever, when freemen shall stand
Between their loved homes and the war's desolation!
Blest with victory and peace, may the heav'n rescued land
Praise the Power that hath made and preserved us a nation
Then conquer we must, when out cause is just,
And this be our motto:"In God is our trust."
And the star-spangled banner in triumph shall wave
O'er the land of the free and the home of the brave!

Ⅱ. The Declaration of Independence

When in the course of human events, it becomes necessary for one people to dissolve the political bonds which have connected them with another, and to assume among the Powers of the earth, the separate and equal station to which the Laws of Nature and of Nature's God entitle them, a decent respect to the opinions of mankind requires that they should declare the causes which impel them to the separation.

We hold these truths to be self-evident, that all men are created equal, that they are endowed by their Creator with certain unalienable Rights, that among these are Life, Liberty and the pursuit of Happiness. That to secure these rights. Governments are instituted among Men, deriving their just powers from the consent of the governed, that whenever any Form of Government becomes destructive to these ends, it is the Right of the People to alter or to abolish it, and to institute new Government, laying its foundation on such principles and organizing its powers in such form, as to them shall seem most likely to effect their Safety and Happiness, Prudence, indeed, will dictate that Governments long established should not be changed for light and transient causes, and accordingly all experience hath shown, that mankind are more disposed to suffer, while evils are sufferable, than to right themselves by abolishing the forms to which they are accustomed. When a long train of abuses and usurpations, pursuing invariably the same Object evinces a design to reduce them under absolute Despotism, it is their right, it is their duty, to throw off such Government. and to provide new Guards for their future security. —Such has been the patient sufferance of these Colonies, and such is now the necessity which constrains them to alter their former Systems of Government. The history of the present King of Great Britain is a history of repeated injuries and usurpations, all having in direct object the establishment of an absolute Tyranny over these States. To prove this, let Facts be submitted to a candid world.

He has refused his Assent to Laws, the most wholesome and necessary for the public good.

He has forbidden his Governors to pass Laws of immediate and pressing importance, unless suspended in their operation till his Assent should be obtained; and when so suspended, he has utterly neglected to attend to them.

He has refused to pass other Laws for the accommodation of large districts of people, unless those people would relinquish the right of Representation in the Legislature, a right inestimable to them and formidable to tyrants only.

He has called together legislative bodies at places unusual, uncomfortable, and distant from the depository of their Public Records, for the sole purpose of fatiguing them into compliance with his measures.

He has dissolved Representative Houses repeatedly, for opposing with manly firmness his invasions on the rights of the people.

He has refused for a long time, after such dissolutions, to cause others to be elected; whereby the Legislative Powers, incapable of Annihilation, have returned to the People at large for their exercise; the State remaining in the mean time exposed to all the dangers of invasion from without, and convulsions within.

He has endeavored to prevent the population of these States; for that purpose obstructing the Laws of Naturalization of Foreigners; refusing to pass others to encourage their migration hither, and raising the conditions of new Appropriations of Lands.

He has obstructed the Administration of Justice, by refusing his Assent to Laws for establishing Judiciary Powers.

He has made Judges dependent on his Will alone for the tenure of their offices, and the amount and payment of their salaries.

He has erected a multitude of New Offices, and sent hither swarms of Officers to harass our people, and eat out their substance.

He has kept among us, in times of peace, Standing Armies without the Consent of our legislature.

He has affected to render the Military independent of and superior to the Civil Power.

He has combined with others to subject us to a jurisdiction foreign to our constitution, and unacknowledged by our laws, giving his Assent to their acts of pretended legislation.

For quartering large bodies of armed troops among us.

For protecting them, by a mock Trial, from Punishment for any Murders which they should commit on the Inhabitants of these states.

For cutting off our Trade with all parts of the world.

For imposing taxes on us without our Consent.

For depriving us in many cases, of the benefits of Trial by Jury.

For transporting us beyond Seas to be tried for pretended offences.

For abolishing the free System of English Laws in a neighboring Province, establishing therein an Arbitrary government, and enlarging its Boundaries so as to render it at once an example and fit instrument for introducing the same absolute rule into these Colonies.

For taking away our Charters, abolishing our most valuable Laws, and altering fundamentally the Forms of our Governments.

For suspending our own Legislature, and declaring themselves invested with Power to legislate for us in all cases whatsoever.

He has abdicated Government here, by declaring us out of his Protection and waging War against us.

He has plundered our seas, ravaged our Coasts, burnt our towns, and destroyed the lives of our people.

He is at this time transporting large armies of foreign mercenaries to complete the works of death, desolation and tyranny, already begun with circumstances of Cruelty & Perfidy scarcely paralleled in the most barbarous ages, and totally unworthy the Head of a civilized nation.

He has constrained our fellow Citizens taken Captive on the high Seas to bear Arms against their Country, to become the executioners of their friends and Brethren, or to fall themselves by their Hands.

He has excited domestic insurrections amongst us, and has endeavored to bring on the inhabitants of our frontiers, the merciless Indian Savages, whose known rule of warfare, is an undistinguished destruction of all ages, sexes and conditions.

In every state of these Oppressions We have Petitioned for Redress in the most humble terms: Our repeated Petitions have been answered only by repeated injury. A prince, whose character is thus marked by every act which may define a Tyrant, is unfit to be the ruler of a free People.

Nor have We been wanting in attention to our British brethren. We have warned them from time to time of attempts by their legislature to extend an unwarrantable jurisdiction over us. We have reminded them of the circumstances of our emigration and settlement here. We have appealed to their native justice and magnanimity, and we have conjured them by the ties of our common kindred to disavow these usurpations, which, would inevitably interrupt our connections and correspondence. They too have been deaf to the voice of justice and of consanguinity. We must, therefore, acquiesce in the necessity, which denounces our Separation, and hold them, as we hold the rest of mankind, Enemies in War, in Peace Friends.

We, therefore, the Representatives of the United States of America, in General Congress, Assembled, appealing to the Supreme Judge of the world for the rectitude of our intentions, do, in the Name, and by Authority of the good People of these Colonies, solemnly publish and declare, That these United Colonies are, and of Right ought to be Free and Independent States, that they are Absolved from all Allegiance to the British Crown, and that all political connection between them and the State of Great Britain, is and ought to be totally dissolved; and that as Free and Independent States, they have full Power to levy War, conclude Peace, contract Alliances, establish Commerce, and to do all other Acts and Things which Independent States may of right do. And for the support of this Declaration, with a firm reliance on the Protection of Divine Providence, we mutually pledge to each other our Lives, our Fortunes, and our sacred Honor.

Ⅲ. The 50 States of America

States	Dates of Admission	Capitals
Alabama	1819	Montgomery
阿拉巴马		蒙哥马利
Alaska	1959	Juneau
阿拉斯加		朱诺
Arizona	1912	Phoenix
亚利桑那		菲尼克斯
Arkansas	1836	Little Rock
阿肯色		小石城
California	1850	Sacramento
加利福尼亚		萨克拉门托
Colorado	1876	Denver
科罗拉多		丹佛
Connecticut	1788	Hartford
康涅狄格		哈特福德
Delaware	1787	Dover
特拉华		多佛
Florida	1845	Tallahassee
佛罗里达		塔拉哈

Georgia	1788	Atlanta
佐治亚		亚特兰达
Nevada	1864	Carson City
内华达		卡森城
New York	1788	Albany
纽约		奥尔巴尼
North Carolina	1789	Raleigh
北卡罗来纳		罗利
North Dakota	1889	Bismarck
北达科塔		俾斯麦
Ohio	1803	Columbus
俄亥俄		哥伦布
Oklahoma	1907	Oklahoma City
俄克拉荷马		俄克拉荷马城
Oregon	1859	Salem
俄勒冈		赛勒姆
Pennsylvania	1787	Harrisburg
宾夕法尼亚		哈里斯堡
Rhode Island	1790	Providence
罗得岛		普罗维顿斯
South Carolina	1788	Columbia
南卡罗来纳		哥伦比亚
South Dakota	1889	Pierre
南达科他		皮尔
Maryland	1788	Annapolis
马里兰		安纳波利斯
Massachusetts	1788	Boston
马萨诸塞		波士顿
Michigan	1837	Lansing
密执安		兰辛
Minnesota	1858	St. Paul
明尼苏达		圣保罗
Mississippi	1817	Jackson
密西西比		杰克逊
Missouri	1821	Jefferson City

密苏里		杰斐逊城
Montana	1889	Helena
蒙大拿		赫勒纳
Nebraska	1867	Lincoln
内布拉斯加		林肯
New Hampshire	1788	Concord
新罕布什尔		康科德
New Jersey	1787	Trenton
新泽西		特伦顿
New Mexico	1912	Santa Fe
新墨西哥		圣大菲
Hawaii	1959	Honolulu
夏威夷		火奴鲁鲁
Idaho	1890	Boise
爱达荷		博伊西
Illinois	1818	Springfield
伊利诺斯		斯普林菲尔德
Indiana	1816	Indianapolis
印第安纳		印第安纳波利斯
Iowa	1846	Des Moines
艾奥瓦		得梅因
Kansas	1861	Topeka
堪萨斯		托皮卡
Kentucky	1792	Frankfort
肯塔基		法兰克福
Louisiana	1812	Baton Rouge
路易斯安那		巴吞鲁日
Maine	1820	Augusta
缅因		奥古斯塔
Tennessee	1796	Nashville
田纳西		纳什维尔
Texas	1845	Austin
得克萨斯		奥斯丁
Utah	1896	Salt Lake City
犹他		盐湖城

Vermont 佛蒙特	1791	Montpelier 蒙彼利埃
Virginia 弗吉尼亚	1788	Richmond 里士满
Washington 华盛顿	1889	Olympia 奥林匹亚
West Virginia 西弗吉尼亚	1863	Charleston 查尔斯顿
Wisconsin 威斯康星	1848	Madison 麦迪逊
Wyoming 怀俄明	1890	Cheyenne 夏延

Ⅳ. Presidents of the United States

1. George Washington(1789.4.30—1797.3.3) 乔治·华盛顿 Federalist 联邦主义者
2. John Adams(1797.3.4—1801.3.3) 约翰·亚当斯 Fed.联邦主义者
3. Thomas Jefferson(1801.3.4—1809.3.3) 托马斯·杰斐逊 Democratic Republican 民主共和党
4. James Madison(1809.3.4—1817.3.3) 詹姆斯·麦迪逊 Dem-Rep.民主共和党
5. James Monroe(1817.3.4—1825.3.3) 詹姆斯·门罗 Dem-Rep.民生共和党
6. John Quincy Adams(1825.3.4—1829.3.3) 约翰·昆西·亚当斯 Dem-Rep.民主共和党
7. Andrew Jackson(1829.3.4—1837.3.3) 安德鲁·杰克逊 Democratic.民主党
8. Martin Van Buren(1837.3.4—1841.3.3) 马丁·范·比伦 Dem.民主党
9. William H. Harrison(1841.3.4—1841.4.4) 威廉·H.哈里森(died in office) Whig 辉格党
10. John Tyler(1841.4.6—1845.3.3) 约翰·泰勒 Whig 辉格党

11. James K. Polk(1845.3.4—1849.3.3) 詹姆斯·K.波尔克 Dem.民主党
12. Zachary Tayler(1849.3.4—1850.7.9) 扎卡里·泰勒 Whig 辉格党
13. Millard Fillmore(1850.7.10—1853.3.3) 米勒德·弗尔摩尔 Whig 辉格党
14. Franklin Pierce(1853.3.4—1857.3.3) 富兰克林·皮尔斯 Dem.民主党
15. James Buchanan(1857.3.4—1861.3.3) 詹姆斯·布坎南 Dem.民主党
16. Abraham Lincoln(1861.3.4—1865.4.15 assassinated) 亚伯拉罕·林肯 Rep.共和党
17. Andrew Johnson(1865.4.15—1869.3.3) 安德鲁·约翰逊 Rep.共和党
18. Ulysses S. Grant(1869.3.4—1877.3.3) 尤利塞斯·S.格兰特 Rep.共和党
19. Rutherford B. Hayes(1877.3.4—1881.3.3) 拉瑟福得·B.海斯 Rep.共和党
20. James A. Garfield(1881.3.4—1881.9.19) 詹姆斯·A.加菲尔德(assassinated) Rep.共和党
21. Chester A. Arthur(1881.9.20—1885.3.3) 切斯特·阿瑟 Rep.共和党
22. Grover Cleveland(1885.3.4—1889.3.3) 格罗佛·克里夫兰 Dem.民主党
23. Benjamin Harrison(1889.3.4—1893.3.3) 本杰明·哈里森 Rep.共和党
24. Grover Cleveland(1893.3.4—1897.3.3) 格罗弗·克里夫兰 Dem.民主党
25. William McKinley(1897.3.4—1901.9.14) 威廉·麦金莱(assassinated) Rep.共和党
26. Theodore Roosevelt(1901.9.14—1909.3.3) 西奥多·罗斯福 Rep.共和党
27. William Howard Taft(1909.3.4—1913.3.3) 威廉·霍华德·塔夫脱 Rep.共和党
28. Woodrow Wilson(1913.3.4—1921.3.3) 伍德罗·威尔逊 Dem.民

主党

29. Warren G. Harding（1921.3.4—1923.8.2） 沃伦·G.哈丁（died in office） Rep.共和党

30. Calvin Coolidge（1923.8.3—1929.3.3） 卡尔文·柯立之 Rep.共和党

31. Herbert C. Hoover（1929.3.4—1933.3.3） 赫伯特·C.胡佛 Rep.共和党

32. Franklin D. Roosevelt（1933.3.4—1945.4.12） 富兰克林·D.罗斯福（died in office） Dem.民主党

33. Harry S. Truman（1945.4.12—1953.1.20） 哈里·S.杜鲁门 Dem.民主党

34. Dwight D. Eisenhower（1953.1.20—1961.1.20） 德怀特·D.艾森豪威尔 Rep.共和党

35. John F. Kennedy（1961.1.20—1963.11.22） 约翰·F.肯尼迪（assassinated） Dem.民主党

36. Lyndon B. Johnson（1963.11.22—1969.1.20） 林登·B.约翰逊 Dem.民主党

37. Richard M. Nixon（1969.1.20—1974.8.9） 理查德·M.尼克松（resigned office） Rep.共和党

38. Gerald R. Ford（1974.8.9—1977.1.20） 杰拉尔德·B.福特 Rep.共和党

39. Jimmy Carter（1977.1.20—1981.1.20） 吉米·卡特 Dem.民主党

40. Ronald Reagan（1981.1.20—1989.1.20） 罗纳德·里根 Rep.共和党

41. George Bush（1989.1.20—1993.1.20） 乔治·布什 Rep.共和党

42. Bill Clinton（1993.1.20—2001.1.20） 比尔·克林顿 Dem.民主党

43. George W. Bush（2001.1.20—2009.1.20） 乔治·W.布什 Rep.共和党

44. Barack H. Obama（2009.1.20— ） 贝拉克·H.奥巴马 Dem.民主党

The Development of American Political Parties

This paper is a brief study of American political parties. It covers three sections: 1) a brief development of American political parties, 2) a short account of minor third parties, 3) a brief analysis of the American party system.

Section Ⅰ introduces factors that lead to formation of political parties, how they develop, function and shape into the two-party system as time and circumstances change, and what their program and purposes are.

Section Ⅱ deals with minor third parties, giving a classification of parties and introduction to their purposes and functions.

Section Ⅲ gives a brief analysis of the American party system—the election system, some characteristics and nature of the system.

Section Ⅰ
A Brief Development of American Political Parties

The United States has a history of more than 200 years. Since the establishment of the first political parties in about 1789, they have undergone a process of development full of tests and practices. According to different contents and for convenience's sake in study, it is divided into three stages: 1) Federalists vs. Democratic Republicans from 1789 to 1827, 2) Democrats vs National Republicans from 1828 to 1860, and 3) Democrats vs Republicans from 1860 to the present.

(1)Federalists vs Democratic Republicans (1789—1827)

The first American political parties, the Federalists and the Democratic Republicans, came into being before the end of Washington's presidential term. The initial stirrings of party formation appeared when Alexander Hamilton began to force connections with members of George Washington's Cabinet and Congress. His factional activities inevitably led to opposition first by James Madison, then Thomas Jefferson. An increasingly sharp conflict over issues of foreign policy divided them further. As they viewed the French Revolution differently, Hamilton and his cohorts plumped for monarchical England while Madison and Jefferson for republican France. Controversy over the Jay Treaty with England in 1795 brought the initial stage of party formation to virtual completion—Federalists led by Hamilton and the Democratic Republicans by Jefferson.

From the founding of the United States government in 1789 to 1800, the government was firmly controlled by the Federalists headed by Hamilton. Federalists policies were based on Hamilton's view that governments had to be ruled by gentlemen, and by his conviction that American progress depended on bringing the wealthy and well-born to the firm support of the new government. He distrusted the ordinary people and emphasized the need to restrain them. He believed in a powerful central government and a strong executive with the active participation of government in finance, commerce and manufacturing. He shared the view of prior development of industry and commerce to that of agriculture. He favored funding at face value the debts of both the national and state governments. He introduced the first protective tariff into the first Congress. The first bank was established, excise taxes on Whisky were levied, sale of public land in large tracts was fixed and a pro-English foreign policy was formulated. In short, Hamilton's program was designed to bind the wealthy classes to the central government. As Washington was an aegis very essential for Hamilton's purposes, Hamilton and his cohorts were decisive in policy-making and administration both in the Cabinet and Congress. Thereby Hamilton's political program laid down the basis for the shaping of the future of the United States and determined the nature of the country—a country under the rule of a highly centralized government of the capitalist class. The Federalist policies, in conformity with the interests of industrialists and businessmen, facilitated the accumulation of capital and high profits.

Yet Jefferson favored a decentralized, democratic government with power endowed in the people. He believed in the leadership of "a natural aristocracy" based on talent and intelligence instead of on wealth and gentle birth. As he considered agriculture as the foundation of economy, he preferred prior agricultural development to that of industry and commerce. He opposed the establishment of the U.S. bank. In foreign affairs, they leaned towards France and favored a free trade with all nations. Thus, his political program laid down the basis for another type of the shaping of the future of the United States and determined the nature of the country—a country under the rule of a decentralized democratic government of the plantation landowners.

Federalist policies went against the interests of the broad masses of workers, farmers and planters. As they were put into practice step by step, they met with growing resistance. The scratches between Hamilton and Jefferson developed into wounds. The crescendo of their discord threatened the very existence of the nation. Their conflicts culminated in the Whisky Rebellion in 1794, the Jay Treaty in 1795, the XYZ affair in 1797, the Alien and Sedition Acts in 1798. The military suppression of the Whisky Rebellion by the Federalists pushed their opponents to a blind alley. In response, Jeffersonians accepted the challenge. They organized themselves into an anti-Federalist political party, the Democratic Republican party.

Meanwhile, the Federalists became badly disintegrated in the national tension between 1794 and 1800. The conflict began in Hamilton's defection from John Adams in the campaign of 1796. Hamilton won greater favor of High Federalists in the Cabinet and had greater influence in both Houses than Adams did. The nomination for a new envoy to Paris for peace mission brought them to open split. This contributed greatly to the loss of the Federalists' Presidential election in 1800. This electoral failure marked the beginning of the decline of the Federalists and it brought about the first fundamental change of leaders, a shift from the Federalists to the Democratic Republican in the first stage of the American party history. The Federalists died out in about 1820.

The Democratic Republican party's ideal was "a wise and frugal government, which shall restrain men from injuring each other ... and leave them otherwise free to regulate their own pursuits of industry and improvements".

After Jefferson took office, he removed many Federalist office-holders and appointed Democratic Republicans instead, so as to ensure the implementation of the Republican policies. He repealed the excise taxes along with other internal taxes, returned the public debts through revenues from import duties, sale of public land through rigid government economy and reduction of government and military expenditures. But he did not tamper with such Hamilton-initiated programs as the bank of the U.S., funding and assuming the national debts. In violation of his own concept of limited government and strict interpretation of the Constitution, he purchased Louisiana from France with $15 million which added substantially to the national debt.

Jefferson adjusted some of his political and economic principles to the life of the American people and converted many rank-and-file Federalists to Democratic Republican, but he could not manage to appease his opponents and bring party politics to an end. Groups of disgruntled older Federalists such as the Essex Junto appeared. They could not reconcile themselves to Jeffersonian Republicanism and even urged that the Union dissolved. Younger Federalists also appeared. They worked to build party organizations and tried to win election. Though they failed, they made an important contribution to the development of two-party politics.

Within the Democratic Republican party, there appeared a local third-party movement. Personal and patronage disputes in New York and Pennsylvania produced the "Tertium Quids". States righters headed by Randolph criticized Jefferson severely for having compromised too much with Federalist aims and policies.

Like Jefferson, Madison was forced time and again to compromise traditional Republicanism. He revived Hamilton's program of internal improvements, protective tariffs, the second national bank and defence. Monroe continued Madison's program and John Quincy Adams pushed it even further. Neo-Federalism was fully restored.

For several years after the War of 1812, the national economy flourished. Southern cotton-planters regained their European markets. Western farmers found their markets in the South, Northeast and overseas. Farm commodity prices were good. Transportation grew rapidly. Settlers swarmed into the West and within a few years after the Treaty of Ghent, five more states entered the Union. In the year 1816 when Monroe took office, he found the country in a complaisant mood, everywhere he saw abundant signs of national unity and prosperity. The year 1817 saw America in a prosperous and happy condition with economy booming, political factionalism at a low ebb, and relative harmony among the sections. But the "Era of Good Feeling" did not last long. It came to a sudden end in the middle of his administration.

In the election of 1824, the Democratic Republican party quickly disintegrated as a national political organization with four competing candidates—John Quincy Adams, Henry Clay, William H. Crawford and Andrew Jackson, each attracting different sections and interests. Crawford, a Virginian by birth was a state-rights representative of the planter class. Adams was a nationalist and the favorite of New England. Clay was champion of the American system. Jackson was a military hero with wide popular appeal but rather vague political views. Since none of them polled a majority in the Electoral College, the choice had to be made by the House of Representatives. Clay came in fourth and Crawford gave up the running because of his illness, so the choice was between Adams and Jackson. Thanks to Clay's backing, Adams won the election and Clay became the Secretary of State. They called for vigorous federal action and pursued a more radical program for national economic growth. Hardly had they put into operation their program when they met with hostile enemies in and out of the Cabinet and Congress. The Democratic party led by Andrew Jackson and Van Buren had rallied the forces against Adams' Administration, including those of Crawford and Calhoun. Clay and Webster joined together in the National Republicans. After a bitter contest in the election of 1828, Jackson won the majority. Thus began the second American party system, the Democratic party vs the National Republicans.

(2) The Democratic Party vs the National Republicans (1828—1860)

The fragmentation of the Democratic Republicans brought its dominance to an end. The first party system ended and "a new party system began—one that differed in the willingness of its leaders to abandon the 18th century ideal of social harmony and accept parties and political conflicts as both inevitable and constructive". As vigorous two-party politics developed in all sections of the country, a growing number of voters turned out in national elections seeking. Their own respective interests in public affairs of the country. Throughout the years from 1828 to 1860, there existed first the struggle and conflicts between the Democratic party and the National Republicans, then those between the Democratic party and the Whigs. The Democratic party was dominant while the others were subordinate even though the Whigs won two Presidential elections. Along with the struggles and conflicts between the major parties, there were conflicts among the third minor parties that complicated the party history in this period.

The Democratic party led by Jackson and Van Buren pledged to be faithful to traditional Jeffersonian Republicanism and held broad support from the workers, farmers and entrepreneurs in the South and the West.

As a follower of Jefferson, Jackson promised to use his power to "reform" the civil service and made it more responsive to the public will. He emphasized that the federal government was one of the limited power, favored strict interpretation of the Constitution and state sovereignty. He regarded agricultural interests as superior importance to all others. But he opposed the protective tariff, the rechartering of the national bank and the American antecedents who embraced orthodox Federalist doctrine with an aim at building a strong national defence, establishing a national bank and credit supply, conducting a protective tariff to stimulate domestic manufacturing and create an enlarged domestic market.

During has administration, the country enjoyed a period of glorious prosperity and unprecedented economic growth. However, debts increased, controversies over the protective tariff, the rechartering of the national bank, and territorial expansion were intensified, and slavery became prominent. The National Republicans, northern industrialists and other anti-Jacksonians joined together in resistance against Jackson's administration.

The National Republicans endorsed its republican system, but did not have a specific political program. They represented the interests of industrialists and businessmen in the Northeast. They insisted on the protective tariff, the rechartering of the national bank and federal internal improvements.

In the campaign of 1840, the National Republicans renamed themselves the "Whigs" and sought to take Democratic dominance. They favored the goals of the republican system and struggled for the containment of slavery. In the campaign, Harrison was elected President. For the first time the Whigs organized its administration. But unfortunately Harrison died one month after he took office. His successor Tyler opposed everything most Whigs hoped to achieve. In his administration, the Whigs was badly disintegrated. Then Tyler and Southern allies drifted back to the Democratic party. Bitter struggle over the admission of California hastened the split and the death of the Whigs.

In 1844, the Presidential election exposed a variety of tensions that had been in American history. The long depression that began in 1837 had kept alive the issues of national policy concerning money, banking and public land—issues that sometimes divided labor and capital, sometimes farm and city. "The entrance of the abolitionist crusade into politics had given a sectional difference a moral dimension that made compromise more difficult to achieve." The influence of the doctrine of Manifest destiny and the drive for the westward expansion had become an irresistible force. Brekinridge against Bell in the South and Lincoln against Douglas in the North. The electoral result gave the Republicans an overwhelming majority. The Republicans reaffirmed their stand against the extension of slavery into the territories, laid emphasis on a series of economic proposals. Protective tariffs were stressed in manufacturing states; homestead legislation, land-grant privileges, internal improvements, and a Pacific Railroad was stretched farther west. The foreign-born were reassured of their free election. Lincoln played down the electoral issue and held up the banner of the Union.

Alongside the process of bitter struggles and conflicts between the major parties, the third parties turned out as a striking force.

In the campaign of 1832 appeared the first national third party, the Anti-Masonic party. It focused on opposition to the Society of Freemasons and secret societies in general. It was essentially anti-Jacksonian. In 1831, it held a national convention to nominate William Wirt for President, but it failed. Then most of its leaders joined the National Republican party.

In 1840, a group of abolitionists organized the Liberty party and nominated James G. Birney for the Presidency. It aimed at abolishing slavery. At the outset it favored moral suasion, and then it turned to force. By 1861, abolitionism had helped to win the Northern population morally for the terrible struggle of the Civil War.

In 1848, emerged the Free-Soil party made up of the disgruntled Van

Buren barn burners, Free-Soliers, Conscience Whigs and other political abolitionists which came out flatly for the limitation and discouragement of slavery and took as their slogans: "Free Soil, Free Speech, Free Labor and Free Men."

In this period the Republican party became more and more conservative and reactionary toward the territorial and slavery issues and tried to keep the slavery system by opposing the bourgeois revolution. Therefore the National Republicans, the Whigs and the Republicans rose against it in succession. Besides, the third parties were especially active. Their struggles over the territorial and slavery issues became so acute that they led to the breakout of the Civil War.

(3) The Republicans vs the Democrats (from 1860 to the present)

The Republicans and the Democrats are the two dominant major parties from the Civil War to the present. During this period politics is highly competitive between the Republicans and the Democrats. From 1860 to 1872, the Republicans kept dominance, but from 1876 on the two parties kept on a seesaw in their competitive elections. The margin between victory and defeat was so narrow that neither party could win an easy majority.

It was the decisive issues, the Kansas-Nebraska bill and the election of President Lincoln that led to the breakout of the Civil War. The war lasted four years and through it, split was avoided and the Union was kept safe and sound at the cost of heavy losses of American lives and resources.

Before the start of the war seven Southern states had left the Union to form the Confederate States of American and soon more states seceded and joined the Confederacy under President, Jefferson Davis. It was a decentralized government like that under the Articles of Confederation, maintaining the states rights and slavery system. Protective tariffs and internal improvements were made unconstitutional.

But the North under President Lincoln upheld the banner of the

Union. It reaffirmed the policies concerning the abolition of slavery, protective tariffs, the banking system and internal improvements.

After the Civil War, the antagonistic contradiction between the Republicans, representatives of the northern newborn capitalist class and the Democrats, representatives of the southern landlord class was solved. The Republicans became dominant and they started the rehabilitation of the South. President Lincoln favored full rehabilitation except for the military, political leaders, while Congress opposed it with the Wade-Davis bill. From then on disaffection within the Republicans began to appear. Radicals resented that Lincoln and Johnson had made too much compromise. After the governments of Tennessee, Louisiana and Arkansas were recognized, Congress passed the radical reconstruction plan. The congressional opposition accompanied by people's opposition to the incompetence of Grant's administration and corruption in the government led to the rise of "Liberal Republicans". The Liberal Republicans nominated their own presidential candidates, supported civil service reforms to eliminate corruption and economic measures that did not defer to the interests of the country. Prohibition movement also gained increasing momentum. The election between Hayes and Tildon was in a deadlock. It was only after the compromise of 1877 was made that Hayes was elected President. According to the compromise, "home rule" and other favors for the South were guaranteed. Home rule meant Republican abandonment of freedmen, carpetbaggers, scalawags and Radicals and virtual nullification of the 14th and 15th Amendments and the Civil Rights Act. The Republicans forfeited much of its honor and the fruits of the Civil War. This again indicated the struggle between pro-slavery and anti-slavery, between the radical Republicans and Southern Democrats.

In 1884, the Republicans lost its election because of its intra-party conflicts. A group of liberal reformers called Mugwumps kept up a running crusade against patronage and corruption of the Republican government. They demanded reforms in currence, banking, credit system and public welfare. They refused to support the Republican nominee but supported the Democratic nominee Cleveland instead. The Democrats came to power for the first time after the Civil War.

Cleveland maintained the gold standard and high tariffs. Over these issues the Democratic party was badly split into two sections, one representing the Northern Democrats and the other representing the South and the West. Never before had a president been so detested and abused of his own party as was Cleveland.

As the gold standard, high tariffs and internal improvements were taking greater effect, capitalism had come into full bloom which resulted in fiercer interwoven conflicts and class struggle. Workers, farmers and other poor people rose in their struggle for democracy, liberty, public welfare, etc. On February 22, 1892, delegates from the Farmers' Alliances, the Knights of Labor, the Nationalists, the Single-Taxers, Greenbackers, Prohibitionists and reform groups held a convention and officially founded the People's party, and took part in the presidential election in 1892. They popularized certain reform measures while calling attention to inequities and injustices in the American socio-economic order. The Populists organized the first important movement to insist that laissez-faire economics was not the final solution the industrial problems and that the federal government had some responsibility for social well-being. Although they failed, they still sought to bridge the cleavages between parties, sections, races and classes that kept apart the forces of reform. Though not all their demands were realized, a later generation would find many of their proposals of merit and write them into law. These included the direct election of the U. S. Senators, a graduated income tax, greater railroad regulation, supervision of big business and such measures of direct democracy as the initiative referendum, and recall. The significance of the Populist movement should not be overlooked.

In 1893 started the great depression that brought on a new wave of wage cuts, layoffs and strikes. More workers were thrown out of work by strikes in 1894. The Pullman strike was the most important one. After it failed, Eugene E. Debs became known to the nation. Within a few years, he became the foremost leader of the socialist movement in the country.

As the Democrats were badly eroded, Mckinley was elected President in 1896. His name was synonymous with high tariff. He was for the gold standard. He shared such programs as "duty determines destiny". In his administration he saw the revival of the economy and the end of the long depression. The influx of gold and capital gave impetus to industrial development which in turn touched off a boom in iron and steel. Capitalism had developed into the stage of imperialism; sectional conflicts and class struggles further intensified. In order to cover up these contradictions and transfer the struggles of the working people, Mckinley resorted to foreign expansion. In 1898, he declared war with Spain. The U.S. won and the Treaty of Peace was signed. Cuba was given independence, and Porto Rico Guam and the Philippines were ceded to the United States. The ratification of the treaty stirred up attacks on the Republicans, and they were denounced as imperialist expansionists. Mckinley's administration marked the beginning of the U.S. foreign expansion. Since then America had stepped into fast development of imperialism.

After Mckinley was assassinated in September, 1902, Theodore Roosevelt took office. He tried to moderate to some extent the fierce conflicts and contradictions between classes and sections by advocating the Square Deal, a program of social welfare, federal regulation of business and industry and direct democracy which attracted support from workers, farmers, middle-class Americans, intellectuals and even business managers. He brought both labor and capital to the White House to settle a dispute and got them both to accept the judgement of a commission appointed by the executive. But what President did went against Roosevelt's policies and practice. He relied on the Court to make laws. He was antagonistic to labor unions and direct democracy. As a result, the Republicans became badly eroded. Taft's administration led to the formation of the Progressive Party (Bull Moose) made up of Roosevelt men—workers, farmers, feminists and industrialists.

Meanwhile socialism consistently gained adherents especially in the cities. Middle class, immigrants and intellectuals organized themselves into the Socialist Party headed by Eugene V. Debs in 1900. He employed a stirring rhetoric that mixed Jeffersonian and Marxist principles. He was a continual candidate for President. In 1912, almost one million Americans supported him.

Due to the bad disintegration of the Republicans and the development of the socialist movement, the Democrats won the election in 1912. Woodrow Wilson endorsed New Freedom. He favored states rights, free competition to regulation of big business. What Wilson contributed most to progressive social reforms was the first efficient banking system since Andrew Jackson. World War Ⅰ brought Wilson down from the stage.

After World War Ⅰ, the Republicans, Harding, Coolidge, and Hoover took office, but none of them did anything to prevent the deterioration of social conflicts and class struggles. In Hoover's administration, the Great Depression hit, destroying the faith of the American people in the essential worth of the capitalist system. It caused widespread suffering and profound discontent among all classes in all sections and this in turn revived the progressive movement in full strength.

When in office, Franklin Roosevelt tried to make some reforms. He shared the thesis of inevitable economic concentration instead of laissez-faire free competition and agricultural adjustment. He worked out the National Recovery Act. He shifted financial capital from Wall Street to Washington that directly controlled the volume of money and credit. Roosevelt's New Deal did end the despair of the people but did not produce complete recovery. He met with increasing pressures. The Court fight, the aggressiveness of organized labor and the resumption of spending policy all tended to widen the gap between the liberal and the conservative wings of the Democratic party. Most liberals were Northerners, while most conservative were Southerners. The struggle between pro-reform and anti-reform paralyzed the Democratic party.

World War Ⅱ in 1939 gave rise to new contradictions which divided Americans into isolationists and internationalists. Their struggle cut across party lines. Roosevelt managed to get through great difficulty by pushing the policy for internationalism and a postwar economic bill of rights with federal guarantees to education, employment and expanded social security.

In Truman's administration, the diehard conservative Southern Democrats splintered from the Democratic party and formed the States Rights Democratic party(Dixiecrats) in alliance with liberals and blacks in opposition to Truman's civil-rights bills and Truman Doctrine. Truman Doctrine and the Marshall Plan outraged communist sympathizers in the North as well as liberals like Henry A. Wallace, whose concern for world peace led them to overlook Soviet communists. Therefore the Progressive party was formed in the Presidential campaign with the Republicans, but failed. The Republicans continued to hold office till 1960 after the end of the Korean War.

After the Korean War the U.S. foreign policy became ever aggressive. The U.S. troops occupied Taiwan in China, started aggressive war on Vietnam and war flames quickly spread throughout Indo-China. This policy aroused country-wide opposition and worsened the conflicts between the Republicans and the Democrats. In the presidential campaign of 1960, Kennedy, a Democrat, declared the view of a "world of diversity"—a world of nations various in institutions and creeds, "where every country solves its own problems according to its own traditions and ideals". This view was confirmed by Nixon who contributed to the restoration of the relationship with China and is to some extent continued by Reagan.

It is imperative to note the balance and resilience of the Republican party and the Democratic party since the Civil War. The results of every presidential election were very close and those of Congress were even closer. While from time to time, the parties have lapsed from closely matched competitiveness. They have shown a remarkable facility for restoring balance. The Democrats recovered quickly from the failures of the 1920s and maintained dominant rule throughout the 1930s. Despite the catastrophe of 1964 the Republicans recovered quickly and won the presidency in 1968, 1972, and 1980. At present, there are no signs that show such a competitive balance between the two major parties will be broken in the near future.

Since the Civil War, economic expansion had developed greatly into imperialism by the end of the 19th century. In spite of their serious competitions over a series of issues over civil rights, banking system, protective tariffs, internal improvements, slavery, foreign policies, etc., the Republicans and the Democrats are in common the representatives of the ruling class of different sections. Their common essence is the exploitation and oppression of the people both at home and abroad, conflicts over issues are only minor issues concerning methods.

Section Ⅱ Minor Parties

Along with the major parties, dozens of minor parties appeared in different stages throughout the process of party development in America. The Anti-Masons in the 1820s, the Free Soilers in the 1840s and 1850s, the Populists in the 1890s, the La Follette Progressives in the 1920s and George Wallace's American Independent Party in 1968, etc. But they differ in origins, purposes and functions; some are splinters, some are ideologically-oriented and some are issue-oriented.

Firstly, there are splinters. Splinters are those that have split away from the major parties and formed their own minor parties, partly because of their views and interests different from those of the major parties, and partly because of their own political purposes. The Southern Democratic party of 1860 and the Progressive parties of 1912 and 1924 were splinters of the major parties. These minor parties tend to be highly personalized around a charismatic leader or centered on a section of notable people, such a Brekinridge, head of the Southern Democratic party and Robert La Follette of the Progressive party of 1924. Similarly, the success of the American Independent Party in 1968 represented a personal achievement for George Wallace. His success was not extended to other American Independent Party candidates, nor has the party been able to retain the momentum in succeeding elections without Wallace. As they are either local or regional groupings with some specific interest or purpose, they usually fail in elections by lack of national supports from the people.

Secondly, there are minor parties of ideology. These parties have broad ideological commitments. They have their own political programs to reform or reconstruct new social, economic and political institutions. For instance, the Progressive party of 1948 had a program of social reform and civil liberties with a foreign policy of friendship with the Soviet Union and reduction of Cold War tensions.

Thirdly, there are minor parties around specific critical issues. The Anti-Mason, Free Soil and Prohibition parties were formed as response to specific issues. The Free Soil party campaigned largely on the single issue of the abolition of slavery. These parties have not been viable at the national level for some time. Once the issue is absorbed by one or both of the major parties, these issue-oriented organizations have disappeared.

Though the Populists and the Socialists were quite successful in their movements and electing members to the House of Representatives, most minor parties tend to be transient or limited to the presidential contest. Their efforts to carry their organizations to other levels of government have always met with frustration. Despite the large number of the third parties in the U.S. history, they seldom have received much attention or significant support for their efforts because they have failed in publicizing their ideas and mobilizing enough support for their ideological stands.

They tend either to fade away due to lack of continuing support or to turn inward and become nothing more than interest groups representing a loyal but small corps of members.

The minor parties have failed one after another, but they have to some extent, enjoyed their influence in the U.S. society. Many of their ideas have eventually been incorporated into the programs of the major parties and translated into public policies, such as the progressive ideas on taxation, regulation of railroads and social insurance initially introduced by the Socialist, Populist and Progressive parties. However, they have had a very minor role in shaping policy.

Due to unequal access to the media, restrictive ballot procedures and the electoral process in general, it is very difficult for the minor parties to grow strong enough to compete with the major parties. They can only make themselves a shifting weight between the two parties, finely balanced the major parties.

The U. S. Communist Party was founded in 1919 by Charles E. Ruthenberg on the basis of the Socialist propaganda League formed by the left-wing elements of the American Socialist Party to propagate Marxism among the American workers. After Ruthenberg's death in 1927, Lovestone became the party leader. He held that imperialism still had a long period of "vigorous development" ahead, which touched off inner-party struggles. In 1929 William Z. Foster was elected chairman of the party. Foster became seriously ill in 1932 and the party leadership was usurped by Eart Browder. He declared that U.S. capitalism "retains some of the characteristics of a strong capitalism" and that there is a "common interest" between the proletariat and the big bourgeoisie in the U.S. He pledged to safeguard the system of monopoly trusts and follow a line of class collaboration with monopoly capital, which led to the formation of the Communist Political Association of the U. S. Led by William Foster, the anti-Browder forces met in a special national convention in July 1945 at which Browder was repudiated and the true color of the

U.S. Communist Party was restored.

The decade following World War Ⅱ was a most difficult period for the U.S. Communist Party. It was subjected to frenzied attacks by the U.S. ruling capitalist class. Between the year 1955 and 1956 more than 139 party leaders were arrested under the Smith Act to frame-up charges of "plotting or inciting attempts to overthrow the government by violence". As a result, the party was badly weakened both organizationally and politically. Nevertheless, it continued in the struggle for civil rights of the blacks and the economic betterment of the working class as a whole.

Under the influence of the economic boom after World War Ⅱ and Khrushechov's revisionism, non-Marxist ideas came to the fore again. They held that the party should be transformed into a political or "educational association", and changed the color of the party after Foster's death in 1960.

Following the 22nd congress of the Soviet Party, the American party followed its line closely in violation of the fundamental principles of Marxism-Leninism.

Section Ⅲ The American Party System

Looking back at the development of political parties in America, we can see that the United States has been placed in the two-party system throughout the American history. From 1789 to 1827, the Federalists and the Democratic Republicans maintained the dominant rule, even though the Democratic Republicans kept one-party rule after the Federalists disbanded in about 1820 to 1827. This is the first phase of party development in which the first party system took shape. In this phase, each party tries to keep one-party rule. Then came the second phase of party development. The shift of political center first from the North to the South and then from the South to the West showed the balance of strength of the three different sections. None of the ruling classes of each section could overpower the other easily. Therefore many party leaders began to realize the merits of party organization and saw the two-party system as inevitable and constructive. Van Buren and his cohorts first recognized the value of opposition as a cohesive political force. They welcomed the idea of a permanent opposition. Parties had come into their own as legitimate political organizations. By 1840, the two-party system had been tested and demonstrated to be necessary for the ruling class. Though many changes had taken place since then, they had not altered the concept of parties and the party system.

In 1860, the Lincoln Republicans replaced the Whigs. Since then the Democratic party and the Republican party have become the largest and most competitive organizations in the United States. They have been in rivalry for more than a century. They organized the electorate simply by maintaining the two-party system. Actually no Americans can steer their course between them; they inevitably become Republicans or Democrats. As a consequence, most elected Presidents, Senators, congressmen and officials, state and local, are either Republicans or Democrats. This in turn has made the two-party system become so consolidated that it has survived all assaults in the past years.

The American electoral system favors the major parties. Both the Republicans and the Democrats are electoral organizations and they exist primarily to contest offices and win elections. "In the United States, the President is not a member of Congress and presidential and congressional elections are largely separate. American people not only elect the President, but a host of other executives. They also elect congressmen from single-member district. For example, they elect 435 members of the House of Representatives from 435 districts, one member for each district." Electoral votes are awarded on a winner-take-all basis. This kind of election makes it easy for the major parties to win the majority and maintain their dominant position, but difficult for the minor parties to obtain any chance to win their elections.

Laws in some states also block the way to the entry of the minor parties into presidency. The Ohio law had been passed in 1948 in order to prevent the third-party candidacy of Henry Wallace in that state. The law required that a new unestablished party collect a number of signatures equal to 15 per cent of the votes cast in the last state-wide election—a percentage which required the Wallace forces to muster 433,000 signatures. In addition, the Ohio law required those petitions to be submitted in early February, a time far earlier than most campaigns are mobilized. It also prohibited independent, non-party candidates. The state argued that it had a legitimate interest in preserving the existing two-party system, in preventing a division of the vote among a number of parties and ultimately making sure that minority candidates would not win elections. The discrimination against the third parties was the avowed policy of the state of Ohio. Though the Supreme Court struck down the Ohio law for violating the equal protection cause of the Fourteen Amendment in 1968, still there are such laws that discriminate against and prevent third parties from entering presidency in election.

Finance serves as a very important factor in an election campaign. In running a campaign, large sums of money are needed in mass media and work of mobilization and organization. Most Republican and Democratic candidates are men of wealth and gentry. Backed by active capitalists throughout the country in election affairs, they can manage to raise sums large enough to engage in costly campaigns. It is estimated in "The Capitalist System" by Reich and Weisskopf that "it (the Republicans) commands the allegiance of 80 to 90 percent of American capitalists ... the Democratic candidates receive 45 to 65 percent of their funds from capitalist doners". Therefore financial contributions made by big capitalists to some extent ensure the campaign victories of the two major parties, especially as the scope of the campaign widens from city to nation. Up to present no minor party has been able to raise sums large enough to compete with the major parties in a national campaign. That is one of the reasons that all minor parties have failed in their elections.

In terms of party membership, there are different levels of party involvement. "At the center is a group of leaders which includes precinct committeemen, county and district leaders and state party leaders. These are crucial to the success of any party at all levels." Next to the leaders are party workers. They represent the leaders, and have influence in policy-making and application. Concurrent with the workers are the official party members. "They formally join a party by applying for membership, subscribing to party principles, paying dues, etc." Members of these levels are considered as elements of the parties.

Then come the voters who participate in the election of party nominees by voting the primary. They play an important role in the general election and party activity even though many of them are not active party members. Party identifiers may or may not be associated with actual voting support. Large numbers fail to vote or vote for candidates of the opposing parties. Party affiliation is defined solely on the basis of identification.

Both the Republican and the Democratic parties concentrate on election instead of ideology. "They make very little efforts to educate the public on principles and doctrine. Their survival depends not on a mass of loyal members but on their ability to mobilize votes at each election. In order to mobilize support to win election both major parties are moderate or centrist-oriented." They tend to keep the status quo; seldom do they initiate great changes in social order that would prevent them from attracting a coalition as broad as possible and a support as great as possible. Party unity is often overshadowed by lack of party loyalty and sense of disciplines. Many party members including party bosses betray their own parties and turn to vote for candidates of the opposing party. In 1960, being a Republican, Nelson Rockeffeller supported Kennedy, a Democrat in the election against Nixon. Again in 1972, Nixon got support from a Texas Democrat, John B. Connolly in the election. Cases like these have appeared time and again in American history.

It is interesting to note the changes in the division of allegiance of the Republican and the Democratic parties. A generation ago the party division was along geographical lines. The Republican party drew support chiefly from the northern and western states of the country and the Democratic party from the South. Since 1932 this state has been breaking up and is now being displaced by a national party division. There is an estimate in "The American Party System" by E. B. Schaitschaeider saying: "Between 1924 and 1952 the Republican vote in the South increased sixfold while the Democratic vote in the North increased five-fold. This new tendency was illustrated in the 1960 election in which Kennedy polled less than 40 percent of the vote in only three of the fifty states and more than 60 percent in only two states." Republican Barry Goldwater in 1964 and Nixon in 1972 carried Alabama, Georgia, Lousiana, Mississippi and South Carolina and George Wallace carried all but South Carolina. The once-solid Democratic South is solid no longer. The displacement of the regional party alignment by the national one suggests a great increase in the competitiveness of the major parties, an increase of two-party states but a threat to local minor parties. This change is likely to alter power relations in the national government and bring about a series of vexing social problems to American life and politics, such as intraparty and inter-party conflicts and other social contradictions. It is clear that both the Republicans and the Democrats will contend in a broader, deeper and more complicated way. On the other hand they will by instinct make compromises to maintain the two-party system which in turn will help strengthen and consolidate the rule of the capitalist class they represent.

约翰·洛克的《政府论》及天赋权利思想对美国革命和建国的影响

一、欧洲的启蒙运动

17—18世纪欧洲的启蒙运动标志着在欧洲历史上一个从以上帝为中心的、宗教解说上帝创造人类说和反理性认识的世界观向以自然科学为基础的宇宙观过渡的历史时期的开始。牛顿对启蒙思想的创立做出了重大贡献，他认为宇宙是个巨大的有机体，一切事物都遵循着一些能用数学公式表达的自然规律运行。启蒙运动的思想把宇宙看作一个有规律运转和可以认识的体系。

启蒙运动的思想家不仅相信宇宙像一部巨大的机器在运转，而且相信人类社会也同样受自然规律支配。因此，他们开始运用这种世界观来观察、研究政治和经济问题。

洛克(1632—1704)是运用这种世界观解说政治、经济问题的主要代表人物。他继承和发展了弗朗西斯·培根的唯物主义，详细地论证了知识起源于感觉经验，反对“天赋观念”，认为经验有外部经验(即感觉)和内部经验(即反省)之分，后者是通过心灵内部活动的体验而来的。在政治上他赞成君主立宪制，主张国家权力应分为立法权、行政权和处理外交事务的权利。其中，立法权是最高权力，应属议会，执行权和对外权则属于国王。他强调国家的主要任务是保护私有财产。他的思想对英国和美国民主思想的发展及美国早期政治运动有深远影响。他在1689—1690年写了两篇《政府论》，阐明了组织政府的目的、形成和权力范围。

二、洛克的思想对美国革命的影响

洛克的思想对美国革命产生了深远影响，它启迪人民应该摆脱英国君主政权的统治，争取民主、自由、平等和独立。洛克说："为了正确地理解政治权力，并追溯它的起源，我们必须研究人类原来自然地处在什么状态。那是一种完美的自由状态，他们在自然法的范围内，如他们认为合适的话，决定他们的行动和处置他们的财产和人身，而无须得到任何人的认可或听命于任何人的意志。"他又说："自然状态有一种为人人所应遵守的自然法对它起支配作用；而理性，也就是自然法，教导着有意遵从理性的全人类：人们既然都是平等和独立的，任何人就不得侵害他人的生命、健康、自由或财产。"

美国第二任总统约翰·亚当斯说："革命在战前就开始了。革命隐藏在人民的心里和思想里。"他还说："引导美洲人反叛的因素和情绪应该追溯到两百年前，追溯到第一个美洲种植园建立以后的历史。"

美洲第一个种植园詹姆斯敦建立于 1607 年，到 1776 年美国独立战争胜利共经历了 169 年时间，这段时间可分为两个时期：1607—1763 年的"有益疏忽"时期和 1763—1776 年的美国独立战争时期。

詹姆斯敦建立于 1607 年 6 月 12 日，建立初期移民们遇到了难以想象的困难，缺乏粮食，没有住房，可怕的蚊子、细菌、野兽严重威胁着他们的生命安全，印第安人也经常袭击他们。虽然英女皇授权一个七人的弗吉尼亚议会管理统辖詹姆斯敦的政务，但他们远离英国，不能直接行使女皇的权威和命令，议员遇到问题经常有意见分歧，不团结。此议会实属虚设。为了生存和立足，约翰·史密斯挺身而出，果敢地挑起了移民们的重托，带领他们造房盖屋，垦荒种地，修筑城堡。随着生产经济的发展，移民们看到自治的必要，于是建立了第一个议会(the House of Burgesses)，承认习惯法所保障的人民自由，并承袭英国人为争取政治自由而进行长期斗争的经验，把传统的自由观念写进了弗吉尼亚的第一个特许状，规定移民享有一切自由、特权和豁免，就像"他们出生和生长在英国本土一样"。其他各州移民的情况也类似，虽然有的是因政治或宗教的迫害到美洲避难定居的，有的是英皇特许的王爵达官到美洲建立私人殖民地的，但他们都远离母国，经受了长期、严峻的困难和考验，先后建立了各州的议会或会议制的自治政府，创造了自己的历史。要求摆脱英国的殖民统治，建立一个自由、民主、独立的资产阶级民主共和国的思想开始萌芽。

在"有益疏忽"的时期里，英国一直处于内部的宗教纷争和与法国争夺欧洲和世界霸权的战争之中。国内清教徒运动此起彼伏，波澜壮阔，猛烈地冲击了国教和王室政权；圈地运动导致大批农民失业和反叛斗争兴起；资产阶级的兴起动摇了英国的封建专制王朝。英法争夺欧洲和世界霸权的战争进行了一百多年，17 世纪 50 年代它们的争夺到了白热化程度。正当英国人在北美洲大西洋沿岸建立 13 个殖民地的时候，法国人在北美洲建立了一个从魁北克沿俄亥俄河和密西西比河流域到新奥尔良的半月形帝国，形成了英法争霸北美洲的相持局面。为了争夺俄亥俄流域，英法爆发了七年战争，结果英国胜利，夺取了法国在美洲几乎所有的属地，此后英国便成了北美洲的唯一霸主。

英国在内争外夺的 150 多年的岁月里，无力顾及对北美洲殖民地的直接统治，这有利于北美洲各殖民地依靠自身的力量发展壮大，从经济上和政治上都取得了独立于母国之外的能力，他们不仅有了自治政府，而且他们的民主自由思想得到了空前提高，相信他们的天赋权利——人生、自由和财产，是神圣不可剥夺的，因此他们称这段时期为"有益疏忽"时期。

七年战争胜利后，英国不仅成了美洲的霸主，而且成了世界头号霸主。它在全球拥有 33 个殖民地，它的海军游弋于各大海洋，它的足迹遍布世界各地，成了一时的"日不落国"。它负债累累，维持大英帝国的经费比战前猛增五倍之多。为了减轻经济负担，英国开始对美洲殖民地采取帝国主义政策，即重商主义政策。

重商主义是英国资产阶级长期奉行的经济理论和经济政策，其手段是采取行政和立法措施，变殖民地为母国的商品市场和原料来源地，并限制和母国的工业竞争，以达到母国繁荣富裕的目的。早在 1651 年，英国制定的第一个法令——《航海法令》就是重商主义政策的典型，它规定，除了英国之外，禁止一切国家和美洲殖民地通商。从 1763 年开始，英国在短短的两三年内制定了一系列强调性法令（coercive acts），如《食粮法》《货币法》《驻军法》《印花税票法》等。这些法令严重地触犯了殖民地人民的基本权利和利益，议会、商人、激进分子和各界人士纷纷提出抗议和斗争。塞缪尔·亚当斯提出了"没有代表权便没有征税权"（no taxation without representation）

的口号，以动员美洲爱国者起来进行反课税斗争。

当《印花税票法》于1765年一颁布，殖民地各界人士，包括商人、记者、律师、教士和企业家等立即行动起来进行斗争，他们组织了“自由之子社”(Sons of Liberty)，捣毁邮电所，烧毁印花税票，抵制英货，并于1765年10月在纽约召开了第一次由美洲人倡议的反《印花税票法》会议，通过一项决议，严正宣布“除由各殖民地议会自行决定者以外，从来不曾有，亦不可能有任何符合宪法的课税”，《印花税票法》具有“破坏殖民地人民的权利和自由的目的”。由于殖民地人民的强烈反对和抵制，英国议会被迫于1766年废除《印花税票法》。

但时隔不到一年，英国财政大臣查尔斯·汤森奉命制订了一项新的财政计划，加强海关管理，并对出口殖民地的纸张、玻璃、铅条、茶叶等征税。汤森法的颁布又一次掀起了反英浪潮。波士顿人民的反英情绪尤为高涨，他们围攻、殴打收税的海关人员。为此，英国派军保护海关人员，英军的到达更加激起了波士顿人民的仇恨，他们成群结队袭击英军，英军便下令开枪，结果发生了“波士顿惨案”。

由于殖民地人民的强烈反抗和斗争，英国议会再次被迫废止除茶叶税外的所有汤森税。此后，局势似乎平静了一些，但“激进分子”明白，只要茶叶税继续存在，英国议会就有权力继续向殖民地课税，殖民地人民的自由权利就会继续遭到危害。著名的激进分子塞缪尔·亚当斯连续发表文章、演说，激发人民起来为彻底废除课税和争取完全的自由、民主、平等而斗争。在他和托马斯·杰斐逊等激进分子的倡导下，各殖民地于1772年成立了“通讯委员会”，互通情报，联合行动，以防英政府可能挑起的新事端。

不出所料，1773年东印度公司因财政困难求助于英政府，获准向殖民地出口茶叶的垄断权。该公司把茶叶价压到市价以下，垄断了茶叶市场，危害了茶商的利益，茶商便和爱国者联合起来进行斗争，有的茶叶被迫退回英国，有的被封存在仓库里。在波士顿，有一群爱国者在亚当斯的领导下化装为印第安人，登上三艘停泊在波士顿港的英国船，把全部茶叶倒入海中，这就是美国革命前夕著名的爱国运动——波士顿倾茶事件，从此殖民地人民便开始了有组织有领导的反殖民主义的暴力斗争。

爱国者的革命行动触怒了英政府，他们的革命活动被诬为强盗行为，因此英政府采取强制措施，封锁波士顿港，改组马萨诸塞的自治议会，并派军进驻，妄图镇压马萨诸塞人民，使他们就范。

面对英政府的强制手段，各殖民地人民派出代表于1774年9月在费城召开了第一次大陆会议，研究形势，制订对策，通过了《权利宣言》和《怨由陈情书》，重申他们享有生命、自由和财产的权利，并向英政府宣告只有他们自己选出的议会才有权向他们课税。大陆会议成立了"联合会"，在"联合会"的领导下，各殖民地人民纷纷组织起来抵制英货，打击各地的王室权威。与此同时，马萨诸塞的爱国者开始组织民兵，并在离波士顿仅32千米的小镇康科德搜集火药和军需品，盖茨将军闻讯后立即派遣一支强大的支队前往没收军火，并准备逮捕审讯亚当斯和其他领导人，但武装民兵早有准备，在莱克星顿伏击了行进的英军。英军伤亡惨重，被迫撤回波士顿。在莱克星顿打响了独立战争的第一枪之后，新英格兰各州的殖民地人民同仇敌忾，两万大军奋起包围了波士顿。

在这紧急关头，各殖民地人民派出代表于1775年5月在费城召开了第二次大陆会议，发表了《关于拿起武器的原因和必要的公告》，通过了一份对英皇的请愿书，郑重声明他们同英国平等的地位，必要时他们要拿起武器保卫自己的自由；大会决定把民兵改编为大陆军，任命乔治·华盛顿为总司令，发行纸币支付军备和行政费用。英皇对此惊恐万状，当即宣布殖民地处于叛乱状态，并派重兵前往镇压。

当殖民地人民的严正立场和正当要求再三遭到拒绝后，他们决定要求完全的独立。1776年初托马斯·佩恩发表了《常识》，在列举了大量事实说明推翻王室政权，建立共和国的必要性之后，他说："所有正确或合理的事物都要求脱离英国。被害者的血，自然界的哭泣声在呼喊，'是分离的时候了！'""作为最后手段的武装决定这场斗争的成败；使用武装是皇帝的选择，大陆已经接受这个挑战。"这本小册子轰动了整个美洲大陆，对号召和动员全美洲人民拿起武器进行独立战争起了重要作用。美洲人民由此认识到，要取得彻底的民主、自由和独立，他们必须与英国脱离关系，进行坚决的武装斗争。于是他们于1776年发布了《独立宣言》，庄严宣告美利坚合众国的诞生，并经过六年的浴血奋战获得了真正的独立。

《独立宣言》是托马斯·杰斐逊负责起草，13个州议会签署批准的。洛克的天赋权利思想被明确地写进了《独立宣言》里。《独立宣言》写道："……人类生而平等，造物者赋予他们若干不能出让的权利，其中如生命、自由和幸福的追求。为了保障这些权利，人类才在他们之间建立政府，而政府之正当权力是经被统治者的同意而产生的。任何政府一破坏这些目的，人民便有权力把它政变或废除，以建立一个新的政府。”这段话是《独立宣言》这部纲领性文献的核心思想，阐明了美国人民组建政府的目的，阐明了人民与政府之间的关系，是美国人民组建政府的根本指导思想，成了美国人民的基本哲学思想，至今还有深远的影响。

三、洛克的思想对美国建国的影响

在革命胜利后，美国人民开始以洛克的哲学思想为基础组建政府，先是制定《邦联条例》，组建邦联政府；后是制定宪法，组建中央政府。

1. 制定《邦联条例》和组建邦联政府

洛克说：“人们参加社会的理由在于保护他们的财产；他们选择一个立法机关并授以权力的目的，是希望由此可以制定法律、树立准则，以保卫社会一切成员的财产，限制社会各部分和各成员的权力并调节他们之间的统辖权。”他又说：“立法机关一旦侵犯了社会这个基本原则，并因野心、恐惧、愚蠢或腐败，力图恢复已握有或给予任何其他人以一种绝对的权力，来支配人民的生命、权利和产业时，他们就由于这种背弃委托的行为而丧失了人民为了极不相同的目的曾给予他们的权力。这一权力便归属人民，人民享有恢复他们原来的自由的权利，并通过建立他们认为合适的新立法机关以谋求他们的安全和保障，而这些正是他们所以加入社会的目的。”

美国宣布独立后立即于 1727 年指定一个委员会草拟《邦联条例》，并于同年 12 月提交各州议会签署，但到 1781 年才获批准，其原因是西部土地问题没有得到及时解决，有边界关系的大州提出了广泛乃至相同的西部土地要求，无边界关系的小州认为西部土地应归国有，由大陆议会划分若干自由和独立的政府管辖区，经讨论协商和议会的建议，前者才放弃了土地要求，并把西部土地归合众国统一处理。西部土地问题解决后，议会通过了《邦联条例》，并按条例精神组建邦联政府。邦联政府成立后，制定了《西北法令》，把西北土地（即西部土地）划分为三至五个州，当每个州的居民超过六万时，它可以组织自己的政府，并享有与原来各州同等的权力加入联邦。这个法令为美国解决西部新开拓土地的国有化和接纳新州的政策奠定了基础，对迅速完成西部开拓起了重要作用。

邦联政府是个松散的邦联组织，没有权威对各州施加影响和统辖，产生了许多严重问题，如战后的经济困难，民族纠纷，边界争端，州际的关税、贸易、货币等矛盾，邦联政府都无权也无法处理。另外，邦联政府无权向各州课税，调整和统辖对内对外贸易，因此在国防安全、外交、财政等方面都发生了严重困难和危机，且有日趋恶化之势。这一系列问题引起了群众的广泛不满，尤其是负债的农民，他们面临负债入狱和破产的危险。在谢司的领导下农民发生了暴动。这一暴动唤醒了有见识的政治家，他们看到了邦联政府的弱点，认为有必要建立有权威的中央政府，因而召开了制宪会议。

2.制宪会议和组建中央政府

洛克说："虽然人们在参加社会时放弃他们在自然状态中所享有的平等、自由和执行权，而把它们交给社会，由立法机关按社会的利益所要求的程度加以处理，但是这只是出于个人为了更好地保护自己、他的自由和财产的动机，社会或由他们组成的立法机关的权力绝不容许扩张到超出公众福利的需要，而是必须保障每个人的财产，以防止上述三种使自然状态很不安全、很不方便的缺点。所以，谁握有国家的立法权或最高权力，谁就应该以既定的、向全国人民公布周知的、经常有效的法律，而不是以临时的命令来实行统治；应该由公正无私的法官根据这些法律来裁判纠纷；并且只是对内为了执行这些法律，对外为了防止或索偿外国所造成的损害，以及为了保障社会不受入侵和侵略时，才能使用社会的力量，而这一切都没有别的目的，只是为了人民的和平、安全和公众福利。"

制宪会议于1787年召开，参加会议的有55个代表，他们都是来自各州(除罗得岛外)的知名人士、学者、政治家和英雄；他们对洛克的思想和孟德斯鸠的均权政治学说(Montesquient's concept of the balance of power in politics)都很熟悉，一致同意政府设立平等的但又相互制衡的行政、立法和司法部门，而且同意国会设上、下两院，参议院和众议院(the Senate and the House of Representatives)。但他们在研究解决具体问题时，产生了尖锐矛盾，大州主张各州在联邦政府中的代表人数按各州的人口比例决定，而小州则主张按州决定名额，因此双方争论不休，最后采取一个折中的方案：在众议院里各州的代表名额按人口比例决定，在参议院里则各州名额相等。他们对代表的选举产生、黑人的代表权、税制、经济、货币，以及总统的权力、任期和选举方法等政策问题都产生过激烈争论，经长时间的辩论、协商后才一一得到了解决。矛盾解决后，于 1787 年 9 月大会通过了美国宪法，后送各州签署批准，但各州在讨论签署中又产生了许多类似的尖锐矛盾，经过长时间的辩论达到妥协后，美国宪法才于 1789 年 3 月被多数州签署生效。

各州在辩论中对宪法没有明文写进人权反应强烈，在他们的一致要求下，宪法增补了十条修正案，明确规定美国人民享有的基本人身权利受宪法保护，不受任何地方、州或中央政府的迫害。

宪法批准生效后，美国于 1789 年 4 月 30 日建立了以乔治·华盛顿为总统的第一届中央政府。宪法规定政府设行政、立法和司法三个部门，总统行使行政权，国会行使立法权，最高法院行使司法权，三权分立但又相互制衡，以防任何一个部门独揽大权。宪法还明文规定了中央政府和州政府的权力范围，即中央政府有权统辖全国各州，但各州也享有相对的独立性，从而妥善处理了州和中央政权之间的关系。

按宪法组建的中央政府比按《邦联条例》组建的政府前进了一大步，它更加健全、更加完善、更有权威，掌握着国家的政治、经济、军事、财政和外交大权，能组织和领导社会各阶层的力量把国家建设得更加美丽富强，能有效地抵御外部的入侵和侵略，保障人民的利益，维护国家安全和国际威望，这对美国此后的迅速发展壮大具有深远的历史意义。

但美国宪法是一部资产阶级的宪法，它决定了美国的国家性质是资产阶级的民主共和国。因此，我们不能抽掉美国宪法为资产阶级统治服务的阶级本质而抽象地谈论美国是个何等民主、自由和平等的国家，洛克的天赋权利思想不过是为资产阶级统治服务的工具而已。

洛克的《政府论》和天赋权利思想不仅对美国的独立战争和建国有过重要的影响和作用，而且对美国各个阶段的历史发展、各大领域都有深刻的影响和作用。到了 19 世纪 60 年代西部开拓完成以后，洛克的资产阶级民主思想发展到了高峰，其影响和作用更深、更广、更大；19 世纪下半叶以后，他的思想便成了美国帝国主义发展的哲学思想基础。

西进运动及其主要政治哲学思想

西进运动是欧洲殖民者在北美大陆大西洋沿岸定居之后，不断地从东到西向太平洋沿岸移居，开拓和逐步完成美国国土扩张的运动。它早在殖民时期就已开始，但较大规模的西进运动始于独立战争之后，结束于19世纪中叶，为美利坚合众国的统一和成长奠定了基础，是美国人民的壮举，谱写了美国史上光辉的一页。本文初析西进运动及其主要政治哲学思想，内容分三部分：第一，西进运动梗概；第二，西进运动中的主要政治哲学思想及剖析；第三，结束语。

一、西进运动梗概

1607年首批英国殖民者在大西洋沿岸建立了第一个殖民地詹姆斯敦，接着一批又一批的英国殖民者相继来到大西洋沿岸建立了13个殖民地，最后一个殖民地佐治亚，于1733年成立。殖民地建立以后，政治、经济、文化、教育等发展很快，与宗主国之间的矛盾日益加深。为了摆脱宗主国的压迫和自身的发展，移民开始向西部迁移。在北部，他们从纽约经哈得逊河和莫霍克河进入西部大草原；在中部，他们从宾夕法尼亚西部沿俄亥俄河进入西部；在南部，他们从弗吉尼亚穿过昆布兰山口进入西南地区，越过阿巴拉契亚山脉慢慢地进入西部大草原。

1781年美国独立之后，成批的移民开始涌向西北地区，不久这地区就被开发起来了。

为了控制和开发密西西比河沿岸地区和新奥尔良港，杰斐逊政府于1803年向法国购买了路易斯安那邦，把西部边疆延伸到落基山脚下，使美国的领土增加了一倍。

1810年美国出兵侵占西佛罗里达，1818年向西班牙购买了东佛罗里达，消除了外国在东部的势力；1846年美国迫使英国放弃了俄勒冈地区，把美国的版图扩展到太平洋沿岸；紧接着美国发动了1846—1848年墨西哥战争，吞并了加利福尼亚、新墨西哥和亚利桑那，把太平洋沿岸的大片地区归入美国版图。此外，美国还于1867年向沙俄购买了阿拉斯加。至此，美国在一个多世纪里经过战争、契约和收买等办法完成了美洲大陆的西进运动，把建国时的13个殖民地的面积扩大了10倍，规模之大、速度之快在世界历史上都是罕见的。有人预言，完成大陆的西进运动至少需要500年，甚至2000年，但美国只用一个多世纪的时间就完成了这一人间奇迹、世界壮举。

伴随着大面积西部土地开拓的是大工业的崛起。商业、工厂、矿山到处出现，铁路、公路、电报线像蜘蛛网一样遍布美国。1860—1894年美国的工业总产值增长了4倍，从世界第四位一跃而居首位，在不到半个世纪的时间里，美国从一个落后的农业国迅速发展成为工业强国。

西进运动的进程是美利坚民族形成和发展的过程。1812年战争激发了美国民众的爱国热忱，增强了美国民众的民族主义精神、民族尊严和自信心，他们相信他们将成为一个伟大的民族，矗立于世界民族之林。亚伯拉罕·林肯是个伟大的民族主义者，在内战中，他高举民族团结、统一的旗帜，为维护美利坚合众国的统一与美利坚民族的形成和发展，建立了不朽功勋，从此以后，美国的进步和发展进入了一个历史新时期。

西进运动的开拓者是猎人、皮货商、牛仔、淘金者和印第安人，他们在深山野林追踪珍贵皮毛动物，在大草原驱赶牛群，为了保卫自己的财产与殖民者展开殊死搏斗。这一系列的真人真事形成了美国西部地区独特的文化，为美国西部文学的形成和发展提供了社会源泉，这不仅对美国政治、经济的发展具有重要意义，也对美国民族文化的形成和发展产生了巨大影响。

二、西进运动中的主要政治哲学思想

美国的西进运动是一个长期、复杂的历史发展过程，是由许多政治、经济、文化、自然条件等所决定的，现就政治哲学思想——J.洛克的天赋权利思想、个人主义、自由竞争和社会达尔文主义等对西进运动的作用和影响谈谈我的粗浅看法。

首先,美国人民具有浓厚的J.洛克的天赋权利思想。

自1781年独立战争胜利后,美国人民虽然获得了民主、自由和独立,但国家安全、民族尊严、外交和国际通商还经常受到世界强国的威胁和破坏。英国蓄意封锁美国海岸线,违法扣留和搜查美国船只,索回英国逃兵或强令美国公民为英国服役。此外,美国经常受到来自加拿大境内受英国武装策划的印第安人的骚扰和袭击。西班牙还占领着佛罗里达和密西西比河以西的大片土地。由于上述种种原因,美国发动了1812年战争,虽然美国没有达到预期的战争目的——从英国夺取加拿大和从西班牙夺取佛罗里达,但在巴尔的摩要塞的保卫战和夺取新奥尔良的战斗中,美国军队击败了现代化武装的强大的英国军队,取得了辉煌胜利,洗刷了民族耻辱,维护了民族尊严,增强了民族团结和民族自信心,提高了国际威望,巩固了国防,因此,美国人又称这次战争为第二次独立战争,从此以后,他们便致力于国内建设和西部开拓运动。

19世纪30年代,命定说促进了西进运动。美国人相信他们是上帝优选的民族,向大陆西部,甚至整个美洲大陆扩张,是为了保卫人类自由。他们认为与上帝的沟通是靠个人的信仰,努力实现上帝赋予他们的权利。美国记者约翰 L.奥沙立文于1845年在《纽约晨报》(*New York Morning News*)里写道:"……我们天赋的命运就是要遍布并占有上帝赋予我们的整个自由大陆,联邦自治政府的大陆,犹如一株树有权占有空间和土地以利于它自身的充分发展——犹如溪流流过渠道自然地不断增加它的流水量。"他们凭借这种教义像流水般地涌向得克萨斯、俄勒冈、新墨西哥、亚利桑那和加利福尼亚,他们在沿途建立居民点、教堂、学校、法院和自治政府,逐渐侵吞和排斥了英国和墨西哥在这些辽阔地区的统治势力,实现了上帝赋予他们的使命——对大陆西部或整个美洲大陆的扩张和统治。

其次,美国人民具有强烈的个人主义思想。

以J.洛克的天赋权利和个人政治平等为理论基础的个人主义是一种政治哲学思想,按斯坦福大学社会心理学教授英克尔斯(Alex Inkeles)的解释,个人主义的含义是"个人有决定自己的生活和前途的自由和权利"。个人主义强调个人自由、自我支配、自我控制,个人的尊严和价值应受到他人的尊重;反对任何人对个人的干预或控制,尤其反对任何权威或政府对个人的各种支配。美国著名作家和诗人爱默生在《依靠自己》(*Self-Reliance*)一文中指出:"我应做的一切都是与我有关的,不是人们认为我要做的事。"个人主义主张一切个人都是平等的,即任何人都享有均等的权利和自由去选择自己的宗教信仰、前途和目标,享有均等的权利和机会去获得个人政治和经济上的成就;它强调竞争,通过自由竞争达到个人的最大成就和社会进步。美国人都有坚定的信念,认为人生最重要的是自我认识,实现自我价值,以期上帝的恩宠——荣升天堂,免罚下狱。个人主义带有浓厚的宗教色彩,它把基督教神学和资产阶级个人主义世界观融合在一起。它不同于利己主义或自私自利,利己主义主张追求个人利益和幸福是至高无上的,但两者同属于资产阶级世界观的范畴,为资产阶级服务。

西进运动最大限度地激发了个人主义,而个人主义促进了西进运动的迅速发展和完成。

1812 年战争之后,美国才在国际大家庭中取得真正的独立、民主和平等的地位。革命以来,美国所经历的种种严重困难,已大部克服了,经济已开始恢复,社会秩序井然,一大片处女地等待开发,一幅美好的前景——和平、繁荣和社会进步正展现在美国人民面前。在这人定心欢、万物待兴的时刻,美国政治家霍勒斯·格里申于 1851 年号召"青年人,到西部去,和国家共同发展成长"。在他的召唤下,成千上万的拓荒者,尤其是青年,从东部沿岸越过阿巴拉契亚山脉涌向西部大草原。首先到达的是一批狩猎者,他们吃苦、耐劳、勇敢,过着狩猎、经营皮货的艰苦危险的生活;接踵而来的是一批拓荒者,他们开荒、种地、放牧、狩猎、劈林、盖房、造路、建家园;再接着是一批又一批的巧匠、医师、牧师、律师、店主、编辑和政治家,他们每到一地就建造商店、工厂、学校、教堂、公路、农场和仓库,而且带来了文化、教育和科学技术。在短短的二三十年内,西北地区发生了翻天覆地的变化,俄亥俄的人口从 1800 年的 4.5 万猛增到 1840 年的 150 万;1810 年伊利诺的人口只有 1.2 万,1840 年增长到 47.6 万;1830 年还是一个小商镇的芝加哥,很快就发展成为一个拥有大量人口的繁荣都市。农业生产的发展也是惊人的,玉米从 1849 年的 5.92 亿蒲式耳增长到 1859 年的 8.39 亿蒲式耳,小麦从 10 亿蒲式耳增长到 17.3 亿蒲式耳,西北平原已发展成为美国主要的农业基地,其重要地位已日益明显。

1849年加利福尼亚淘金热大大加快了西部开拓，1850年有约11.5万淘金者经历千辛万苦来到人口稀少的加利福尼亚，原来还是一个小镇的旧金山一夜间变成了一个拥挤不堪的城市。她的繁荣加快了周围地区的发展，丹佛、盐湖城相继诞生，太平洋沿岸各州已不再是一片沉睡的处女地，政治、经济都有了举足轻重的发展，影响深远。

1869年横贯美洲大陆的第一条铁路建成了，接着在二三十年内又有四条横贯大陆的铁路相继竣工，西部铁路网的形成标志着西进运动进入了一个崭新的阶段，荒无人烟的西部大草原和终年积雪、令人望而生畏的落基山脉渐渐被拓荒者征服了，漫山遍野的牛群、羚羊源源不断地从西部运往东部，大批农业机械、铁丝网和风车从东部运往西部，红色印第安人、牛仔们的野外放牧生活渐渐被大农场、大牧场的生活所代替；常年风沙成灾、枯竭干旱的“沙漠大盆地”变成了放牧、产粮的绿洲，落基山脉成了拓荒者寻金采宝的要地。

西部开拓者一无政府、法律的约束，二无传统文化观念的束缚，凭借他们的勤苦、耐劳、勇敢、机智在这广阔富饶的西部荒野里开创了他们想要建立的富有传奇性的生活，展现在他们面前的一幅美好的前景——和平、繁荣和社会进步逐步变为现实，而这美好的前景抚育、激发了他们的个人主义思想，J.洛克的天赋权利思想也在西进运动的伟大试验中获得了升华。

另外，自由竞争推动了西进运动，并导致了垄断资本。自由竞争是美国人民的一种品格，他们认为自由竞争是获得个人发展和成就的重要手段，也是获得社会进步的重要途径，美国在政治、经济、文化、教育、科学，甚至日常生活的各个领域都存在自由竞争，他们的理论根据是社会达尔文主义，认为“强存弱汰”是不可违抗的自然规律。为了个人的生存和发展，人人勤奋努力，拼搏向上去创造个人的最大成就，这对西进运动的完成、废奴运动的兴起、地区冲突的发展及内战后的经济起飞都起了重要作用。但这也是对美国历史的反动，盎格鲁-撒克逊自奉为优选的民族，对少数民族外侨、天主教徒、黑人和印第安人进行了惨无人道的歧视、压榨，甚至灭绝人种的迫害。

随着西进运动的发展，南、北之间在政治、经济、文化上的差别越来越大，矛盾越来越深，竞争愈演愈烈，最后爆发了南北战争。在北部，工业迅速发展，新兴的工业资产阶级要解放奴隶，支持保护税；而南部封建奴隶主阶级则依靠奴隶发展种植园经济，维护封建奴隶制；在西部，工农业发展很快，需要劳力，他们反对奴隶制和保护税，但拥护政府资助西部建设。随着西进运动的发展，地区和阶级间的各种矛盾激化了，其中最突出、最敏感的是奴隶问题。南部奴隶主为了本阶级的利益，顽固坚持把奴隶扩展到西部任何地方，但北部新兴的资产阶级则坚决反对。19 世纪下半叶，日益增多的自由州加入了合众国，奴隶主渐渐失去了在国会里的多数票和控制权，他们从合众国分裂出去，成立了南部邦联。1860 年新当选的林肯总统代表北部工业资产阶级的利益，维护合众国的团结和统一，支持保护税，反对奴隶制，支持废奴运动，从而爆发了南北战争。战争的结果是代表先进生产力和生产关系的北部工业资产阶级打败了代表没落、腐朽生产力和生产关系的封建奴隶主阶级，解放了黑奴，消除了资本主义发展的障碍，为美国资本主义的飞速发展铺平了道路。

内战结束后，美国的经济开始起飞，从农业国一跃成为工业国，自由竞争被垄断所替代。内战前，美国多数企业是小型的、私营的，充满着竞争，但战后企业家为了发展生产，提高利润，削减成本，限制竞争，集中人力、物力、财力进行有效的生产，开辟了相应的市场，银行和交通运输等实行综合联营，因而出现了安德鲁·卡内基这样的钢铁大王，标准石油公司、摩尔根财团等托拉斯企业，这对美国生产力的加速发展及战后的经济腾飞起了积极作用和影响。1860 年，美国还是一个世界第二流的工业国，工业总产值低于英、法、德三国；但到了 1890 年，美国已成为第一流的工业强国，工业总产值相当于英、法、德三国产值的总和。但垄断导致了阶级的两极分化，分工运动和种种社会弊病不断出现，为了缓和各种社会矛盾和斗争，美国政府制定了一系列限制垄断活动的法律和法令，如《谢尔曼反托拉斯法》等，但均未奏效，因为，这些都是美国资本主义制度，即生产资料私有制内部所固有的弊病，无法克服。

三、结束语

综上所述，J. 洛克的天赋权利思想、个人主义、自由竞争、社会达尔文主义对西进运动的完成和战后经济的腾飞都起了重要作用，但这些思想也为垄断资产阶级服务。